LOUIS D'ALTON AND THE ABBEY THEATRE

To dear
Gabs with
Love from
Louis

Louis D'Alton and the Abbey Theatre

CIARA O'FARRELL

FOUR COURTS PRESS

Set in 11.5 on 13.5 point Centaur
FOUR COURTS PRESS LTD
7 Malpas Street, Dublin 8, Ireland
e-mail: info@four-courts-press.ie
http://www.four-courts-press.ie
and in North America
FOUR COURTS PRESS
c/o ISBS, 920 N.E. 58th Avenue, Suite 300, Portland, OR 97213.

A catalogue record for this title
is available from the British Library.

ISBN 1–85182–868–0

SPECIAL ACKNOWLEDGMENT

This publication received a grant in aid of publication from the Arts Council/An Chomhairle Ealaíon.

Printed in Great Britain
by MPG Books Ltd, Bodmin, Cornwall.

For my father and mother, with love

Contents

Illustrations

The illustration section appears between pages 128 and 129.

Preface

To research the life of a neglected playwright so influenced by his experience in an equally neglected aspect of Irish theatre – fit-up theatre – posed many methodological difficulties. The lack of directly relevant secondary criticism meant that I had to locate, read and analyze substantial amounts of unpublished source material. For making this work available I am indebted to all those who were so generous and supportive in both their time and in the loan of documents. They include: Cathleen Barrington; Lori-Ann Burke; Robert Carrickford; Brendan Connellan; Eileen Connellan; Seamus de Burca; Mairead Delaney; Martin Fahy; Pauline Flanagan; Robert Hogan; Garry Hynes; Vikki Jackson; David Judge; John Kenny; Margot McCambridge; Michael McClaffrey; Tua McCormick; Ken McCracken; Denis Murphy; Michael Neary; Andy O'Callaghan; Nancy Quinn; Patricia Richardson; Kevin Rockett; Susan Shreibman. I would also like to thank the staff of the following libraries and archives: Abbey Theatre Archive; Archives Department, University College Dublin; British Film Institute; British Library; Imperial War Museum, London; Irish Theatre Archive; National Library of Ireland; Theatre Museum, London; University College Dublin Library.

I owe special thanks to Louis D'Alton's wonderful sister, the late Babs D'Alton, who befriended me, granted me numerous interviews and gave me all of Louis' remaining personal documents and photographs. I am also indebted to D'Alton's late daughter Sheila, to his grandchildren Kenneth McCracken and Sharon Folkes, and to his second wife Eithne Mulhall, for all their support and help.

I am deeply grateful to Gearóid O'Brien who loaned me the personal papers of his late father Brendan O'Brien which detailed fit-up activity in Athlone from 1830 to 1940, and which were of enormous benefit in allowing me to gauge the range, quality and number of fit-up performances in Ireland during this period.

My sincere thanks also to those actors whom I interviewed or corresponded with who worked with Louis D'Alton: Phyllis Ryan, the late John Cowley, Barry Cassin, and Shela Ward were more than generous with their time and knowledge; thanks also to Micheál Ó hAodha, Milo O'Shea and the late Cyril Cusack. I would also like to pay special thanks to those fit-up actors who loaned me documents and who talked to me in great detail about this area of Irish theatre, particularly Paddy Dooley and David Costello. Without their generosity in placing knowledge of Louis D'Alton and the fit-ups at my disposal, this book would not have been possible. My particular thanks are due to Professor Christopher Murray of the English Department, University College Dublin. I owe a great debt to him for his invaluable guidance and support throughout my PhD.

My personal thanks to Sue Norton for reading so thoroughly whatever I threw her way, and to her, Moynagh Sullivan, and John Barrett for being so much more than academic colleagues. Thanks also to Ann and Bo Lantorp, for putting me up during all those research trips to London.

Despite his observation that my manuscript was, 'a cure for chronic insomnia', my love and special thanks to my husband, Paul Holland, for his love and humorous support during the transition of this book from my PhD. In the ups and downs of the book-writing period, he was definitely one of the ups.

Finally, my most special thanks to my parents, for their constant support and encouragement throughout my years of research. This book is dedicated to them.

Introduction

Pasted in a small scrapbook that belonged to Louis D'Alton's brother, Noel, is an untitled, undated, yellowed newspaper report. In this anecdotal clipping, the writer describes his visit to the Father Mathew Hall where Louis D'Alton was adjudicating the annual amateur drama competition:

> High up on the balcony, all by himself, screened off with a backcloth, in front of a table on which the shaded lamp spread a bright light, sat the adjudicator, Louis D'Alton. I found him, after fifteen successive nights of uninterrupted play judging for the award of Independent, Abbey Theatre and Universe Cups, not weary, as I had imagined, but in completely arrested attention, his eyebrows knitted, one arm over the balustrade holding a currant bun from the tea tray just provided by a helping hand. It was some minutes before he became aware of both myself and the bun – then I got a friendly smile, the bun a hungry bite.

This image of D'Alton is interesting for a number of reasons. Our introduction to him, secluded high up on the balcony, reflects his shy nature, which was often mistaken for insipidness. And the friendly smile he afforded the reporter points to another facet of Louis D'Alton's personality that his granite-face and sea-cold grey eyes belied – an unwavering kindness, which reputedly was yielded to all he knew. As a producer and manager, D'Alton's reputation for being supportive and propitious was well known, a fact that earned him great respect, especially from young actors starting out in the theatre business.

D'Alton's 'completely arrested attention' during the amateur performance at the Father Mathew Hall is hardly surprising, given the love he had not only for city theatre but for small-town provincial drama. It is not difficult to picture him savouring the ambience of this amateur drama festival, complete with all its pitfalls and despite its lack of sophistication, as it was precisely this lack of urbanity that D'Alton felt at home with. Having grown up in the precarious and unstable world of fit-up drama, he progressed to become one of the

Abbey Theatre's most prolific and popular dramatists of his day. However, as we shall see, he never managed to cut himself off from his touring roots – or, indeed, desired to. Even when D'Alton's popularity as a playwright was peaking, he continued to adjudicate amateur drama competitions all over Ireland.

In May 1941, when *The Money Doesn't Matter* was playing in the Abbey to great acclaim, D'Alton adjudicated the amateur drama festival in the Father Mathew Hall. At the beginning of the month, Gabriel Fallon had urged his readers to attend at the Abbey play, saying, 'Go and see the finest play that has been presented there for a long, long time';[1] yet less than a month later D'Alton was immersed in amateur drama advising amateur producers, directors and actors about their craft. The extent of his involvement can be seen from the following report by Gabriel Fallon in *The Standard* of 23 May 1941:

> Having accomplished the in-itself commendable feat of speaking for over three and a half hours, having filled each minute of that period with sixty seconds' worth of sound practical theatre advice, Louis D'Alton, player, producer and playwright, found himself forced by flying time to bring his adjudication of the Father Mathew Festival to a hurried close when last Monday evening was five minutes old.
>
> Naming the winners, he departed, leaving behind him a legacy of over one hundred and twenty pages of closely-written painstaking notes. To the competing groups these should be invaluable, for Mr D'Alton is an adjudicator who knows his theatre through the experience of having mastered every job in it. Consequently, when Mr D'Alton found fault with a piece of acting in the festival, he not only told us the reasons why he did find fault, but he furnished practical illustration of the right and wrong of it in a manner which both delighted and enlightened his audience. So too with production; the stage became a rehearsal call, and Mr D'Alton moved and positioned players as if the players were already there.
>
> His comments on the dramaturgy of the works presented revealed a wide knowledge and a deep sympathetic insight free from any of that lily-literary pretentiousness which so often marks and mars the work of an adjudicator at drama festivals. In a long experience of adjudicating, Louis D'Alton claims a high place.

Fallon's appraisal of D'Alton helps us form a picture of a man who not only undertook his duties with a great deal of professionalism , but who obviously received enormous satisfaction in helping those who had not yet achieved his level of theatrical craftsmanship. He remained indebted to the small towns and villages that proffered him both a welcome and an income when launching his career as a playwright and producer; and he never forgot that the vision of provincial Ireland he portrayed in his plays, making them so accessible to Irish audiences, was afforded in no small way by his experiences travelling with fit-up drama.

Louis D'Alton's Abbey Theatre career began in 1937 when his first play, *The Man in the Cloak*, was produced there. After this, eight more D'Alton plays received their premieres at the Abbey, three of them produced posthumously (his final play, *Cafflin' Johnny*, as much as eight years after his death). Yet theatre at the Abbey during these two decades is generally criticized as being rather desolate. Sean O'Casey, a friend and correspondent of D'Alton's, had made his name there in the 1920s, and it was well after D'Alton's success that the plays of Behan, Beckett and Friel began to capture Irish audiences. Still, D'Alton's contemporaries included the likes of Lennox Robinson, St John Ervine, George Shiels, Teresa Deevy, Paul Vincent Carroll, Joseph Tomelty, M.J. Molloy, and Walter Macken – all of whom were important to the Abbey during his theatrical career – but because little has been written about them, it is not surprising that the Abbey is perceived as having been in the doldrums during this time.[2]

The main policymakers of the Abbey Theatre at this time have also been criticized for generating theatre that was sterile and dull. By far the most influential policymaker during D'Alton's time was Ernest Blythe, invited by Yeats to join the Abbey board of directors in 1935, and appointed managing director in 1941, a position he held until his retirement in 1967. He was, despite his length of service, not a popular administrator. Tomas MacAnna recounts that he was 'utterly ruthless, a fanatic for the Irish language, with little or no artistic judgement, and certainly the decisive influence that had brought the once-famous theatre to its ever-present lamentable state'.[3] He was even accused of engaging players for their knowledge of the Irish language rather than for their acting abilities,[4] of rejecting good plays, of focusing on kitchen comedies so as to inflate box-office receipts, and of encouraging long runs and revivals of popular plays at the cost of introducing new drama to the Irish stage. An article in the *Irish Times* on 8 November 1952 sums up the attitude many had towards Blythe:

> The cold grey eyes, the flat Northern voice conceal a personality that is forceful by its pertinacity … It is impossible not to look to him when good plays are discarded after a week's run; when bad plays are revived endlessly; when recruitment is based on the principle (in his own words) 'not to take on any new junior players who are not able

> to perform in both Irish and English'; when standards of acting appear to be judged by a player's dexterity in differentiating between the broad and slender consonant in the Munster dialect.
>
> This single-minded devotion to the cause of the language is not what won the Abbey fame. It is hardly likely to increase that fame, or even maintain it. There is no doubt, the pursuit of an ideal; but is it the ideal of Yeats?

Years later, on 4 July 1964, the *Irish Times* published another damning critique of Blythe, this time from Sean O'Casey, who told reporter John Howard, 'What the hell does Blythe know about the drama anyway? He knows nothing about acting or drama. He may be a good manager in a financial sense but he doesn't understand the drama.'

As we shall see, even Louis D'Alton, a popular playwright who benefited in many ways from Blythe's policy of long runs and revivals of popular plays, found it difficult to work with him. But it was D'Alton's awareness of Blythe's policies, coupled with his own ambitions to become a successful playwright, which impelled him to write the sort of comedies that would please Abbey audiences and inflate box-office receipts. The title of D'Alton's first such comedy, *The Money Doesn't Matter* is thus loaded with irony. However, as we shall see, D'Alton also had another agenda – to portray his objections to the conservatism that was characteristic not only of the Abbey but of Irish society at large during the 1940s.

In an interview for the *Sunday Express*, 17 May 1964, Blythe attempted to shift the blame for the Abbey's poor reputation away from its board to its playwrights:

> We have had good plays at the Abbey which would have been much better if the authors had had the courage to face up to the questions of religion and morals involved. But they deliberately evaded the issues in order to keep criticism from themselves. The Abbey would not have minded airing these questions fully and clearly.

D'Alton would certainly have taken issue with this. Indeed, in 1941 when *Lovers' Meeting* was in rehearsal at the Abbey, Blythe and D'Alton disagreed strongly about the morals expressed in the play. Phyllis Ryan, who played in this production, remembers that Blythe was particularly upset at D'Alton's insistence at having her portray the heroine of the play (who commits suicide) as being sane. Blythe was incensed that someone who committed the 'sin' of suicide could be seen as sane, and Ryan maintains that her decision to follow D'Alton's direction against Blythe's wishes resulted in her being subsequently 'exiled from the Abbey because, according to Blythe, I did not fit in with its policies'.[5] Considering that *Lovers' Meeting* was the last D'Alton play to be staged at the Abbey for a period of six years, and that his next play, *You Can't Be Too Careful*, was produced in the Olympia Theatre, it is safe to assume that D'Alton's switch of theatre was in direct response to Blythe's policies and attitudes.

While one cannot deny that the Abbey's policies and the quality of its plays were questionable at times, the calibre of the actors and actresses at this time was high. F.J. McCormick played in four of D'Alton's plays, and his final Abbey appearance was during the 1947 run of *They Got What They Wanted.* Cyril Cusack acted in D'Alton's first three Abbey productions, and other actors and actresses of note included Ria Mooney, Denis O'Dea, Michael J. Dolan, Brian O'Higgins, Fred Johnson, Bríd Ní Loinsigh, Eileen Crowe and Maureen Delaney. Even D'Alton himself starred in the first production of *To-Morrow Never Comes* in 1939 when F.J. McCormick had to pull out at the last moment due to illness. Nevertheless, it must be said that while D'Alton began his career as a fit-up actor and received good reviews whenever he played, his talents lay elsewhere.

This book charts the life of Louis D'Alton (1900–51). In its broadest sense this entailed my assembling the fragmented pieces of D'Alton's life to form a picture of a man whose life and work have hitherto largely been neglected. Necessary to this process is an investigation of the whole notion of fit-up drama, another area of Irish theatrical history that deserves much more attention than it has received or indeed than I can do justice to here. I therefore concentrate on D'Alton's writings as being a product of his experience as a fit-up artist. Fit-up theatre, with its emphasis on melodrama, was the only form of drama D'Alton knew intimately before he began writing, and it is reflected strongly in his initial plays and in his novels. Even so, D'Alton's writings transcend melodrama, especially in their obvious battle against the dominant religious, political, social and cultural trends of Ireland during the 1930s and 1940s.

D'Alton wrote to satisfy the tastes of his public, and his involvement in the fit-up world, where pleasing the audience was everything, undoubtedly shaped his attitude towards Abbey Theatre audiences. But it is precisely this playwright–public relationship that posed the greatest dilemma for D'Alton. On the one hand, he wanted to expose the faults he felt were inherent in Ireland at that time, but he also craved success as a playwright and all too soon felt pressured to cater to his audiences' demand for drama that was essentially non-controversial, light-hearted and comic.

This book also investigates the extent to which, and the reasons why, theatregoers dictated the type of drama written for in the Abbey in the 1940s. Because the Abbey Theatre was going through one of its most difficult periods during this time, commercial success was vital. Blythe's policy that 'a play's a failure if it doesn't ultimately draw an audience. It's a miserable failure, in fact,'[6] further served to heighten the power of the audience. D'Alton eventually chose a middle ground where he could express his opinions to those audiences who were willing to listen, and at the same time satisfy the desires of those who wanted nothing more than to be entertained.

When Louis D'Alton died in 1951, he was described in an obituary in the *Irish Times* as being 'more than a playwright – he was a craftsman of the theatre'.[7] I hope that this book not only re-discovers D'Alton's craft, and evaluates D'Alton as a playwright/producer, but also commemorates D'Alton the man.

CHAPTER ONE

Descending from the stage

Louis Francis Joseph D'Alton[1] was born on 24 May 1900, at 14, Turlough Terrace in Fairview, Dublin, the first of Frank and Catherine Dalton's five children. With a background steeped in theatrical tradition – his father, mother, aunts and uncles had all travelled Ireland and England playing with various fit-up theatrical companies – it is hardly surprising that Louis, along with his brother and sister, became directly involved in theatre.

Though registered as an 'Irish comedian' on Louis' birth certificate, Frank Dalton was better known in Ireland and England as an actor/producer, and worked in such notable theatres as the Royal and the Queen's as well as travelling throughout Ireland, England, Scotland and America as a fit-up artist. Frank graduated at the old Theatre Royal in Dublin's Brunswick Street (now Pearse Street) where the stage director was C.W. Granby; it was, he said, 'the best possible school of its time for an all-round actor'.[2] His apprenticeship there took place in the early 1870s, a time of gas-light, stage Irishmen, pathos, patriotism and sensationalism where the primary function of drama was to satisfy the tastes of a largely unsophisticated audience.

Fifty years later, in 1923, Frank wrote of his early experiences in the Theatre Royal in the *Dublin Magazine.* He recalled that it was with 'a boyish insouciance, fortified by much inquisitiveness' that he took part in his first rehearsal there; he was no stranger to the Royal, having seen Shakespeare performed there on many occasions, but this was a day that was to remain firmly etched in his memory as it was the first time he worked with the actors he so admired. The article, 'Ghosts of "Old Royal"', captures the mixture of anticipation, awe and fear that he felt, and depicts his first impressions of Guido Linders, the stage director 'who could produce and prompt without book or script any play, tragedy or old comedy', and of the actors he would work with – Faucett Saville, Agnes Markham, Bessie Rignold, Mrs Huntley, Minnie Harford, Frank Huntley, Davy Byng, Sam Johnson and C.W. Granby.[3]

Frank subsequently joined the first stock company at the Gaiety, playing with actors such as Charles Matthews, J.L. Toole, Lal Brough, George Belmore and Ada Cavendish, before taking to the road performing with the fit-up company of Charles Dillon where he played the parts of Horatio and

Young Lorenzo, among others. After Dillon, Frank joined another tragedian, T.C. King, and then became associated in the Shakespearean line with Barry Sullivan, Charles Calvert, Irving, Lorraine and others. From here he then went on to play with Boucicault's company at York, where, we're told, 'I dropped the "Young Lorenzo's" and started the "Harvey Duffs" in which I rather unfortunately scored too well, and so became identified with such parts which at an age of specialism meant that I could get little else.'[4]

Nonetheless, Frank's admiration of Boucicault was immense. This is well documented in two sources, the first being a letter he wrote to the editor of the *Freeman's Journal* in 1906 in response to an address to an Abbey audience on 13 October 1906 in which W.B. Yeats outlined how he intended to create 'a genuine and new art for the theatre' by incorporating into the Abbey's repertoire translations of foreign plays that mirrored the peasant life of Ireland. Dalton urged Yeats to 'produce good native plays wherever he can get them', and not to ignore Irish playwrights; he singled out Boucicault, and quoted Dickens as describing *The Colleen Bawn* as '*The Vicar of Wakefield* of the stage'. 'Could the National Theatre', he concluded, 'provide us with another such, many of them would be quite content to let them shelve a very large proportion of their present stock.'[5]

In a second article written for the *Dublin Magazine* entitled 'Small Change and Boucicault', Frank reminisces about the Theatre Royal. Even though seventeen years had passed since his *Freeman's Journal* letter, this article is in line with his earlier criticism of Yeats: 'The utility of change, even small-change, is unquestionable, as the alternative means moral, mental, or physical stagnation; yet change merely for its own sake is neurotic, unbalanced, and, however small, will inevitably entail results out of all proportion and expectancy.'[6] Again he speaks up for Boucicault ('Our pride would be lowered, our dignity abated, should the name of Dion Boucicault be forgotten in the sociable city – Old Dublin') – perhaps not as a great actor, but certainly as 'a great retoucher', 'the master magician of stagecraft':

> An ill-balanced picture was a torture; gas he disliked; a dozen wax candles was his chosen light; even his name troubled him, and did not escape retouching. At school he was Bourciquoit; on his early productions it is Bourcicault; and later he expunged the letter 'r' – possibly to worry the Londoners. (282)

Dalton also details Boucicault's physical appearance, his personal style, his character, his acting abilities and his writing skills. A 'typical Dubliner', Boucicault's style of dress and physique were, however, distinctive and he 'would have appeared Parisienne [*sic*] to anyone who didn't know his Dublin.' He 'just miss[ed] being great' as an actor, but in artistry 'he was unexcelled'.

Clearly Dalton admired Boucicault and learned much from him about stage craft that would later stand to him when he toured and produced plays; however, his apprenticeship with Boucicault ended when Hubert O'Grady saw him play with the company in York and lured him away. The earliest written account of Frank touring with Hubert O'Grady's Original Irish Company relates to 1880 when he performed in *Eviction,* a play by O'Grady dealing with the strained relationships between landlords and tenants, dramatizing the consequences of the failure of the potato crop in 1878.

Eviction, which received its debut in 1880, was regularly performed at the Queen's Theatre over the following three years, and also toured Ireland. The *Irish Times* review of the Queen's production noted that the crowded house responded with 'warm applause' which, though frequent, was 'in some portions ... simply enthusiastic'. The audience, however, was obviously roused by the plot of the play which dealt with the fiery relationship between a landlord and tenant: when the actors came before the curtain, 'those who were considered to have acted cruelly were loudly hissed, the bailiff [Frank Dalton] crossing the stage amid a storm of hisses groans and cries'. Hubert O'Grady received acclaim for his role of Dermot McMahon, as did Mrs O'Grady who 'played with much merit' the part of Molly, his sweetheart. Frank Dalton was singled out for credit for acting his part as Rooney the bailiff.[7]

Soon after this, *Eviction* was taken to the United States. According to his daughter Babs, it was not long before Frank was fired from the company because he spoke up on behalf of his fellow actors about conditions of pay; however, Frank's version of events is much tamer: 'The tour suddenly finished when, with great good fortune, I met a dear friend, Frank Clements [who] introduced me to a Colonel Sims, manager of the Brooklyn Theatre, [and] I plunged from "Rooney" the bailiff into a round of French comedies and society plays, with Rose Eytinge, an American actress of the highest class, with whom I toured two hundred leading cities.'[8] There is no written proof to suggest that Frank's 'great good fortune' in meeting Frank Clements was because he had lost his job with the O'Grady Company, though Babs D'Alton remembers him telling her that Mrs O'Grady had fired him with the words, 'Be gone, needle-nose!' She also remembers Frank recounting that after two years working for Colonel Sims he was promoted to the position of stage manager where his duties had included collecting fines from actors who were not punctual, but because Frank did not like to do this, he was demoted again and so left the company and travelled America and Canada for a further four years, working for various theatre companies.[9]

Whatever version of events is true, by 1887 Frank had returned to Ireland 'homesick'[10] and had begun working with his sister Mrs Charlie Sullivan (née Marian Dalton) and her Irish Combination. Frank seems to have made his first appearance with the company in Tuam in early June of that year, when it was announced that Mrs Sullivan would be 'supported by the favourite comedian of the Dublin, London, American and Canadian theatres, Mr Frank Dalton'.[11] Originally trained as a teacher, Frank's sister Marian, had married actor-comedian Charles Sullivan in May 1886, his first wife, Margaret Seymour (sister of fit-up manager Guilfoyle Seymour) having died five years previously. Sullivan was one of Ireland's most respected actor-managers of his time. Having started his career working for companies such as Wybert's Dublin Gaiety Company and Fitzroy Wallace's 'Highly Successful Musical and Dramatical Cosmopolitan Company', in 1876 he decided to form his own ensemble. On 4 December 1876, Black's Hotel in Galway was the venue for the starting point of a tour managed by Sullivan; it was, he claimed, the first tour in Ireland of Boucicault's *The Shaughraun.*

The 18-strong company formed specifically to perform this play on the Irish fit-up circuit quickly became a success, and while some of its actors, including Mr and Mrs Cooke and Charles Dobell, went on to become well-known fit-up actors and even to set up companies of their own, it was Charles Sullivan who was most esteemed by critics and audiences alike. For example, the *Clare Journal* states on 22 June 1876 that as a delineator of Irish character, Sullivan 'has few equals on the stage and few better than he … His manner is easy and natural and wanting entirely in the forced and vulgar style so often assumed by characters when representing Irish life in the olden time'. The same paper five months later goes as far as admitting that the 'liberties' Sullivan takes with his *Shaughraun* are often improvements: 'the author himself could scarcely quarrel with the additions, not to say improvements introduced by this most amusing Irish Comedian' (10 November 1976).

Less than a year after their inaugural performance, Charles and Margaret were playing the lead roles of *The Shaughraun* at the Adelphi Theatre in London, and Sullivan's company, complete with new scenery, mechanical and lime lighting effects, elaborate costumes and original vocal and instrumental music by a string band, had made its name in Ireland, where local newspapers such as the *Waterford Mail* were dubbing the troupe's collective performance as 'the best of the kind yet presented to a Waterford audience' (9 April 1877).

The company had also successfully toured the States, and by 1881 Charles and Margaret had inaugurated a twelve-month engagement with the Queen's Theatre.

However, a year later Margaret Sullivan died of blood poisoning. This was 'a heavy trial' to Sullivan,[12] 'a terrible blow',[13] but he kept on touring and furthered his status in the profession, first by fulfilling a highly successful engagement at the Gaiety with Shiel Barry in 1884, and in 1885, in what must have been the highlight of his career, by playing at the Adelphi in London to a 'crowded house' who had gathered 'to witness his incomparable representations in Irish Drama'.[14]

The first mention of Marian Dalton playing in Sullivan's company is on 22 March 1886 when the *Freeman's Journal* reports that 'Miss Dalton was good' in her role of Moya in *The Shaughraun*, which had opened in the Gaiety Theatre. By this stage Marian had obviously waived her job as an English teacher in favour of the theatre, and in April 1886 she and Charles were married, although their marriage was a short one as ten months later, on 26 February 1887, Charles died in Liverpool, of Bright's disease. Charles left three children from his first marriage, and less than two months after his death it was announced that his children – Charles, an actor; Sarah, a harpist; and Ella, a pianist – would be taken on tour with Marian, by the children's uncle, Guilfoil Seymour, under the amended name of 'The Sullivan Irish Combination'.[15] It was soon after this that Frank Dalton joined the company, a move that must have been mutually satisfactory for the two, as Marian would surely have welcomed the support of her brother at this time, and Frank would have been attracted by the status of Charles Sullivan's company. For Seymour, it made eminent sense: for the troupe to continue its success, a suitable replacement had to be found for Charles Sullivan.

The company began its tour in May 1887 and it soon became clear that the new partnership was to flourish. Audiences, instantly keen to support the Sullivan family, attended the shows in large numbers, and it was Frank who captured the admiration of audiences and critics; they had 'no hesitation in saying that he could be favourably compared with Boucicault, Sullivan or Toole'.[16] Frank had thus immediately established himself as a worthy successor to Charles. A week later, the Sullivan Irish Combination played *Kerry* and *The Colleen Bawn* in the Queen's and returned there in September to perform *Arrah-na-Pogue* and *The Colleen Bawn* with 'real horses and cars' as part of their scenic effects.[17] The company toured Ireland until 1890, playing regularly at the Queen's, although Frank did make appearances on stage with other touring companies. Why Frank and Marion eventually left the Sullivan Irish Combination is unclear; the company was maintaining a high level of success and Charles Sullivan's eldest son was making a name for himself as a successor to his father. However, for a period in 1889, Frank and Marion played with James O'Brien's dramatic company, and while they may have simply grasped the opportunity to once again perform Boucicault at the Queen's, the move may well have been symptomatic of an uneasy relationship that was developing between the Dalton and Sullivan families.

It was in another fit-up company, Lacy-O'Brien's, that Frank was first introduced to a 17-year-old apprentice, W.G. Fay, who had just begun to tour with fit-up artists for the first time. Fay acknowledges in his autobiography that it was Frank Dalton, 'the best character actor of his time', who first impressed on him 'what a fine calling' the acting profession was.[18] Having accepted Fay as an apprentice, Frank taught him many performance techniques which would later greatly affect the acting style of the Irish National Theatre Society and the Abbey Theatre. Here is how Fay describes what he learned from Frank:

> He [Frank] was certain that one should study a part thoroughly before attempting to create it. He told me many a thing – as never to speak a line that did not mean something to me personally, always to think first of the audience, then of the play and my comrades who were playing in it. He showed me how to use inflexion when there was no other way to get variety, how to hold the attention of the audience when I was the speaker, and how to fade out when it was someone else's turn. Above all and everything he insisted that the audience had paid to see us perform, and that therefore every honest actor should see to it that they got value for their money. I never forgot this and I never will. Frank Dalton had himself in a lesser degree that great gift that Sir Charles Hawtrey in pre-eminence possessed, of holding your attention every second he was on the stage.[19]

This quotation not only shows us the methodology that Frank used; it also stresses the beliefs he adhered to, and it allows the modern critic to gauge the principles that lay behind the whole notion of fit-up drama, its primary one being to cater for the tastes of the mass audience. What Dalton stressed to Fay was an aspiration to give an audience a performance they could understand and appreciate; whether or not they understood the finer points of acting technique or dramaturgy was secondary. The audience would return if they felt they got good value for money, and for the fit-up actor/producer, there was simply no room for magniloquent dramatic experiment. Fay's remarks also show that Frank had very clear-cut ideas on performance technique, choice of material, and consideration of the audience.

In 1891 Frank and Marian joined McMahon and Liddle's Company where during the Easter season *Aladdin* was performed. A week later, the company was re-named McMahon and Dalton, but the partnership was short-lived as no further mention of Dalton is made in newspaper advertisements. (Interestingly, it was Frank's progression into production that associated him with another great Irish theatrical figure – Sean O'Casey. O'Casey's first steps into the theatre took place in 1895 when he acted the part of Father Dolan in *The Shaughraun* which Frank Dalton was producing at the Mechanics Theatre in Abbey Street. Frank's touring company was due to give this performance but at the last minute one of the actors became ill, and the 15-year-old O'Casey was asked to step into his role as he knew the play by heart.)[20]

By 1898, having toured with various fit-up companies, Dalton again decided to set-up his own company, 'Mr Frank Dalton's Dramatic and Unequalled Combination', headed by the 'leading actress Mrs Charles Sullivan'.[21] It played such stock dramas as *The Colleen Bawn* and *Wolfe Tone*, but it never became a touring success. A year later, in June 1899, Frank married Catherine Lynch. He had first met her at his sister's second wedding seven years previously when Marian had married a Northern Irish newspaper editor, John McAdam. Frank's friend Billy Lynch, with whom he had toured for a while, was Catherine's brother, and he had brought Catherine to the wedding. Catherine came from a conservative background. Her father, William Lynch, a furniture broker, was a wealthy man who owned a shop in Liffey Street, and a house on the North Circular Road. His eldest daughter, Anna, supposedly disgraced her father by eloping, and Billy, whom his father had expected to become a priest, left Maynooth Seminary at eighteen to tour with Frank Dalton.

The old man had died seven years before Catherine married Frank. A deeply religious man, and a strict Catholic, no doubt he would have disapproved of the kind of unconventional life Catherine would lead as the wife of a strolling player. Catherine's mother, however, was a kindly person and when Catherine gave birth to Louis, her mother minded him for two years while his parents toured England and Scotland. Babs, Frank and Catherine's daughter, remembers her mother telling her that she felt she just could not cope with a new baby on top of everything else, and so it was that Louis spent his first years at 14 Turlough Terrace, Fairview. However, when a second son, Noel, was born in Oldham two years later, Catherine and Frank returned for Louis. They continued to tour England, and had two other children, both of whom died as babies, before their only daughter was born on 26 September 1905 – Mary Catherine, known as Baby and later Babs.

Details about Louis' childhood are very sparse. His parents travelled so much that they rarely settled long enough in one place for the children to form lasting friendships. Because of this, Louis, Noel and Babs were very close, not surprisingly choosing to play with each other rather than trying to make friends with children they would soon have to part from. Indeed, in later life, Louis would always retain a certain distance from people, and consequently acquired the reputation of being slightly aloof. His novel about fit-up life, *Rags and Sticks,* mirrors the loneliness Louis he have experienced when travelling as a child. Ellie, the heroine of the novel, is particularly interesting as she is described by the narrator as a 'member of a restricted commonwealth of eight to ten people cut off by the circumstances of a nomad life from intercourse with the external world!':

> there were girlfriends with whom at times she kept up a desultory correspondence. These correspondences began with fine enthusiasm, waned rapidly and perished early, for the excellent reason that there was nothing to keep them alive. They had no communal interests to discuss, no matters of mutual concern. Once the company passed on, the brief seven days' friendship was severed and years might pass before they met again. Such friendships but served to emphasise the loneliness of her life.[22]

Louis, Noel and Babs must have led a similar life, attending various schools in England, but never for very long. Louis was apparently very good at Mathematics, and was told by one of his teachers to concentrate on this area and he would go far! However, his real interest was in drama, and from an early age he would write plays which he, Noel and Babs would act in, performing for their parents and any neighbours who were interested.

In 1912 Catherine Dalton returned home to Dublin for a few months with the three children. Frank continued to tour the English theatre circuit, but as many English companies took in Dublin, Belfast and Cork as part of their tour, he was able to visit his family during this time. Later that year he began to tour with John Brownson's Company and, some weeks after his joining, sent news to Catherine that one of the actresses had fallen ill. As Catherine had had some previous experience acting with Frank, on impulse she decided to join the company in England. Babs D'Alton remembers this time well. Louis, though only 12, volunteered to look after 10-year-old Frank, and 7-year-old Babs, until all three would join his parents a few days later. Babs remembers how Louis washed and packed their clothes and how all three got on the boat to go to Holyhead. From there, they were to take a coach to the train station and to travel to Manchester where Frank would meet them. However, when the children arrived at Holyhead there was no coach, so they had to walk to the train station, arriving when their train was just about to depart. When they got to Manchester, there was no sign of Frank, and after a couple of hours Louis left Babs and Noel and began to look at all the advertising hoardings until he found the name of the theatre where his parents were playing. He then went there, found out where they were lodging, returned to the train station and brought the children there. Frank had been waiting at the wrong station – it seems that Louis, at twelve, had more foresight and maturity than his father ...

During this time Frank and Catherine were performing in *Secrets,* a 'Celebrated Oriental Spectacular Play'[23] by Max Goldberg, originally entitled *Secrets of the Harem.* However, by the time the play reached the Lyceum Theatre in Gillingham on 11 March 1912 where it was to play twice nightly, disaster struck: the Lyceum, which had only recently been fitted-out, was totally destroyed by the fire. Babs D'Alton remembers her mother entering the bedroom in the lodgings where the children were staying, and telling them to get up. Such was the intensity of the fire that Babs thought it was morning, the front room of their lodgings down the road from the theatre being lit up by the flames.

A newspaper report covering the fire stated that the cast of *Secrets,* who had been playing a card game in a local house when the fire broke out, stood 'looking on as if they were stupefied'. Well they might have, as all their properties were in the theatre dressing rooms. The troupe of fourteen, which included an orchestra, lost £60 of property; none of it was covered by insurance, and an appeal was launched by a Dr Lord who was quoted as saying that 'many of those who cater for our amusement live almost hand to mouth, and it is impossible to aggravate the magnitude of this disaster to the particular individuals concerned'.[24] The appeal managed to raise enough to pay one week's salary per artist.

For the next couple of years, Frank continued to tour England primarily, with Frank Thorn's fit-up company. By now he had settled his family in Southend, where he would visit as often as possible at weekends. Once war broke out, travelling became more difficult and Frank began to experience the drawbacks of touring with a young family. In 1915, fearing that Louis might be conscripted, and concerned for the safety of his other children, the whole family went home to Ireland. However, Frank immediately returned to England to continue working. Catherine and the three children lodged in a house in Brunswick Street, and Louis secured his first job walking dogs for a lady who lived in Palmerstown, though soon after this, in early 1916, he was accepted to work in the Civil Service. He was fifteen years old, thus just qualifying the lower age limit for a position in the Civil Service, but it is unlikely that he worked as a boy clerk as his name is not recorded in any of the official records; his family maintain that he worked in the Barracks in Linen Hall, Islandbridge.

Not surprisingly, by far the most influential event of this time for Louis was the Easter rising of April 1916 (it would be the subject of his first novel, *Death Is So Fair,* published twenty years later). Louis was leaving work, accompanied by a friend of his called Gargan, to return home on a new bicycle, when they were unwittingly caught in the first throes of the rebellion. For years to come, Louis would relate to his family the horrific sights he witnessed, including the dead and injured lying on the streets, as he abandoned his bicycle and negotiated his way home among the sounds of shooting. Crossing over the Halfpenny Bridge, where he had to hide behind an advertising boarding to dodge bullets, he then ran down Liffey Street, crossed O'Connell Street, took off down the Lower Quays, crossed over to Ringsend, and made his way back up to Brunswick Street. How much of this event is accurately portrayed in the opening scenes of *Death Is So Fair* is difficult to say, but it is likely that much of what I quote here is taken directly from personal experience. Louis witnessed the following event (according to Babs) as he made his way to work on the morning of the rebellion:

> The tram rumbled citywards, stopping at Westland Row. Here a strange thing occurred; it was the precursor of events still more astounding. Half a dozen boys of varying ages, from fifteen to twenty, surrounded the tram. They wore a sort of uniform and were led by a young man wearing a Sam Browne belt, a slouch hat reminiscent of those worn by the Boer guerrillas of De Wet, and carrying a sabre of antique pattern. He was accompanied by a young lieutenant, similarly garbed, and armed with a nine-foot pike which he directed gravely at the tram, sentinel fashion, to bar its way. (2)

The narrator goes on to describe the disbelief of the passengers who are 'convulsed with joy', thinking it was a flag day or 'the Trinity students ... or the medicals ... they do always be great gas'. Even when the lieutenant, 'surrendering his pike to one of the youths, boarded the tram', the occupants are still slow to realize that this was not a prank:

> He drew a long-barrelled pistol from his holster and placed it at the big man's head, remarking as his did so: 'C'm'on. Get offa the thr-a-m, before ye're took f'r resistin' the aut'ority of the Republic. This is no joke.' The man rose hurriedly. He was heard to remark as he left the vehicle that if it wasn't a joke he'd be damned if he knew what it was.

> The bewildered passengers followed his example, the reluctant, protesting element being assisted with jabs of the blunt sabre … The tram emptied of passengers, a sharp altercation took place with the aggrieved driver, who opined that jokes were all right, but that business was business and he didn't want to get the sack for an Easter gift. A whispered conversation took place between him and the sword bearer, at the end of which the latter individual stepped off the tram and it began to move back from whence it had come. (4)

The narrator later describes a journey home that is remarkably similar to the sequence of events that Louis described to his family in 1916. Where the journey varies, it is possible that Louis includes here his friend Gargan's experiences, as they had lost each other in the furore, Gargan making his way up Grafton Street before seeking refuge in the Shelbourne Hotel.

> Towards four of the afternoon Mr Moody, crossing the Liffey by the Metal Bridge, was startled by the sudden screaming of machine-gun bullets, immediately overhead. He dropped upon one knee behind a large metal plate, which advertised a patent food. He listened, his heart pumping rapidly, to the metallic impact of the bullets against his shelter.
>
> They were firing … at him! Who they were he did not know.
>
> Glancing around he observed a crowd of men, women and children racing in dead silence along the quays … members of this crowd detached themselves and dived into laneways and by-streets …
>
> Feeling that he could no longer endure to be sniped at, with only a small steel plate to screen him, a solitary figure on a deserted bridge, suspended over the middle of the Liffey, he ran swiftly and gaining the Quay entered the shelter of Fleet Street, panting. (10–11)

This sense of urgency and fear continues to percolate the narrative. Moody hears machine-guns and rifles 'barking' from Trinity College, more machine guns 'drumming horribly' from Dublin Castle; in fact, the 'loud, shattering, insistent volleys' seem to follow him. This is all effectively contrasted to the silence of the white-faced crowds flying past him. Arriving in Grafton Street alone, Moody sees a man lying on the ground, writhing, and passes swollen horses that give out 'a horrible stench'. Then:

> A sharp cry rang out behind him, followed by a report. He glanced back and saw a solitary figure in civilian clothes spinning dizzily with

> arms akimbo. He seemed to be executing the fantastic steps of a negro dance, to the accompaniment of a brisk, staccato rattling ... He toppled abruptly. (12)

Moving on to Merrion Square, the narrator recounts 'the blurred nightmare of Red Cross nurses, ambulances, heavy firing, khaki-clad figures who pushed him along into safety, and people moaning in pain.' (12) By the time Moody had reached home, he was thankful to be still alive.

For Louis, who had undertaken a similar journey to his fictional character, the relief must also have been immense. Negotiating Pearse Street was dangerous, as snipers were in force here, but he eventually reached his house and found the family in the basement where the back kitchen was. Babs D'Alton remembers the days the family spent huddled in the kitchen and how, when Frank turned on a light, the house was fired at. So, they sat by candlelight and, once the candles were finished, Frank and Catherine tore up old vegetable boxes and used these to light a fire. Frank wanted to leave the house to see what was happening, but Catherine would not let him so, instead, he entertained the children with stories of his youth and with songs and ditties. However, the severity of the situation did not escape even the younger children. Babs, just eleven years old then, remembers looking out a window and seeing two women who had made it over to Boland's Flour Mills to look for some bread, but who were shot at on their journey back. Injured, they had to wait on the bridge for four hours – until they were rescued when the sniping ceased.[25]

Babs also remembers that their landlady called to the house with a basin of flour, some margarine and a two-pound tin of pineapples she had looted from 'Hunts', the local shop. The landlady also brought over some rum that she had taken, and Babs recounts how her mother 'slept for the day'. It was then that Frank, accompanied by Louis, took the opportunity to leave the house to see for himself the furore outside. The following passages from *Death Is So Fair* are probably based on fact:

> Curiosity again rose uppermost in his [Moody's] breast and he became an interested spectator outside of the sacking of a provision store, which was in the process of being looted. A tall, red-haired fellow led the dregs of slumdom in their predatory lust ... They were like famished rats that, rushing up out of the bowels of earth, and rid of their fear of the swift retribution of the law, fed frenziedly upon the prostrate body of the public.
>
> There ensued a pandemonium of destruction. Boxes and packing cases were torn down and splintered with bars of iron. Mounds of

> dried fruits strewed the ground and were trodden underfoot ... Tea-chests were torn open and sacks of sugar ripped up. Cakes of soap and cases of butter were trodden into the ground. Women fell and were trampled, shrieking, whilst others fought like a stampeding herd above them.
>
> The strongest battlers took what they wanted and made off with their spoil. Sometimes in their greed to derive the most from this unique occasion, they would drag whole cases away, which, proving too much for their strength, they would be compelled to abandon and dart back into the turmoil.
>
> Women, with hair streaming, fought and clawed each other for possession of certain coveted prizes.
>
> Some, filling sacks and pillowslips with food, stuffed their mouths with dried fruits, endeavoring to assuage their present hunger and secure their future needs at the same time. Everybody ate ravenously. Even the women who fought with torn faces, streaming sweat and blood, stuffed their mouths in the intervals of conflict ... A young woman, her blouse torn away, was stripped naked to the waist ... Her strong arms clutched her spoils pressing them to her round breasts. She laughed with mad joy and rolled her black eyes. Children writhed between the legs of the combatants and escaping destruction by a miracle, ate the foods that strewed the stone floor. The din was deafening. Screaming, cursing and reviling uprose everywhere. (13–15)

Another passage describes how sacks of flour were poured onto the ground, the crowd filling 'buckets, baths and utensils of all kinds with it', and how a large barrel of undiluted Jamaican rum, 'hundred percent proof' was rolled into the centre of the store – probably the same flour and rum that made its way to the Dalton residence. (15) Thus, it seems certain that young Louis' experiences of the Rising, and its consequences, shaped the opening chapter of his first novel. Moody, the central figure makes a comment that surely echoes D'Alton's sentiments: 'He would never see the like of this again ... never. He would see it all. In years to come he would talk of it.' (14) But for Louis, his memories would also hold one moment of jubilation. Passing by Boland's Flour Mills, Frank Dalton suddenly decided to help himself to the tricolour that flew from the flagpole above the building. Frank and Louis ascended the stairs only to find another man there with the same idea, but as the flag was too high for one person to reach, a compromise was struck whereby Louis stood on the man's shoulder and took down the flag. However, when handing the flag over, Louis suddenly thought that this man was about to grab the flag from him, and so he pulled it back, an action that resulted in the flag being torn in two. Both parties left with half a flag, and for years after the rebellion, when Frank toured Ireland as a fit-up, he brought his half with him, narrating the story and showing it proudly to his audiences.

The following year, Babs began touring with her parents as a child actress, and Noel joined the company when he left school. Both toured Ireland with the small family company until 1918. In the meantime, Louis continued to work in the Civil Service until 1921 when he left, apparently because he did not want to take the oath of allegiance to King George. He subsequently studied art at the Slade School on Kildare Street, contributed satirical cartoons to such publications as *Dublin Opinion* and worked as a bookkeeper for a short time in a small motor company. It was not until approximately 1923, that he finally followed in the footsteps of his brother and sister, and joined his first touring fit-up company, headed by Victor O'Donovan Power. Power, a native of Co. Wexford, wrote plays, short stories and novels, and acted and produced his own melodramatic plays, touring the provinces with them throughout the 1920s.

Louis played with various companies in the 1920s, probably the best known being Carrickford's Company, although he only stayed six months with this troupe. It was when travelling with Mark Wynne's Company that he met his first wife, actress Anne Mulhall. They were married when Louis was twenty-four, in the cathedral of the Assumption in Carlow on 9 February 1925. After his marriage, Louis became more and more immersed in fit-up life, setting up his own company with Anne which he called the 'Bohemian Players'. John Cowley remembers:

> Money must have been scarce because I often heard Anne tell about her father lending Louis ten shillings ... It was a case of sink or swim. If the people came in it meant they could pay the company, and move on to the next date with money in pocket.[26]

A report written at the time of the Irish cinema tragedy at Drumcollogher, Co. Limerick in September 1926 where over fifty lives were lost in a fire in a cinema mentioned that Louis D'Alton had been playing at the same hall for the first part of the week 'but business being bad, he moved out before the weekend'.[27] It was also at this time that the actor Charles Carey joined D'Alton's company, as confirmed by a telegram from Louis to Carey from the Abbeyfeale post office in Dromcollogher, saying, 'Offer two ten. Join Monday.'[28]

Soon after forming his company, Louis began to write his own plays. At first, these were stock melodramas, but according to John Cowley his company 'grew into a great success' because this 'made a big difference from all the other companies, who were all doing the same old melodramas'.[29] Eventually, Louis began to write plays that were good enough to be performed in Dublin's Abbey Theatre, many of them reflecting, in both style and content, the type of entertainment preferred by the largely unsophisticated audiences that fit-up artists played to. To illustrate the world Louis was so involved in, the next two chapters will detail the various aspects of fit-up life, an area of Irish theatrical history that remains largely unexplored by historians and theatre critics alike.

CHAPTER TWO

Fitting-up

In a letter written to Louis D'Alton in 1943, Sean O'Casey remarked, 'It is odd how Ireland likes the strolling player.'[1] Yet despite the popularity of fit-up theatre in Ireland, the real place of strolling players in the history of Irish theatre has yet to be established, let alone fully explored. Strolling players form an important part of Irish dramatic history, and an extremely unusual and interesting one at that, as the customs and traditions of previous ages were preserved in the many fit-up companies that toured Ireland during D'Alton's time. Because strollers were the most conservative of all players, the lifestyles and routines of many of the companies that toured the provinces during this time were in many ways contemporary reproductions of traditional strolling customs. And the staging and dramatic conventions remained with them long after new fashions in professional stage drama had come and gone.

In a similar fashion, the melodramas and farces which characterized fit-up drama long after Dublin stages had moved on to new genres may be of little intrinsic or literary merit in themselves, but any remaining repertoires of these companies merit examination as manifestations of popular taste. And though they may *seem* archaic and out of place, even for the times when they were performed, when studied alongside the contemporary social, cultural and political contexts, they can be understood and evaluated critically.

It is impossible to estimate accurately how many strolling companies toured Ireland in the nineteenth and twentieth centuries. However, I have deduced that during this time there were at least 250 such troupes, and probably many more.[2] The origins of strolling players can be traced as far back as Thespis who, according to tradition, took his actors around in a cart in 534 BC, which formed their stage. However, strolling players did not begin to become commonplace until the sixth century when the barbarian invasions closed the Roman theatres, and the dispossessed players had to wander around, entertaining in local markets (or wherever they could gather a crowd), singing, dancing, clowning, juggling and performing acrobatics.

The fourteenth-century Anglo-Saxon gleeman also could be considered an early link, although gleemen were of a higher class and were more respected for their poetic *songs* about local tribal history. However, it was not until the fifteenth century that travelling entertainers began to add plays to their repertoire. Usually consisted of four or five men and a boy to play female parts, companies performed mystery, miracle or morality plays. These plays became extremely popular, and as a result troubadours and jugglers diverted their talents to this new form of performance. This could be said to be the beginning of the fit-ups, as for the first time, strollers had to transport and erect temporary stages wherever they performed.

Travelling players were originally referred to as 'itinerant players', the title 'strolling players' coming into use sometime between the closing of English theatres in 1642 and early Restoration times. It wasn't until the nineteenth century that the term 'fit-up' became widely used, but there are many similarities between the travelling troupes of the seventeenth and eighteenth century and the fit-up companies that toured Ireland in the first half of the twentieth century.

For the most part, the quality and production of the fit-up plays performed in Ireland were far from city theatre standard. Quality was not, in fact, a particular of goal of strolling players, and while there were obviously different levels and calibres among the many companies that toured, the essence of these players lay not in their adeptness in imitating 'legitimate' drama (they simply had not the resources to do so), but in their ability to entertain those that had no other access to theatre. An article in the *Irish Independent* in 1956 encapsulates the basic nature of such players:

> Ireland is a land of strolling players, of little family companies who roam the countryside with fare at which the city sophisticate would look down his nose, but which pleases its audience mightily. These little companies never come near the cities, and seldom touch even towns, particularly the bigger ones. Outside of the areas they tour, they are often unknown. However, they fulfill a need, and often do it with surprising ability, for most of them, however humble the 'fit-up' have a streak of the artist in them.[3]

The term 'fit-up' refers to such strolling companies who travelled around with their own temporary stages, prosceniums and equipment for converting a space into a theatre, the name deriving from the fact that they erected or 'fitted-up' their own stage. An early Irish reference to a fit-up can be seen on an Ormonde Dramatic Society programme, dated December 1897, which reads:

> To Amateurs: First-class fit-up and Scenery for hire. Terms Moderate. Apply W.G. Fay, 2 Mander's Terrace, Ranelagh.[4]

Thus, the Ormonde Dramatic Society performed with the use of a fit-up stage, which Willie Fay describes, in an unpublished essay, as comprising a frame–proscenium with a landscape and wings to match, and a couple of interior scenes: 'These were for ourselves, but by hiring them out to other clubs that had none of their own I earned myself a few odd pounds during the winter.'[5] Indeed, seven years earlier, Fay had started his dramatic career touring with the fit-ups, but even before this he was obviously impressed with this way of life:

> My youthful indiscretion in trying to inflict plays upon an innocent public began at home in the 'Theatre Royal' back drawing-room. I made a fit-up stage for it with the necessary wings, and a black cloth, which I painted by tacking a canvas on the wall of the room where I was supposed to occupy my time studying for the civil service.[6]

As well as touring Ireland, Fay also produced plays for the travelling company, 'The Arts League of Service' in the 1920s, choosing one-act plays that were most likely to appeal to rural audiences. Evidently, his experience with the Irish fit-ups was a great help, noted by Eleanor Elder, founder of the Arts League of Service, 'It was he who urged us to ask for hospitality for our company on tour and laughed at our doubts. The Irish Players had done it in the past, and, as he pointed out, we could not hope to make both ends meet on the receipts from village halls without it.'[7]

In his autobiography, Fay explains the term fit-up as referring to travelling companies who: 'carried with them all the scenery and other "props" that they needed for their performances, and they fitted up a temporary stage or platform in any town hall, market hall, court house or other building at their disposal, in which there was seating accommodation for an audience'.[8] However, by the 1930s, many companies had begun to tour with their own 'booths' or portable theatres, wooden structures which, when pitched, had three walls and a canvas roof or 'tilt', which sometimes not only housed the stage but the auditorium as well. Erecting the fit-up was no easy job: Bob Bickerdike explains that it could take up to seven hours to fit-up the booth, and Paddy Dooley, who travelled mainly in the 1950s, noted that the problem with booths was that they were quite small: he remembers that he was taller than the front border, so that while the audience could see him, he could not see them.[9]

Travelling with the fit-up was also a challenge. Charles Brookfield, in his book *The Green Room*, paints an attractive picture of touring by train in 1879, where the carpet-slippered leading man would travel first-class.[10] However, travelling conditions were generally far worse than this, and some companies went so far as to travel with their belongings on their shoulders because they could not afford to hire a vehicle to convey their stock from town to town. O'Keeffe lists the various types of transport used by nineteenth-century Irish strollers as, 'the port chaise, the gig, the whiskey, the noddy, the single horse, the double horse, the car and St Francis' mules',[11] though strolling players of D'Alton's time found it easier to travel, and generally used trains or motor vehicles. One of the most unwieldy jobs was to load the lorry properly. Eleanor Elder, whose company travelled throughout England from 1919 to 1937, and visited Ireland twice during this time, describes the art of loading and travelling:

> Hermione and I usually travelled on the top of a large theatre basket, well under the canvas cover which was all the protection we had from the weather, and we were quite unable to see anything of the beauty of the country we were passing through ... The theatre ladders and battens were tied on the outside over the wheels, and on wet days had to be scraped clean of mud before they could be taken on to the stage.[12]

The 'fit-up' usually consisted of a large 'frame', a device which when erected, would facilitate the hanging of scenes and tabs (i.e. curtains). Companies would also have 'flats' which when tied together would make a room or interior setting of some kind. In *Rags and Sticks,* D'Alton's fictional account of the fit-up world, the narrator describes the art of transporting both the company and its effects. This account differs little from Eleanor Elder's experience in England:

> The piano and wardrobe baskets were arranged neatly on the floor of the lorry. Upon these were superimposed the rolled-up scenes and upon these again a dozen or so 'flats' or oblong wooden frames covered with painted canvas each ten feet high and four feet wide. On top of this erection the members of the company seated themselves.[13]

In a document entitled 'Report on Prospective Provincial tour', Ernest Blythe sets out plans for the 1940 Abbey provincial tour; under the heading, 'Fit-Up', he writes:

> To enable us to put on plays in a presentable manner in halls inadequately equipped for stage productions, it is necessary that we should utilise a fit-up; such a fit-up is to consist of, a light portable frame of eight pieces which can be erected on any stage to give an opening of

> 16 to 18 feet. It would also require a portable proscenium, wings, and tableau curtains. The material needed for the making of the curtain and the frame would, in the opinion of Mr D'Alton, cost about five or six pounds. Mr D'Alton would be prepared to supervise the making of the fit-up, and in his opinion all the incidentals and accessories for the fit-up would not cost more than ten pounds, including curtain and frame.[14]

Thus, the old art of fitting-up had changed little. Indeed, the routine of travelling, fitting-up for a few days, then travelling to the next town and fitting-up again, was also a standard practice over the centuries. The actress Shela Ward, who acted in the Abbey production of D'Alton's *The Man in the Cloak,* and toured with Louis D'Alton's Players in 1942, describes life on the road as 'primitive', remembering long journeys with the players jammed into lorries laden with sets and personal belongings, and setting off at four in the morning during turf-digging time because the lorry was needed to cut the turf.[15]

When a fit-up company would arrive in a town or a village, the actors first had to find lodgings, often having to walk around, knocking on doors. The more established touring actors would carry with them a record of the accommodation where price, quality and service would all be noted, along with whether or not the house was 'a good get in', that is if it could easily accommodate the big skip baskets actors had to carry with them. Often it was quite difficult to find lodgings. As Ward says, 'Some towns didn't like the players – they thought we were a queer lot.' As far back as 1881, the *Clare Freeman* saw the need to stress in a newspaper report reviewing the visit of Maggie Morton's company on 3 December 1881, 'We may add that the conduct of everyone of the numerous company during their stay in the town has been exemplary.'

It was not uncommon to sleep two or three people to a bed, and if board could not be found in local houses, the players would sleep on the stage. Ward remembers sleeping on ARP stretchers in town halls during the war, noting that this was often more comfortable than some of the lodgings they stayed in. Conditions in rooming houses often left a lot to be desired – Babs D'Alton remembers sheets which had not been changed, still stained with make up from the previous touring company, and Ward recalls how dinner was once served to her in a jug and bowl set taken from the wash-stand! Sanitary facilities were, of course, poorer then: in most houses the only toilet was the field at the back, and you had to go the local hotel for a bath, a luxury which cost a shilling, though it was cheaper if you brought your own soap.[16]

Once the travelling strollers arrived at their destination, or had decided their next port of call, the first step was to advertise their presence. In Elizabethan times, the bill-poster or publicity man would often arrange for circus-like processions through the towns to announce the players as they arrived. In nineteenth- and twentieth-century Ireland, some towns had their own billposters, but generally the baggage man travelled ahead of the company, erecting posters and booking halls. This tradition stretches back to the sixteenth century when English strolling players had to obtain a licence from the mayor or magistrate of every village visited. Then, two actors were sent ahead to circulate handbills and to 'take the town', as it was known (that is to get leave to play and to hire the barns or halls for the performance). We see a direct reference to this in O'Keeffe's *Wild Oats* where Lamb tells Rover that Mr Trap, the 'treasurer' of the strolling company has to 'take towns' as one of his duties.[17]

The actors who were sent on ahead were known as 'orators' and when the company arrived in the town, they would beat a large drum and distribute playbills to the crowds that gathered. The biographer of one strolling actress, Miss Farren, ascribes the tradition of drum beating to financial reasons:

> A very small number of Bills are made to answer the purpose of Announcing the intended Representations ... To make amends for this defect ... they distribute their Bills by beat of Drum, in order that their arrival and intentions may be known to every inhabitant. A Drum, on this account, always makes a part of the property of a Country Company.

He adds: 'Some companies which wish to appear very respectable add at the bottom of their printed Bills, "N.B., The Company does not use a Drum".'[18] However, it was much more common for companies to beat drums to advertise their arrival in a town. We see this practice in *All's Well That Ends Well* where Parolles talks of a soldier who has 'led the drum before the English Tragedians'[19] and in O'Keeffe's *Wild Oats* we are told that Lamb's strolling company, 'trumpeted' the companies' fame 'ten miles round the country.'[20] *Chambers's Journal* also provides evidence of this, where the portable booth manager 'fetched out a big drum, and thumping on it as hard as he could with one drumstick ... played the ghost of a tune on a shrill whistle' at the same time, in order to 'drum-up' clientele.[21]

In Ireland, the arrival of a company could also be announced by a bellman – normally the baggage/poster man. Bob Bickerdike remembers this tradition when travelling with his father, Professor Presto, who would book a venue for two or three days, cycling the second day to the next village or small town to book and bill that one. The larger towns had special bell men who would announce the arrival of a fit-up company, town-crier like, but their quality according to seasoned fit-up managers, was often unsatisfactory:

> On one occasion my father was so annoyed with the tinkling bell and the mumbling voice that he took the bell ... and bellowed with his voice trained to carry to the back of the theatre auditorium, 'Professor Presto, master of amazement, performing in the hall tonight.'[22]

Professor Presto also adopted a particularly unusual publicity idea by flying a huge kite when the weather was suitable, which carried the message that he would be performing that night. In D'Alton's *Rags and Sticks,* the actor-manager of the Superlative Repertory Players, MacTansey, goes so far to publicize his company as to 'call for mass', where everyone, Catholic and Protestant, is required to attend local mass. The reason:

> It jizzes up the business for the last night – gets ye a good Sunday night. Ye see, when people see the whole company turning up for Mass it makes a good impression. The whole district comes in to Mass and they see us and say we must be a refined, decent company and ought to be supported and then they pack in for last night. (141)

While it is not unlikely that some strolling companies carried out and believed in this practice, D'Alton, an atheist, never attended mass, so it probable that the narrative voice, which immediately undercuts MacTansey's philosophy, reflects D'Alton's views on this matter: 'This, of course, was quite untrue; but repeated disillusionment had not eradicated the idea from MacTansey's mind; it was one of his most potent superstitions' (141).

There are also references made to billing and bell-ringing in *Rags and Sticks* where we are told that MacTansey, determined to become an actor in his youth, had 'attach[ed] himself to a small touring show as baggage manager, bill-poster, property man and advance agent, receiving for these services seventeen and sixpence a week' (19). Perhaps D'Alton based MacTansey's background on that of his father-in-law, Mr Mulhall, a builder in Adare, who worked as a bill poster for D'Alton's touring company in the mid 1920s. D'Alton's first wife, Annie Mulhall, was thus initiated into the fit-up world through her father, and both she, and her sister, Kathleen, went on to became actresses, touring primarily with fit-up companies, including D'Alton's. It was also in D'Alton's company that Bill Costello, who went on to manage the Bohemian Players, a touring company which was at its heyday in the 1950s, started out in the fit-up business as a baggage man.

Willie Fay's first venture into the world of drama was as an advance agent, when he toured with J.W. Lacy's company, earning £1 a week. In his autobiography he writes:

> In most of the small towns, as I have said, there were no hoardings to exhibit posters, so we had to rely on getting as big a window display as possible to attract attention to our forthcoming visit. In the larger towns, there was a special man employed by the theatre called a 'bill inspector' to look after the distribution and display of the 'day-bills' or 'window bills.' He placed them in the same shops each week, and for showing them the shopkeeper got a free pass about once a fortnight. But in the small towns the agent had to do it himself ... The posting or pasting of the bills was a primitive affair before the arrival of the great bill-posting firms who had hoardings everywhere and would post your bills for you ... Instead, during my novitiate, each town had its own bill poster. This benighted individual, who was looked down upon by everybody, even by the sweep, made a precarious living by sticking bills wherever he could ... When there were no bills to post he would drive cattle to the market or pigs home from it.[23]

Fifty years after that time, Blythe also writes of the necessity of hiring an 'advance manager' for the Abbey Theatre tour of the provinces:

> that is, an energetic man who would have to travel one week ahead of the Company during the Tour. His duties would be numerous, mainly concerned with arranging a suitable shop to act as a Booking Office for Advance Booking, to inspect billing and to see that it was done thoroughly, to do publicity work with the local newspapers, to fix up advertising and to secure accommodation for the members of the Company; also to make arrangements regarding trains.[24]

Fit-up advertising was typically sated with hyperbole. Albert Daniels points out that phrases like 'Ireland's Greatest Show' or 'Presented at enormous expense' were common: 'It was always emphasized that the star of the act the audience was about to see, was brought solely for their enjoyment, and without any consideration of cost.'[25] Tatler's 'Leader Page Parade' in the *Irish Independent* on 29 April 1956 confirms that such hyperbole was common not only on posters. He recounts receiving a letter from a company manager who introduced herself as 'the head of the oldest known show people in Europe': 'For reference I was given the old Theatrical Section of the British Museum. The person's ancestors, I was told, built the Brancorvenaux Palace in Vienna, while her present day relations, it was claimed, include one of the most famous and distinguished families in the American theatre.' Tatler concludes the article with the ironic declaration, 'It would seem that not only players but history strolls our Irish Countryside.'

It is clear that competition was rife among fit-up companies. In the late nineteenth century, many companies highlighted, both in bills and newspaper advertisements, how their shows differed from others; for example, Dobell (who invariably publicized his arrival in a town with the rhyme, 'From North to South the cry they swell, Our favourite actor is Dobell'), made specific reference to the fact that a real steam-dredger would be shown at work in his performance of the domestic drama *Our Native Home*,[26] and the Belfast Dramatic Company noted in the *Westmeath Independent* how their show was 'patronised during the winter season in Belfast by the Marquis and Marchioness of Downshire, Lord and Lady Dufferin, officers of the Garrison and leading aristocracy' (who the company then went on to detail, in a bid to attract audiences). However, the same advertisement offers a more telling detail – that half price tickets would be available at 9.30 p.m., supposedly to 'prevent interruption', but it seems more likely that despite the grand patrons who had previously attended the productions, the company had difficulty in filling seats in the rural theatres of Ireland.[27]

An advertisement that is comparable in its lack of subtlety is that of Mr R.B. Lewis's World-renowned American Dramatic Company who visited Athlone for the week beginning 6 August 1894, announcing themselves as:

> 25 Artistes including a number of Real Freed Slaves who have appeared in all the principal theatres of America, Australia, New Zealand, India, Egypt, Japan, Holy Land etc. … Real Negroes – freed slaves, Mulattos, Quadroons, Octoroons and Creoles (Male and Female) in their Negro Songs and Dances, Jubilee Songs, Banjo Solos, Camp Shouts and Plantation Break-downs.
>
> The celebrated American Bloodhounds 'Sam and Kerry'[28]

In 1896 Dobell boasted 'new scenery and original mechanical effects' when he visited Ennis, although what is more esoteric about this announcement is the fact that it is stated 'Firearms and explosives are not used in Mr Dobell's performance'![29] A surviving 1926 programme of his astounding 48th year of 'uninterrupted' tour notes that 'an efficient actor is retained as understudy to Mr Dobell' – definitely a rarity among fit-up companies; moreover, – 'all intoxicating liquors [are] strictly prohibited on premises during business hours. No intoxication or disorderly persons are admitted, and very strict silence and order are maintained during the performance.' The programme is also interesting because it contains an advertisement for 'Clarkson's Lillie Powder for complexion' available from 'W. Clarkson, wig-maker, 41 and 43 Wardour Street (nearly opposite the Apollo Theatre, London)' and used by 'the ladies of the company' – a clever marketing device which not only highlighted an obvious sponsor of the tour, but also pointed out the cross-channel profile of the company, a fact which would have surely impressed rural Irish audiences.[30]

Thus, fit-up advertising was considered a crucial crowd-drawing stratagem, and was taken very seriously by travelling managers. However, if a report in the *Athlone Times* is to be believed, it seems that newspaper advertising was the most vital form of publicity for travelling fit-up companies. The article refers to R.B. Lewis's American Dramatic Company ('of more than average ability') who played to very poor houses in Ballinasloe in November 1892:

> the inevitable result of not advertising in the local newspaper … Managers of such companies have evidently yet to learn that the people who can patronize them so as to make their visit a pecuniary success do not stand at public house windows to read play bills. They look to local papers for them.[31]

However, most companies placed an equal emphasis on both newspaper advertisements *and* play bills, and the following re-productions of fit-up posters offer an accurate description of the type of bills circulated by Irish strolling companies. The first poster dates from the 1950s and provides a good example of such advertising strategies:

> COMING TO YOUR TOWN
> WILLIAM COSTELLO'S
> * PORTABLE THEATRE *
> In which he presents
> THE BOHEMIAN PLAYERS
>
> Please note that this is the only Modern Mobile Theatre of its kind in Ireland, and on all Irish Concern. Everything for your Comfort and Entertainment which includes the cream of Irish and International Talent in Dramatic Plays and 1st-class Variety.[32]

The poster goes on to list the 'Entirely Original and Comprehensive Repertoire of Plays, Concert items and Sketches'[33] and continues:

Several Others too Numerous to Mention. Each Play lavishly Dressed and Presented in First-class Settings, with up-to-date Lighting, including Unique Infra-Red Luminous Effects. Each Play Preceded by:

A FIRST-CLASS VARIETY PROGRAMME

And Terminated with A LAUGHABLE FARCE.

COMPANY INCLUDES: Kathleen Mulhall, Famous Dramatic and Comedy actress of the late Louis D'Alton's Company; William Costello, David Costello, The Outstanding Child Actor, Rachel Glynn, Vocalist and Dramatic Actress; Eddie Mack, BBC and TV Yodler and Guitarist; Tom Farrell, Vocalist and Actor, late Anew MacMaster's Company; Leyland Vincent, well known Actor and Monologist; Jacqueline Larblestier, the clever young Actress from Jersey; Moira Desmont, Pianist and Character Actress.

There are many other examples of poster advertisements like this. For example, the 'Richard Carrickford Repertory Company' billed a poster which boasted: 'Every play is presented in a manner befitting any city Theatre, all costumes and uniforms being authentic. Special scenery and lighting effects, and played in the Carrickford manner – earnestly, attention to detail, nothing ship-shod, by Artistes from Theatres of repute';[34] and the 'People's Popular Players', with whom Babs D'Alton performed, claims in a bill that its show was 'the finest and most perfectly balanced Company of first-class artistes that has ever toured Ireland'.[35] Perhaps one of the more innovative posters, however, was printed for 'Roberto Lena and his New Cosmo Players.' It reads:

£20 REWARD
WANTED FOR MURDER!
DEAD OR ALIVE.
What? Why? Who?
is
THE INFORMER
Roberto Lena and his New Cosmo Players
Present
THE PLAY OF THE CENTURY
To-Night at the Temperance Hall, 9.15
You may never again have this opportunity of seeing this Grim and stark Epic Story of Love, Hate, Cowardice and Sacrifice.
It Grips! It Thrills! It Amazes![36]

In *Rags and Sticks*, the Superlative Repertory Players advertise themselves on a bill that is modest in comparison:

> They are Coming!!!
> THE
> SUPERLATIVE REPERTORY
> PLAYERS
> featuring
> Ireland's Greatest Actor
> BARNEY MacTANSEY
> in
> a new repertoire of Plays, Farces,
> and Concert items.
> All Star Cast.
> List of Plays includes:
> MOTHER O'MINE
> A CONVICT'S DAUGHTER
> A MAN'S WORST FRIEND
> A WOMAN'S HATE
> POOR BUT HONEST
> THE IRISH PATRIOT
> And many others, etc.
> !!!RAFFLE FOR £1 EACH NIGHT!!!
> !!!YOU MAY BE THE WINNER!!![37]

D'Alton's fictional poster is interesting in that it highlights a raffle, which was a staple feature of most shows. Indeed, David Costello remembers that often the raffle would take in more money than the show itself, although Shela Ward asserts that when D'Alton toured in the early 1940s, he refrained from holding a raffle in order to elevate his show to the status of Dublin theatre where no raffles took place.[38]

Gallagher, the ventriloquist, placed particular emphasis on the raffle. In 1837, he advertised that a plumb cake, valued at one guinea, would be raffled,[39] and from 1855 regularly held 'Grand Prize Nights' where such treasures as 'a concertina, [a] half dozen silver spoons and [a] ladies work box' could be won by those seated in reserved seats and galleries, while those in the body of the hall could procure for themselves items such as 'a serviceable shawl, a fine hat and a handsome dress'.[40] He also raffled gold and silver watches – the gold watches valued at £8 given to reserved seats and galleries, and the silver one, worth four pounds, offered to the body of the hall. However, these prize nights often created controversy, and Gallagher had to advertise that 'two gentlemen from those present will be selected as "Drawers" and the tenth number drawn by these gentlemen will be declared the Prize for whatever part of the house the Drawing may be given.' However, the same newspaper reported the following week that:[41]

> Contrary to the pledge given in the public advertisement and to ourselves personally, did not call upon a committee of the audience to superintend the drawing – his own servant drew the prizes and no others besides himself were on the stage – for the watch (after the draw for the hats and shawls). Mrs McCabe of the theatre was found to be the fortunate possessor. From whatever cause considerable dissatisfaction was expressed by the parties in the house. We are not at all saying that there was anything unfair practiced but this much we do say, that Mr Gallagher should have fulfilled his promises.[42]

The likelihood is that the raffle was indeed fixed, as the advertisement of the previous week had announced that the watch could be viewed at Mrs McCabe's of the theatre. Gallagher discontinued this practice until 1859 when he one again began to advertise regularly his prize nights.

Gallagher, was not the only one to spark controversy through his prize nights; in 1851, the *Freeman's Journal* wrote that Pablo's Fanque's Circus was holding a conundrum night where a car and harness was to be given away, valued at thirty guineas, to the sender of the best conundrum. The circus had advertised in advance that if the winner was not present, the car would be auctioned and the proceeds given to charity. It transpired that the prize was won by fit-up actress-manager Emma Stanley, who had recently played in the Theatre Royal and who had submitted a conundrum: 'Why is Pablo Fanque's prize pony and car like a new laid egg? Because it contains a good yolk.' It had just been announced that Miss Stanley was not present to collect the prize, so it would therefore go to charity, when suddenly she arrived and 'proceeded to take possession of the car amidst a scene of terrific uproar' although in the end 'the fair lady [was] obliged to the firm decision of Monsieur Pablo'.[43]

Another travelling theatrical company to incur trouble over their raffles was Samuel Wild's father's show, which toured England. Wild remembers in the 1820s his father being surcharged by the taxman for not registering their horses and carriages, and so he began to give shows in the open air where there was no admission fee. However, tickets *were* sold for raffle prizes, and it was through this means that the family made their living from the profits –

that is until the authorities found out and Wild (senior) was sent to the Wakefield Correction for three months.[44] Generally, however, raffles did not cause so much contention. Babs D'Alton recounts how everything and anything would be raffled during the interval of a show, and indeed it was not uncommon for livestock to be raffled. She remembers a pig escaping during a raffle at the interval of one of D'Alton's shows, causing havoc as it ran amok squealing around the hall, knocking over the paraffin lamps at the front of the stage, almost causing a fire.[45]

Despite such calamities, raffles were to remain an integral part of the Irish fit-up show, generally taking place after the drama and before the 'laughable farce'. Bill Costello's son, David, remembers selling raffle tickets during his father's shows in the 1950s, for four for a shilling or ten for ten pence:

> My father used to have a display of the various prizes on offer at the top of the hall beside the piano. All sorts of gadgets were raffled, but the most popular of these were two inch high silver horses which contained a cigarette lighter in the saddles. Alcohol was never raffled, as the local priests, whose support fit-up companies were dependent on, would not have approved.[46]

Of course, keeping in favour with the local priest was important, as it was quite common for fit-up companies to use the local town hall as their theatre. In the strolling existence, historically almost any space would serve as a theatre: inns, town halls and other public rooms housed the more reputable companies, while the poorer travellers often had to make do with barns, stables and cowsheds. In fact, so many eighteenth-century touring companies played, and sought shelter, in barns, that they became known as 'Barnstormers'. By the eighteenth century, strolling players had taken advantage of the swift growth in the public's taste for dramatic amusement, and the most popular place for travelling actors to perform, especially in England, was at fairs. Fairs were popular all over England and many strollers wandered from fair to fair setting up booths and performing their 'drolls', as did professional players from theatres who performed during seasonal breaks when theatres were closed.

Fairs were common in nineteenth-century Ireland, and judging from Hogart's painting, 'Donnybrook Fair', there are many similarities between Irish fairs and their British counterparts.[47] In this painting, the only entertainment Hogart depicts is Irish dancing, though it is interesting to note the many drinking booths at Donnybrook Fair, which is probably what has led to the fighting we see. However, *Bentley's Miscellany* informs that some theatrical activity did take place at the fair in 1841, the year it was suppressed, though he describes the dramatic entertainment provided by the 'miserably poor' strollers (an incomprehensible rhyming tragedy followed by a lady in dirty white trousers performing a dance) as 'wretchedly fitted up'.[48]

It was around this time also that Samuel Wild visited Donnybrook Fair. He recounts performing there at his brother-in-law's circus, with his own brother, James Wild, who was a clown, and notes how receipts of the circus amounted to a staggering £125 for the first half day alone. He tells how the fair 'commenced on Sunday, immediately after morning service, and continued with unabated vigour until the Saturday evening following', and from his short account of his time at the fair, we can suppose that it did indeed have a reputation for roughness and drinking, for he specifically mentions that he did 'not remember to have seen a single blow struck during the whole time I was at Donnybrook'.[49]

The eighteenth century also saw a marked growth in the building of provincial theatres in Ireland and England, and since many of these did not have resident acting companies, travelling troupes could make use of them, although, for the most part, conditions remained very poor. The following Belfast theatergoer's depiction of a theatre is probably an accurate reflection of county theatres in the eighteenth century:

> It is impossible for ladies to go in full or half dress without the chance of their clothes being soiled or totally destroyed by the quantities of dirt and dust ... The gallery is so ill ceiled that quantities of punch and other liquors fall in copious showers on the unfolding heads in the boxes. The seats consist of ill-planned boards, destitute of covering. In short, everything in the boxes is finished in the shabbiest style.[50]

A century later in Ireland, many of the local towns halls were still inadequate to the needs of strolling companies and, in county towns there was often strife between townsfolk who demanded a new theatrical space and the authorities who resisted. For instance, the Athlone town hall was described in 1887 as 'repulsive and dirty looking' and 'falling into decay', and as far back as 1871 was deemed 'unsuitable for any kind of stage performance'. In 1888, it was declared that, as a result, 'strolling players or itinerant concert parties pass by Athlone being cautious of the fact that few entertainments draw a hall that would pay', a view iterated by the following comment made during a public meeting in 1880, 'We know of several companies who never survived a visit to this "ancient and historic borough"'.[51]

However, it did not follow that declaring halls in larger towns were of better quality, as we can see from notices on bills or in newspapers that local theatres would be well-aired or even disinfected. In fact, when a theatre space was comfortable, it deserved special mention: the *Westmeath Independent* on 6 January 1849 commented that the theatre where Mr Leonard was to make a guest appearance with Charles Cooke's company had 'cushioned seats, warm stoves, chandeliers, tastefully decorated walls and suitable scenery' which made it 'exceedingly comfortable', but it pointed out that this was unusual as 'many [companies] are prevented from visiting theatrical entertainments in provincial towns in consequence of the unsuitable accommodation that is offered.'

Provincial theatrical venues were still inadequate right up to the late 1950s: Bob Bickerdike recalls his company performing in the largest room of an empty house in a village in Co. Carlow, and on one occasion his father staging his One Man Show in a blacksmith's forge.[52] Billy Hayden remembers playing in one venue which was supposed to be a hall but when they got there it was full of potatoes; and Shela Ward recalls playing in a local hall that was so run down that one wet night, 'when the curtain went up for the play to start, the audience were sitting there with their umbrellas up'.[53] Similarly, Daniels recounts that a shed owner would normally use the shed for byre but when the fit-ups came to town he would 'evict the cows for a week and rent the shed to a touring show ... The seats were made up of butter boxes and beer cases with planks across. The stage was a couple of hay bogeys lashed together ... He also had a pub in the yard so everyone was happy.'[54] But for strolling companies who fitted-up in halls, the disadvantages were many:

> The majority of country halls left a lot to be desired. Most were in poor condition, cold, short of seating. Indeed, some had no seating of any sort. I witnessed the members of a company going around borrowing seats from the local people to help seat the hall for the duration of their visit.[55]

Right up to the demise of the fit-up companies, seats of different prices could be booked, even in run-down halls, barns and small booths where it probably made little difference where you sat. We see this practice in Hardy's *Far from the Madding Crowd* in the 'Royal Hippodrome' company's visit to the sheep fair, where Bathsheba is seated in a 'reserved seat' in the circus tent:

> This feature consisted of one raised bench in a very conspicuous part of the circle, covered with red cloth, and floored with a piece of carpet ... The rest of the crowded spectators [were] one and all

> standing on their legs on the borders of the arena, where they got twice as good a view of the performance for half the money.[56]

Up until the early nineteenth century it was customary, at special performances, to seat guests of honour at the back of the stage, where rising tiers of boards, placed in the form of an amphitheatre, accommodated them. An example of this, referred to in Clark, is when the local freemasons attended a performance in Cashel in February 1771. The masons, fully decked out in their formal attire, sat at the back of the stage, and the master mason occupied pride of place in 'a throne covered with a canopy of purple velvet edged with ermine.'[57] However, as Wilkinson remarked, such seating arrangements were not always ideal: 'Their heads reached the theatrical cloudings; their seats were closed in with dirty, worn out scenery, to enclose the painted round from the first wing; the main entrance from the amphitheatre being up the steps from the middle of the back scene.'[58] It seemed that pomp was more important to comfort for such men. Nonetheless, class structures continued to affect fit-up theatre right up to its demise. Carl Falb in his study of perhaps the most famous fit-up actor, Anew McMaster, states that when Mac played in the smaller county towns in Ireland, the local gentry would arrive by car and sit at the front of the house, whereas the townsfolk or those from the surrounding countryside would sit on benches further back. Then, at the back of the hall, it was common to see a group of men standing, as in church.[59]

Louis D'Alton describes a typical fit-up hall in *Rags and Sticks*, where MacTansey endeavours to instil similar pomp into the fit-up:

> At eight-thirty that evening MacTansey opened the door of Tubbermore's concert hall. By great exertions the fit-up had been erected in record time. The hall was long and narrow with seating accommodation for a hundred and fifty people. The cheaper patrons were expected to stand. The stage, which occupied the end of the hall furthest from the entrance, was a solid structure stretching from wall to wall. Upon it MacTansey's fit-up appeared to unusual advantage. The front scene or act drop (in fit-up terminology 'The Rag') was an ornate colourful conception depicting an Irish Wolfhound reposing at the base of a Round Tower and backed by a flamboyant sunset. Billowing painted curtains swooped down, partly obscuring the scene and were caught up in voluptuous folds by heavy gold ropes, from which hung huge tassels. (87)

This description is an accurate portrayal of a fit-up; however, it is also interesting to note how the narrative voice in *Rags and Sticks* interjects irony into such descriptions in order to present a more realistic picture. Thus, these billowing, ornate, curtains merely allude to grandeur, since they are only painted; protruding from behind this camouflage is the more humble reality: 'The space on either side of the act drop was masked with dusty velvet curtains.' However, we cannot deny the escapism that was provided by the fit-ups and their plays, and although the settings, costumes and props may not have been first-class, the audiences were easily impressed, and it is little wonder, as for many people, the arrival of a group of strolling players would be the only diversion for months on end. The glamour of the stage fitted-up in a normally dusty, neglected hall must have been quite a sight. D'Alton creates this atmosphere in *Rags and Sticks* by having a 'little brown-eyed boy gaze wistfully' at the stage from the back of the hall:

> Lit with a dozen paraffin lamps for footlights it presented an effect of tawdry magnificence and opulent colour. All the light was concentrated upon the scene, there being no other illumination in the hall. The act drop glowed like a jewel at the bottom of a dark pit. (87)

If turning a dirty space into a theatrical venue was one thing, providing suitable costumes for all the troupe members was quite another. The shabbily-dressed strolling player Goldsmith encountered and wrote about in his Essay XXI, identifies the general deficiency in costumes:

> We had figures enough, but the difficulty was to dress them. The same coat that served Romeo, turned with the blue lining outwards, served for his friend Mercutio: a large piece of crepe sufficed at once for Juliet's petticoat and pall: a pestle and mortar from a neighbouring apothecary's answered all the purposes of a bell: and our landlord's own family, wrapped in white sheets, served to fill up the procession.[60]

In the nineteenth century, many companies would stress in their advertisements or bills the superior quality of their costuming. Thus, advertisements such as Maggie Morton's 'Magnificent and costly dresses' or Colonel Reid's 'with historical dresses', were not uncommon.[61] Great care was taken of all the costumes because of their scarcity, a point emphasized by the strolling comedian Peter Paterson who notes in his memoirs, 'It is often difficult to procure the necessary dresses and ornaments out of the scanty salary obtained at a country theatre; hence each article of attire is rigorously looked after.'[62]

Almost a century later, the same problems faced Irish fit-ups. Larger companies like Anew McMaster's, whose repertoire consisted mainly of Shakespeare, could use the same costumes in all the plays, and Mac always attired himself, and where possible his company, in elaborate and elegant ensembles. Indeed, in the mid-1950s one of Desdemona's costumes served as a wedding dress for his daughter-in-law…[63] However, most of the smaller companies had to make do with costumes that were neither lavish nor plentiful. Shela Ward remembers wearing a dress which the leading lady had to wear in the next scene, and having it almost torn off her in the wings,[64] and in a well known fit-up incident which took place in Bushmills, Co. Antrim, around 1930, related here by Daniels, we see what happened when actors Charlie Doyle, Pat McEntee and their wives decided to produce an excerpt from the popular fit-up play, *Napoleon and Josephine,* complete with borrowed costumes:

> Charlie, to put it mildly, was a very rotund figure of a man, Pat was very slight, and when the uniforms were brought in they couldn't get one to fit properly. Pat's coat and trousers were baggy. Charlie's coat was tight and came halfway down his chest. The pants came half way up, leaving a space in between. This was covered by wrapping an orange sash around his middle. With bands-men's hats on their heads, they cut a most peculiar sight …
>
> The lights were switched on the stage, the audience went quiet, all was ready, and Pat, as a senior general in Napoleon's army, marched on to make the opening speech. That was as far as he got. The audience collapsed in uncontrollable laughter. Pat could only stand and stare at them and the more he did the more they laughed. Finally when they stopped for a moment, he stepped forward, and struggling for words, he came out with, 'Right, laugh, laugh at me, but wait till you bloody well see Napoleon!'[65]

The insufficiency of costumes and props can be accounted for two reasons; obviously the poor financial situation of many of the fit-up companies meant that costumes and props could not be treated as a priority, but we also cannot forget the constant travelling fit-up companies had to undertake. And while some of the companies could afford to travel in lorries, most of them had to travel by train where everything was packed in large baskets, one per actor, thus ensuring props and costumes be kept to a minimum. Nonetheless, certain companies prided themselves on an elaborate fit-up, special-effect props or extravagant scenery, and it can be seen from programmes and bills in the nineteenth century that competition between the various companies was obviously widespread. An 1883 advertisement in the *Kilkenny Journal* on 3 November 1883, announcing Maggie Morton's visit to Kilkenny, notes, 'Miss Morton has constructed the most magnificent new portable stage ever seen on tour. It is complete with traps and machinery and is so arranged that everything can be seen and heard equally distinctly from all parts of the house.' Seven years later, Rose Melville's company boasted in the *Ballina Journal* on 8 December 1890, they had 'toured successfully for a number of years and carry the most elaborate and complete Fit-up ever seen.' And a similar note carried at the bottom of an advertisement of Jennie Le Tellier's company in the *Kilkenny Journal*, 25 January 1888, boldly states 'N.B. The company carries their own portable stage, fit-up and scenery, suitable to the requirements of any hall, made with the latest improvements and effects, so as to be able to represent all the pieces in the same adequate manner as they do in first class theatres.'

Scenic effects were also a sure way of enticing an audience to a performance, and perhaps the most famous entrepreneur of special effects was Professor John Henry Pepper (1821–1900), one-time professor of Chemistry at the Royal Polytechnic, London, who devised for stage use a transparent ghost which was produced by means of mirrors and special lighting. The first appearance of a ghost illusion in Ireland was in September 1863, and the idea quickly caught on. That same year Poole and Young showed their Ghost around Ireland, their advertisement brimming with the usual fit-up hyperbole:

> Go to the Assembly Rooms, Imperial Hotel Cork and see The Wondrous Spectral Illusion The Ghost. The Great Scientific Marvel. The Ghost. The marvellous Apparition. The Ghost. The Wonder of the 19th century. The Ghost. The Astonishing Phenomena. The Ghost. The Great Scientific Triumph. The Ghost. The talking Ghost. The singing Ghost. The walking Ghost. The serious Ghost. The funny Ghost. The Mischievous Ghost. The riotous Ghost. The pugilistic Ghost. The Ghost that drinks. The Ghost that receives a flower from a living person. (*Western Star*, 6 August 1864)

Touring Ghost shows remained popular until the end of the century, and forged in provincial audiences a desire to see sensation on stage. But while some larger companies were able to present plays that demanded special stage effects, like Ghost shows or Dobell's 'realistic raft scene [or] the engine rushing along the rails',[66] the majority of both nineteenth and twentieth-century fit-up productions were far from technically proficient. Much more likely was the kind of set described by Hal Roach who remembers playing in shows where the set consisted of a table and two chairs, and when the scene switched to a castle or somewhere more exotic than the village cottage set, covers were simply put on the chairs, a table cloth over the table, and drapes in the background.[67]

Obviously the limited space in trucks or trains prohibited the amount of accessories that could be carried so, as Eleanor Elder remembers, it was common that 'a few folding chairs and tables turned up blatantly in every play'. She notes how a rostrum, six feet by two and a half, played many parts in its time, 'including a bed, a boat, a bunk, a table, a shop counter, a stretcher, a Roman wall, the seat of a railway carriage, a mountain top, to say nothing of heaven itself'.[68] However, a more common practice was for the actors to knock on doors wherever the company was playing, and to ask for whatever dressings for the stage was needed, ranging from tables and chairs to pictures for the walls, and even carpets, if required. In return for this, the providers, and often their families, would be offered free admission to the show. According to Daniels, this was a wily move: 'It meant that the entire family of the house, and their relations would attend the show, just to see their furniture on stage, and to hear their names mentioned when the boss of the show thanked them from the stage for their kindness, and as a rule, wisely compliment them on the quality of the items loaned ... And since only the best items of furniture were offered, the settings looked excellent.'[69] However, such ingenuity was not always successful, as witnessed by Val Vousden during a production of *East Lynne:* 'When Madame Vine threw herself across the dead body of the boy, calling out, "Dead! Dead! and never called me mother!", the bed unfortunately collapsed.'[70]

Lighting for the shows also had to be considered, and although some urban areas had public lighting (gaslight, electricity, or both), rural areas seldom had public supply, so people relied on paraffin oil and candles. In the eighteenth and nineteenth century, lighting was often procured from improvised candles made from linen rolled in tallow and placed in large potatoes, but as times changed the local halls began be lit by oil. Twentieth-century fit-up companies could not rely on this, and many carried their own makeshift lighting sources to augment the often inadequate lamps; and as many performed in sheds and other such make shift theatres, where there was no lighting, it was essential that they had our own lighting basis. Towards the end of the 1950s, lighting techniques had become more advanced. By covering a costume in sequins, and using ultra violet lighting, Paddy Dooley's company could produce special effects when required, such as ghosts or skeletons, as the audience could only see the costumes, and not the actors wearing them.

By the late 1950s, many companies travelled with a large range of different lighting equipment such as reflector lights, gantry lights, pim-wheels, flicker wheels or dimmer boards, the latter being either bought or improvized inventions. As Tony Glass explains, imagination was always employed to create the desired effect, as in the case of the vision of the virgin in his company's production of *A Song for Bernadette*. Here, the black cloth for Bernadette's scene had an opening in it which was covered with gauze so that when the actress stood behind this opening, the lighting would give the effect of a vision. However, lighting difficulties caused by locations that were not suitable for theatrical performances could never be underestimated, as the following anecdote about the British Adelphi Players reveals:

> We were touring remote women's Institutes in Scotland and declared in advance that our only requirement was a 15 amp plug. Arriving at one singularly out of the way spot, we were met by a young woman who, having welcomed us, added that she had met great difficulty in obtaining a plug … but eventually, an expedition into a town some miles away had brought success and here it was; and she held out the plug in her hands. There was no electricity in the village![71]

Despite all these difficulties, fit-up companies somehow got by, their priority being to entertain their audiences as best they could. In an unpublished play, *The Stroller* (also known as *All in the Dark*), Rummage suggests to Sir Frederick that he go back to re-live his early days as a strolling player:

> *Rummage*: Witness when you as a stroller had all the fine women – maids, wives and widows – in every village, ogling, sighing, weeping, fainting and dying for you.[72]

Though this response is somewhat exaggerated, it does, nonetheless, capture the fact that individual fit-up artists and companies were often held in awe by rural inhabitants who did not have access to any other forms of entertainment. When Charles Cooke introduced Mr Leonard, the Irish comedian, to Kilkenny in 1849, the *Kilkenny Journal* announced on May 12, 'the dullness of our city is about to be enlivened' – rather as the *Westmeath Independent* had reported on 18 November 1848: 'We are glad to perceive that the monotony of our town is about to be relieved by the performance of Messrs Cooke and Raymond's Corps Dramatique.' And the *Roscommon Journal*, 13 July 1844: 'Our little town has been much enlivened for this last week by the opening of Mr Stanley's theatre.'

As we shall see disruption of fit-up performances through over zealous audiences was still prominent in provincial Ireland right up to the 1950s, a fact that enlightens us as much about provincial Ireland as it does about fit-up theatre. In Hardy's *Far from the Madding Crowd,* Mr Boldwood, Bathsheba, and farm labourers Jan Coggan and Joseph Poorgrass, attend a production of *Dick Turpin and the Death of Black Bess* in a circus tent at a sheep fair. In a scene where Black Bess and Turpin are pursued by the officers, and the gatekeeper denies that any horseman has passed, Colgan, we are told, 'uttered a broad-chested "Well done!" which could be heard all over the fair above the bleating', and at the death of Tom King, Poorgrass 'could not refrain from seizing Coggan by the hand, and whispering, with tears in his eyes, "Of course he's not really shot Jan – only seemingly."' When the last scene came on, and the body of Bess had to be carried out by volunteers from among the spectators,

> nothing could restrain Poorgrass from lending a hand, exclaiming, as he asked Jan to join him, 'Twill be something to tell of at Warren's in future years, Jan, and hand down to our children.' For many a year in Weatherbury, Joseph told, with the air of a man who had experience in his time, that he touched with his own hand the hoof of Bess as she lay upon the board upon his shoulder.[73]

What is striking here is the unrefined reaction of Poorgrass and Coggan, and their incapacity to distinguish between drama and reality, arguing an ignorance of dramatic convention. Yet this unfamiliarity is typical of many a rural audience who had little or no access to theatrical entertainment beyond the rare visit of a strolling theatre group. Rural Irish audiences, almost a century later, displayed similar reactions to such plays, participating fully, and often inappropriately, in the dramas performed – even in Dublin theatres as late as the early nineteenth century, it was not uncommon for the stagehands to play their part in expressing disapproval. O'Keeffe, when recounting the trials young British acting apprentices had to endure, tells us how:

> In tragedy, if any of these would-be heroes succeeded, and had to die on the stage, the curtain was scarcely dropped, when those behind the scenes rushed forward with smiles and greetings to help them up; but if disapproved of by the audience, they were left to get up themselves, as well as they could.[74]

It was not difficult to gauge audience reaction in the eighteenth and nineteenth century. For example, in Belfast, in 1785, 'nobility and gentry from as far away as Kilkenny and Selkirk, Scotland' crowded into the Rosemary Lane Theatre to see the idol of London theatre-goers, Sarah Siddons, perform in *Venice Preserved*. An enthralled spectator colourfully describes the audience reaction:

> No one was disappointed ... Mother snivelled, Major Leslie cried and damned the play, W. Cunningham rubbed his legs and changed his posture, a Miss Aderton was really taken out in convulsions, and Miss. Lewis, now Mrs Britt, left the house and is present in danger of a miscarriage.

The same spectator describes similar reaction to Siddon's 1785 performance in *The Fatal Marriage*:

> Five ladies were taken out fainting in the last act, and hardly a man could stand it. Sam [i.e. Sam McTier, her husband] cried for half an hour after he went to bed, and many others who withstood it in the house gave up for tears after they went home.[75]

As late as 1927 audiences still immersed themselves fully in the fit-up drama they watched, exemplified in W.G. Fay's account of a performance of *Maria Martin* he attended where the audience numbered 'about two thousand':

> It was amusing to me; to my neighbours it was real life. They cheered, they laughed, they cried, and as they streamed from the theatre on their way home one could feel that to them it had been a very eventful evening.[76]

When placed alongside these two accounts, D'Alton's fictional depiction of the audience's reaction towards the handsome English actor, Eugene Forden, in *Rags and Sticks*, seems, ironically, to be the more realistic of the three. Here is a describtion of the audience response to Forden's portrayal of Marcus Superbus in the popular fit-up play, *Sign of the Cross*:

> An absorbed hush took possession of the audience. It held them to the end of the play ... The audience, more than half of whom had come directly from working in the fields, were moved by the grace and dignity of Forden's bearing. As the play proceeded young girls

> and married women yearned towards him with secret passion and eyes that were veiled with thoughts of love. In the grip of an intense absorption the entire audience seemed to breathe in unison, to sigh and sway in anguish when the tragedy of the play moved them. They were like people dominated by some unfamiliar, sweet but yet agonising experience. At times there was a shuffling sound at the back of the hall when someone who had grown cramped from standing changed feet. It would be stilled at once by an angry hissing 'Hush!' from those about him ...
>
> In a dimly-lit scene they saw the drunken Marcus attempt the rape of Mercia, and so tense was the emotion engendered in many of the women that they could not bear to watch it but bit their lips tightly and closed their swooning eyes. A young girl gripped her breasts in agony and moaned faintly. Men clenched their knotted hands and stared fixedly as if they were in pain ... The curtain fell in an unbroken silence. (115–16)

Indeed, most fit-up veterans could recount many incidences that confirm the extent to which audiences became absorbed in the drama. This was not just an eighteenth- or nineteenth-century phenomenon: fit-up audiences, even in the mid twentieth century, were just as likely to become personally involved in a performance, due to excitement or naïveté. Fred Spangle, who toured in the nineteenth century notes of his audiences, 'Those who had handkerchiefs waved them – those who had umbrellas put them up in their excitement – those who had neither jumped on their seats and stamped their feet, like wild Indians performing a native war dance.'[77]

However, it was not merely the excitement of a travelling theatre company that elicited this response; as twentieth-century fit-up artist Tony Glass observes, 'People really believed what they were seeing.' He remembers playing the role of Kevin Barry alongside Jimmy McFadden who was playing a British Soldier, and who had to beat him up. It was at this point that a woman from the front of the audience mounted the stage and started beating McFadden with her umbrella. He also remembers audiences shouting at the stage, pantomime like, to warn a character of coming dangers, and recounts how an actor playing a Black and Tan was not spoken to by the townspeople after the show.[78]

Similarly, when *A Song for Bernadette* was performed, the audience used to say the rosary,[79] and Treasa Davison, talking about audience reaction to Anew McMaster, noted that audiences accepted Shakespeare as if it was real life. She remembers playing in *Othello* and her landlady chiding her: 'I'm surprised you had anything to do with that fellow.' A similar incident happened to

Vernon Hayden when he was acting in *The Lodger*, a play about Jack the Ripper. After a performance he went back to his digs to find he had been locked out. A window opened and he shouted up, 'I'm only the lodger' to which a voice bellowed down, 'Oh no you're not. I saw you tonight. You couldn't do it if it wasn't in you.' And Hal Roach remembers playing with George Daniels, and lodging about four miles outside Bruree with 'a really old fashioned lady' called Minnie Carroll. Though she had never been to Limerick, or travelled on a train or a bus, he persuaded her to go with him to the show where he was performing as a magician. But, when he got home, he discovered she had locked him out and left his clothes outside, as she 'really believed [he] was a supernatural being that could eat fire and razor blades'. His performance led her to conclude that he was the devil and, according to Roach, she even had the house exorcised because he had stood in it.[80]

The explanation for such credulity must undoubtedly be that, in the remoter parts of Ireland, people were totally unexposed to drama, except for these rare fit-up visits, and thus were more likely to take what they saw at face value. Perhaps Anew McMaster best summed up this susceptibility when he told actress Dorothy Primrose that, often, rural Irish audiences simply had no idea how a Shakespearean play was going to finish. Touring in Ireland, playing the remotest villages, was MacMaster's favourite way of acting, and when audiences shouted advice to him on stage, he was apparently often tempted to take it!

However, audiences were not always appreciative of fit-up drama. Throughout their existence, strolling companies had to battle continually against their own poor reputation caused by puritan opposition or public disapproval. In England, a statute of 1572, which branded unlicensed players 'rogues, vagabonds and sturdy beggars', changed little over two centuries, whereas in Ireland the greatest detractors of fit-up companies were undoubtedly the clergy. Priests had an enormous, though far from popular, hold on Irish fit-up companies in Ireland, especially provincial Ireland. Ironically, it was the clergy who, in the thirteenth century, initiated formal dramatics here through sponsoring simple representations of the Biblical story in order to enliven religious instruction. However, a century later, when such representations had multiplied dramatically, many of the clergy began to regard them with suspicion, even though they were still under the auspices of the Church, and in 1366, the following resolution was passed by the ecclesiastical council of Dublin province:

> We distinctly order all parish priests of our diocese and province to announce publicly in their churches that no one is to presume to

> hold dances, wrestling-matches, or other disgraceful games in our churches and cemeteries, especially on the virgils and feasts of the saints ... [They must also forbid] such theatrical games and frivolous spectacles by which the churches are dishonoured, and the aforesaid priests must warn them [i.e. the offenders], under pain of suspension, and order them in future to abstain from such acts and cease from them, under pain of greater ex-communication.[81]

Thus, whereas in England strolling troupes had to petition for the right to perform, in Ireland it was the Church which held the power, for if a priest condemned a show from the pulpit, the results could be disastrous. It was probably due to this reason that many companies advertised the 'moral' elements of their shows, Gallagher going as far as to emphasize in the majority of his advertisements that his 'theatrical descriptions' were 'particularly calculated to attract the notice and support of those whose religious feelings forbid their participation of a more marked and decisive character', and Professor Pepper's Ghost added a notice to Clergy at the bottom of some of their Christmas season advertisements stating, 'It should be stated that there is nothing throughout this entertainment to hurt the sight or feelings of any religious sect during this holy season'.[82]

It would, however, be misleading to suggest that it was only the Irish Church that found the fit-up lifestyle and its plays unsavoury. In 1823 in England, in a diary written by strolling actor/manager T.H. Wilson, an entry notes the difficulties of counteracting the poor reputation afforded to strollers by the church:

> *1823. May 26th. Derby*: Bible societies religious tract and missionary meetings so debauched the minds of the Derby gentry [...] that forsaking the amusements of the theatre was considered proof of piety. The vile humbugs![83]

And in America, similar steps were taken by strolling players to try to circumvent trouble with the Church. Thus, in the nineteenth and early twentieth centuries, even a circus was never advertised as a 'show' or a 'diversion' of any kind, but as 'a Great Moral and Educational Exhibition'. Further, players would attend church every Sunday no matter where they were, and many even went as far as to paint biblical scenes on the sides of the animal wagons.[84]

It is thus not unsurprising to read in the diary of American strolling player H. Walkins that in 1846 when the young treasurer of the People's Theatre in Louisville, an Irishman, was stabbed to death, his profession worked against him. No priest would even pray for him, let alone allow him to be buried in consecrated ground, and the only person who would conduct a service was a Unitarian preacher. Walkins writes with disgust that during the ceremony, even this preacher 'took it upon himself to slander members of the [acting] profession.' Later that year, Walkins notes that an actor belonging to the American Theatrical Company died, and that there was no minister at the funeral. Instead the theatre manager spoke, 'very feelingly and with more sincerity than a minister would, for the latter would undoubtedly slander the profession'.[85]

One company that incurred the scorn of the clergy in Ireland almost a century later was the *Flash Parade*, a troupe brought to Ireland in 1926 by the male impersonator, Vic Loving. A male impersonator was bad enough; however, the company came complete with a line of bleached blonde chorus girls who quickly became the butt of much criticism from local priests. As Loving's granddaughter Vikki Jackson explains: 'They were the pin-ups of Ireland at the time. The local girls wouldn't be dressed like that.' The slightly risqué nature of some of the costumes made by Vic Loving allowed priests to castigate the show from the altar, referring to the company as 'The Flesh Parade.'[86] As Albert Daniels explains in his book, *Five and Nine*:

> In bringing her shows to Ireland she, unfortunately, had no understanding of the different attitudes of the public in Ireland at that time to the type of entertainment they were prepared to accept ... most of the halls around the 'thirties and onwards were controlled by the clergy. She opened in a small market town in Ireland. The excitement created by the arrival of the show resulted in the hall being packed on opening night. But when the curtains were drawn and the chorus girls revealed ... half the audience left the hall. (30)

In the same book, Daniels recounts a story that further emphasizes the local priest's authority over his parishioners:

> I was in Fermoy when ... Jimmy O'Dea opened to a packed house. The show went down very well ... but some busybody went to the priest and complained about some of the jokes cracked by Jimmy ... the priest spoke at early mass the following morning, and for the rest of the week, the show played to nearly empty houses. (58)

Of course, censorship was prevalent in Ireland during these times. In 1930, fit-up actor Charles Carey, who toured with D'Alton in the early 1940s, wrote a play *The Grass Is Tall*, and submitted it to the Abbey Theatre, which was then under the management of Lennox Robinson. In the author's note, Carey writes:

> Out of courtesy to Mr Montgomery, the [film] censor, scenes four and five are omitted, but they should be indicated on the programme as follows:
> Scene 4: Making whoopee
> Scene 5: Making more whooppee

In provincial Ireland priests were as influential as censors. The staple fit-up play, *The Sign of the Cross,* was undoubtedly part of most company's repertoires for so long because priests welcomed it so. Indeed, when Wilson Barrett first toured with it in 1895, clergymen were said to give sermons on its virtues, presumably due to its strong moral plot of a slave girl who converts a Roman patrician to Christianity, before both are fed to the lions! A poster advertising Annie D'Alton's 'Irish Players' visit to Roscrea in May 1952 (see p. 137 below) shows that even as late as the 1950s, priests were able to prevent the staging of a play they disapproved, as can be seen in a hand-written note etched beside the entry advertising *A Priest in the Family,* which reads, 'Banned by Fr Duffy at the Abbey Hall, but carried on at the Temperance Hall: caused a great sensation – had a packed house.' Indeed, David Costello, who toured with Annie D'Alton's company, remembers that when a priest denounced this play, Annie was so furious that she demanded a meeting with the bishop and indeed met him, though her remonstrations were to no avail.

The play, written by John Tunney and Ciaran Synge, was particularly unpopular with the Church, its plot revolving around an ambitious, single mother, Nora, and her two sons. One son, Sean, wants to become a priest, but Nora forcibly dissuades him from his vocation and he ends up an alcoholic. Her other son, Rory, is in love with a girl she disapproves of, and so she persuades him to join the priesthood in order to end this relationship. Rory eventually turns against his mother and leaves to work in the missions in Africa, despite her pleas for him to remain in the parish, and the play ends with Nora dying a broken woman. Rory returns home to be with her as she dies, and when she asks for his blessing, he gives it to her saying, 'May God forgive you for breaking up the family.' The clergy was more than likely reacting to the fact that Nora's situation as a single mother is unqualified, and that a man should not be seen to join the priesthood without any calling; however, the play was far more critical of the over-powering Irish mother than of the Church. Nonetheless, the local Roscrea priest obviously saw fit to ban it, although judging from the note written on the poster we can gauge that, in this case, the controversy caused did the company no harm at all ...

Another way to secure a local priest's favour was to put on a benefit night for the Church. Benefits for actors and actresses in fit-up companies did not prevail long in the twentieth century; however, the local priest, or 'whid' as he was known in fit-up lingo,[87] expected that a benefit night be held for the church, especially when fit-up companies were playing in local halls. Costello explains that some priests demanded a percentage of the total takings that the company earned during the duration of their stay, and the very least a priest would accept were the opening night takings, usually a Monday, which according to David Costello was a crafty move: 'This meant that he could announce the show from the pulpit the day before, and tell his parishioners that he would expect to see them all at the show the following night.'[88] Fit-up actor, Lawrence Hayes, confirms this practice, saying:

> We wouldn't *offer* a free night to the priest, but we would do it if we were asked ... You could bet though, that if you had a run-in with the priest, the next thing would be a visit from the sergeant. If you were in trouble with the clergy, as sure as anything you had trouble with the law.[89]

According to Babs D'Alton, Louis himself had little respect for priests because of the way they treated fit-up companies. She remembers his disgust at an incident that happened when he was touring with his own company. He was playing in a town at the same time as a local fair, and as a result, his audiences were extremely poor; so he decided to cut his losses and move on to the next town, and called into the local parish priest who had rented him the hall before he left. He explained to the priest that he couldn't pay him the fee for the hall, but assured him he would send it to him the following week. The priest was furious, but Louis explained that he had no other option. When he returned to the hall later that evening to collect the fit-up, he found it locked, the caretaker having been given strict orders not to open it for him. Louis then went to the police, but the local sergeant told him he wouldn't dare cross the parish priest. He kindly offered, however, to loan Louis the money needed, so Louis went back to the priest, gave him the money, and told him that if he had any conscience at all, he would pay the money back to the sergeant himself.[90]

Few show people had time for the clergy, though it cannot be denied that fit-up players occasionally deserved the wrath they incurred from the clergy and indeed the public, as there were a few charlatans who gave the profession a bad name. An example of this can be see in a report in the *Clonmel Chronicle* on 27 September 1877. A mimic, 'The Great Vance', was due to play in Clonmelon. He had been heralded by his agent ('the busiest of men'), who fanned 'public interest into a perfect blaze of excitement.' Vance had apparently won the special patronage of royalty, and was to introduce Miss Eunice Irving, niece of the great tragedian. The largest hall was hired, and on the night he was to play the hall was full to overflowing. Forty minutes late, the curtain went up, and 'out came the aforesaid "agent", now in swallow tails and white kids, bowing rather grotesquely to the audience, but smiling all over in the most gracious manner'. He introduced himself as Vance, apologised for the delay and said that the pianist and another member of his company were unable to attend, being detained in Limerick by a train strike. He had, however secured a local amateur pianist, and the audience, though disappointed, had to settle for this, that is, until Vance began to sing 'in a voice redolent of the very worst of Music Halls'. The audience soon began to complain loudly, and shout out that he was not Vance but an impostor, an accusation vigorously denied from the stage. Unconvinced, the audience demanded their money back, and was told they could get it at the door, but when they tried, there was none there.

What happened next, according to the reporter present, 'baffles description': ladies fainted and a young girl clinging to a bag supposed to be the night's takings, almost choked on the rings she had taken off her fingers and put in her mouth for safety! 'Vance' himself was lynched and pinned by the throat until the girl handed over the bag of money, which the sheriff took charge of, but when it was opened it was found to contain only six pounds: 'the great bulk of the silver must have been adroitly removed before the commencement of this remarkable entertainment'. Meanwhile Vance had escaped over a wall and caught the 3 a.m. mail train to Waterford.

Now, that's entertainment ...

CHAPTER THREE

*Under*standing and *Over*stating

'Nothing is *under*stood, all is *over*stated.'[1]

An eighteenth-century theatregoer attending a performance at one of Dublin's theatres would have expected to view more than just a play, as theatres at that time were not dependent on drama alone. Singing and dancing were included in the programmes, both as entr'acte entertainment and as part of the play itself; each evening's programme began and ended with orchestral music, and most of the full-length plays – comedies, farces and tragedies – contained, or were adapted to contain, songs and dances. This is a practice that Irish strolling players imitated and continued right up to their demise in the 1960s, and though some companies performed *only* dramas or *only* variety, the majority of them combined the two.

A typical fit-up show would run for two to three hours. Those that included both drama and variety would generally commence with an opening chorus, succeeded by variety acts where each actor performed a 'turn' for about five minutes (singing, reciting poetry, dancing etc.). This would take roughly an hour, and after an interval, the drama would be performed. For those companies that performed only drama, a different play would be performed each night the company played in the village or town. In larger villages, or towns, it was common to open doors at eight o'clock, but when fit-ups visited the more rural areas, the times of performances were very much dictated by the locals. Shows often didn't start until eleven at night in the summer months, the locals only arriving when their farming work was complete.

Apart from Holy Week, many companies toured year round, generally travelling on Sunday and performing Monday to Saturday. For these companies, the pace and rigours of such a schedule often meant that rehearsal periods were limited, and when a new play was added to the repertoire, the actors would often rehearse the play all day and stage the show at night. Probably this meant that some of the plays were shortened and, because most of them were hand-transcribed, many different versions were written. So while the basic plots of fit-up plays were the same, parts and lines were cut or added to depending on the requirements of the individual companies. Further, while better known plays such as *East Lynne* were scripted and learned, it was not uncommon for some of the lesser companies to resort to improvization if rehearsal time was against the clock; and while seasoned fit-up actors knew their parts, some new actors joining travelling companies were simply told the outline of a plot and were sent on to the stage to fill out the dialogue as best they could.

Evidence suggests that this practice was neither uncommon, nor frowned upon. In 1940s England, in a letter to Sir Barry Jackson, a Mr Norman Branson remembers a travelling company, Will Power's 'Plays and Players', which visited Middlesex in either 1943 or 1944. Branson notes how surprised he was to find the company paraphrasing the play, and concludes that this method 'obviously made possible the offer which Will Power had announced at the beginning of the season to produce any play anyone cared to ask for, or even to transcribe any novel which may be requested.' Branson then relates a conversation he had with Will Power who had scorned a recruit to the company, a young RADA graduate, who was obviously 'lacking in talent' because 'he had to learn the lines before he could act – he was incapable of improvising or of picking up a cue unless it had been previously learned.'[2]

In smaller companies, doubling of parts was often a necessity. Thaler quotes a letter written in 1748 to Garrick, where the writer noted how he saw a play acted in the country by strollers where 'from a Scarcity of Players, one of the Dramatis Personae has been obliged to act his own part, and read the other concerned with him in the same scene'.[3] Thaler also cites Dibdin, who writes that the stage manager of the strolling company he first played with, Gardner, 'played all the heroes, Falstaff, and the violoncello, set the accompaniments for the orchestra, taught the singers, and sometimes copied the parts, though presumably not at once.'[4] Branson's account of Power's 'Plays and Players' shows that many companies travelling in the 1940s still faced the same problems as their eighteenth-century counterparts:

> I can only recall there being four people in the company – Will Power, a youth, a middle aged woman of large proportions, and another slightly younger woman who had a very husky voice. They arrived in a caravan and trailer and immediately announced that a season of plays would be performed at the Jubilee Hall.[5]

We note the required versatility of the company members, as Branson goes on to relate that, when the pianist was required on stage, she left her piano, said her lines and returned again to her background music. Thus, it is probable that Lamb's summing-up of his role of manager in O'Keeffe's *Wild Oats* is fairly accurate:

> I am manager of the company of comedians that's come down here, and Mr Trap here is my Treasurer – engages the performers, sticks bills, finds proper properties, keeps box book, lights house, prompts play, and takes the towns.[6]

Indeed, this multi-tasking continued as late as the 1950s, as can be seen from an extract of the Century Theatre schedule which lists the various responsibilities the cast members had for the opening of *Othello*:

> *Iago*: also Tours Manager and Driver and Publicity Manager.
> *Cassio*: also a Senator; also member of erection/dismantling crew.
> *Desdemona*: also chief auditorium cleaner; also driver's mate; also on box office rota.[7]

Another characteristic of fit-up repertoire was that the main play was nearly always based upon the fundamental elements of melodrama and farce. In the nineteenth century, melodrama was by far the most popular mainstream dramatic form, but by the twentieth century its decline was evident, firstly in city theatres and some time later in provincial ones. However, fit-up companies in both England and Ireland, toured the countryside playing melodrama right into the 1960s, catering for provincial audiences who enjoyed this genre long after its more sophisticated city audiences had moved on. One possible reason for this is that twentieth-century travelling companies were particularly suited to this form of entertainment, and fit-up actors, like their nineteenth-century counterparts, were capable not only of acting melodrama, but also of singing, miming, dancing and even performing acrobatics if necessary. Of course, the term *melo-drama* means a drama with music, and as fit-up companies were rarely restricted to performing just straight drama, *melo-dramas* suited their talents where singing and even dancing were scripted as part of the play.[8]

Booth describes melodrama as being 'a dream world, inhabited by dream people and dream justice, offering audiences the fulfilment and satisfaction found only in dreams'.[9] He thus captures an important characteristic of melodrama, that it simplifies the world. As de Burca says in his tribute to the Queen's Royal Theatre where many fit-up actors performed melodrama, 'never the intellectual, something of a hedge school mamma you were, showing us the simple picture of right and wrong, giving us simple ideas'.[10] This simplification is largely due to the polarizations that melodrama embodies, to its heightening of emotions and its excessive representations of both situation and character where good invariably conquers evil, and where moral order is invariably eventually restored. There is also a distinct lack of any psychological complexity – as Brooks points out, 'characters represent extremes, and they undergo extremes'.[11] This is all supported by a style of acting that is suitably distended. In his Essay XXI, Goldsmith describes meeting a strolling player who describes the fundamentals of melodramatic acting:

> There is only one rule by which a strolling player may be ever secure of success; that is, in our theatrical way of expressing it, to make a great deal of the character. To speak and act as in common life, is not playing, nor is it what people come to see: natural speaking, like sweet wine, runs glibly over the palate, and scarce leaves any taste behind it; but being high in a part resembles vinegar, which grates upon the taste, and one feels it while he is drinking. To please in town or country, the way is to cry, wring, cringe into attitudes, mark the emphasis, slap the pockets, and labour like one in falling sickness: that is the way to work for applause; that is the way to gain it.[12]

Well over a century later, a similar acting methodology was still practised by Irish fit-ups. Indeed, the discrepancies between the naturalistic technique of acting applied in city theatres and the more melodramatic acting style of strolling players, is ironically portrayed in D'Alton's *Rags and Sticks* when the latest recruit, English theatre actor Eugene Forden, rehearses for the first time with the Superlative Repertory Players:

> It soon became apparent that Forden was completely at sea. He seemed quite incapable of the broad swashbuckling methods of melodrama, with its sweeping movements, its piled-up, declamatory speeches, its startling tableaux and situations. Everything he did was wrong. He spoke confidently and tried to infuse naturalism into the stilted dictions and outworn clichés. He was agonisingly conscious of the smallness of the stage and got in everybody's way. His easy natural attitudes seemed merely the expression of hopeless indifference. His leisurely enunciation slowed down the tempo of the scenes when they should have been crashing to a lurid climax. In vain did Mac Tansey perspire and repeat pathetically that it was easy; that all you had to do was to put a bit o' jizz in it and throw it off your chest. It was dead easy. Up and UP and Up and 'top' Vallance at the end of the act.

> What did 'top' mean? Forden asked.
>
> It was to raise your voice louder than the other actors at each succeeding speech.
>
> The rehearsal became more halting. The company were demoralized by West-end technique. In the end MacTansey dismissed them and hurried away to get a drink.
>
> 'I'm afraid I wasn't what you'd call a howling success just now,' Forden said.
>
> 'Howl louder next time and you'll be alright,' Vallance smiled.
>
> 'You'll get used to this kind of play,' Ellie said encouragingly.
>
> 'I thought this type of play was obsolete,' Forden said.
>
> 'All types of plays are obsolete or very nearly,' Vallance said. 'We are museum pieces.' (102–3)

This passage is interesting for a number of reasons: not only do we see the difference between city theatre and strolling methods of acting, and note the different type of plays performed by fit-up companies, aptly described by Vallance as 'museum pieces', but we also can gauge that while this passage is ironic, it is nonetheless a fairly accurate description of melodramatic acting. In fact, Owen Davis' description of early twentieth-century American melodrama is remarkably similar to the advice Forden is given by MacTansey: 'Instead of avoiding the obvious, you must insist upon it, first, last, and all the time. You must move up the ascending scale of emotions with directness.'[13] William Brady, writing of New York's Bowery Theatre around 1780, recalls the technique villains used when dying on stage – 'elbows stiff, spine rigid, then fall backward square on the back of your head. It took skill to do it right and not kill yourself in earnest'. Apparently, when one actor tried to die more naturally, he was hissed at by the audience until he reverted back to the 'stiffen up and crash method'.[14]

Irish provincial audiences were also used to melodramatic acting, and considered more naturalistic methods, like Forden's in *Rags and Sticks,* as 'bad' acting. Thus, when Grattan Dawson acted in *Othello* on a tour with Cooke's company, it took the theatre reviewer of the *Mullingar Guardian* to point out that 'we could not offer a better critique upon his style of acting than that supplied us by a gentleman who saw him play *Othello* here: "He is too natural, too real and seems to *be* the character he represents."'[15] The play that is being rehearsed by MacTansey's company and the bemused Forden in *Rags and Sticks* is *Mother o' Mine,* a typical tear-jerking, popular fit-up domestic melodrama, and the difference between the realist actor and the actor only used to melodrama, is made clear here:

> 'It's a really fine play – *Mother o' Mine*,' Esther said.
>
> 'I thought it terribly quaint,' Forden said. 'Some of the lines are extradorinarily funny. It must be a scream done seriously.'
>
> There was an icy silence. To refer to the Superlative Repertory Company's most consistently successful production as funny was nothing short of blasphemy.[16]

However, by the 1940s in provincial England (and probably a decade later in rural Ireland), audiences were more familiar with the realist revolution in theatre, and the following playgoer's description of a performance of *Smilin' Thro,* when the Will Power company visited Middlesex in 1943, shows that audiences were beginning to mock rather than revere the typical, struggling fit-up company:

> The orchestra consisted of a stout matron playing upon the upright piano, and Will Power in an open necked shirt banging away upon drums and cymbals.
>
> The set was quite nondescript and one which appeared to be used for every play ... The lighting was most elementary and, to my amusement, was operated personally by Will Power, who simply walked off the stage and manipulated the switches without interrupting his speeches ... Will Power, at one point in the play was apparently so disturbed by the boos and counter cheers which the youth of the village was directing from the back of the hall that he paused in the middle of the action to remonstrate with them in good round terms.[17]

Nonetheless, the audience in this case seem to be amused by the production, if not by the play itself, and that the hall is obviously fairly full, is an indication that such plays still drew in audiences.

The poor quality of the set and lighting in Power's company was another feature of fit-up theatre. City theatres were well-equipped, especially from the mid-nineteenth century when the mechanical innovations so central to melodramas were at their height – revolving stages, sliding trap doors, overhead wires, realistic sets and sound devices. However, most nineteenth and twentieth-century travelling companies lacked the financial resources to reproduce the extravagant staging effects of city theatre melodramas with their train crashes, earthquakes, fires and even naval battles, which in the early twentieth-century Hippodrome productions at London and Bristol were staged in tanks that could hold 100,000 gallons of water! Nevertheless, some of the larger fit-up companies did attempt to emulate the more elaborate city theatre melodramas, and like Maggie Morton's nineteenth-century fit-up, ensured that their stage effects were well marketed. When Morton's company played *Dangers of London* and *Is Life Worth Living?* in the town hall in Ennis in June 1892, she advertised in the *Clare Journal* on 16 June 1892 that the production would include a 'Real Steam Roller, Drawn by Real Steam':

> Five tons of gorgeous costumes, scenery, 20 Artistes. Orchestral band. Real mechanical steamer, an exact model of a Famous Atlantic Liner which sails majestically to the rescue of the Raft Becalmed – passengers dying of hunger and thirst. The Phonograph as a detector of crime, the unsuspected witness with its message from across the seas, testifying to the innocence of the heroine and the confusion of the guilty making the deepest impression of all. Photos of the phonograph and the steamer may be seen in Mr Nono's, Jail Street.

The same company advertised *The White Star* in the *Wexford Independent* on 27 June 1894, saying that Maggie Morton was 'anxious that Wexford should not be the only town to miss seeing her little gold mine', which she boldly described as 'the most perfectly realistic and elaborate scenic production ever placed before an audience'. Interestingly, a short summary of the play is also included in the advertisement, which shows the plot as being an obvious reworking of a typical nautical melodramatic plot, more than likely so as to make use of the same staging devices used by the company in their other productions:

> Steaming peacefully o'er the sea. The collision. Man the life-boat. Meeting of man and wife. Save the child. I'll perish. Struggle for the last life belt. Foundering of the vessel and rescue by the passing American liner 'Vancouver'.

For the most part however, both audiences and fit-up companies accepted that strollers could simply not compete with the larger theatres, and so in the twentieth century, advertisements boasting elaborate staging techniques died out, and companies concentrated instead on promoting the variety popularity of their repertoire.

No Irish fit-up company's repertoire would be complete without a selection of Boucicault melodramas. As far as indigenous Irish melodrama was concerned, Dion Boucicault (1820–90) was by far the most prolific and influential of Irish playwrights, but though his works were long applauded by audiences in the Queen's Theatre (home of Irish melodrama for almost a century), he later became a victim of popular taste, even though the work of some of our most acclaimed Irish dramatists were directly influenced by his dramatic innovations. Shaw and Synge owe a particular debt to Boucicault, as it was he who introduced native Irish drama and, as we have seen, O'Casey, who knew some of Boucicault's plays by heart, had his first theatrical experience in *The Shaughraun*. And while Boucicault undoubtedly painted a highly romanticized version of Irish country life in his dramas, swathed with sensational scenery and melodramatic action, his creation of the Irish Comic Rogue is surely his greatest, and certainly his most lasting achievement. Indeed, the characters of Myles-na-Coppaleen, Shaun the Post and Conn the Shaughraun influenced Irish drama greatly. We know that Frank Dalton was a very vocal admirer of Boucicault, but we shall see in subsequent chapters that Louis was also influenced by Boucicault's works and writing techniques, and that many of his comic rogues, especially the character of Cafflin' Johnny, owe their existence to Boucicault.

Given Boucicault's stature as a popular playwright in the twentieth century, it is hardly surprising that his melodramas were extremely prevalent and popular on the Irish fit-up scene, and continued to be long after his popularity dwindled in city theatres. Indeed, *The Octoroon* (1850), *The Colleen Bawn* (1861), *Arrah-na-Pogue* (1864) and *The Shaughraun* (1874), were staple features of a majority of fit-up repertoires right up until the 1960s, making Boucicault probably the most produced playwright on the Irish fit-up circuit.

However, imported drama was also reproduced by strolling companies in the provinces, and in the late nineteenth century, one of the most popular dramatic adaptations was Beecher Stowe's *Uncle Tom's Cabin*, a play equally favoured in America, so much so, as Rahill points out, that 'Uncle Tomming' became a profession in itself – 'even a hereditary profession like tumbling; children following in the footsteps of their parents'.[18] Indeed, Walkins notes in his diary that in 1852 he saw a production of *Uncle Tom* in New York performed by a travelling company run by a Mr Marsh who had made 'a small fortune with the piece'.[19] Three days later, Walkins attended another performance of the same show where a three-year-old child, playing Little Eva refused to finish her part declaring she did not want to go to heaven! But perhaps the most amusing anecdote is the 1891 advertisement of the same play which announced that alligators would assist the hounds pursuing the fleeing Elizabeth across the ice-blocked Ohio![20]

Domestic murder melodramas were also very favoured in rural Ireland, and while plays based on renounced true life murders like *Sweeney Todd* (George Dibdin Pitt, 1847) or *Murder in the Red Barn* (anonymous, *c.*1840) were staple repertoire right up to the demise of the fit-ups, companies and playwrights would also be quick to dramatize any local murders and perform them for as long as they drew audiences. Thus, the numerous murder melodramas that toured provincial Ireland were often a mixture of fact and fantasy, realism and melodrama. Take, for example, Martin Dobell's company who performed *The Love That Lasts for Ever* in 1912, where Dobell starred as 'the French Barber', a play probably based on *Sweeney Todd* as it was billed as introducing 'methods which are not quite compatible with one's idea of a comfortable shave'.[21] Norman S. Chantry and Company played Athlone for six nights from 29 August 1910, advertising their drama, 'The Beautiful Story of Mona – *Ben-Ma-Chree*', in the *Westmeath Independent*, imploring the local townsfolk to:

> See the mistaken brother. See the heart-broken Bishop. See the murder unpremeditated. See the mound. The sentence of perpetual silence. See the beautifully decorated altar. 'Worth in itself the price of admission.'[22]

We should not forget that while most touring companies performed in order to entertain, some performances placed their emphasis on instruction. Temperance melodrama certainly fitted into this category, and many plays concerned with the evil of drink toured the countryside regularly, although the motives behind some of these plays must be questioned – after all, the local clergy would certainly be more approving of temperance drama, and fit-up travellers found it easier to play in the many rural temperance halls if such a play was included in their repertoire. Maggie Morton's Comedie Anglaise company, who toured Ireland primarily in the 1880s, included one such play in their repertoire – 'Two Wives', described by the *Carlow Nationalist* as 'a drama admirably calculated to impress with the evils of drink', and by the *Kilkenny Journal* as 'one of the best temperance sermons that could be preached'.[23]

However, perhaps the most enduring and popular of all melodramas to tour the fit-up circuits in America, England and Ireland was the domestic melodrama *East Lynne*. Inspired by Ellen Wood's book of 1861, the first adaptation was produced in America in 1864, although most of the Irish productions would have followed T.A. Palmer's adaptation. The plot of *East Lynne* follows melodrama's usual paradigm. The heroine, Lady Isobel, duped by the evil Levison into believing her husband is having an affair, abandons both husband and children and leads a dismal life until she returns years later, disguised as a nurse, in order to see her children once again. However, her son promptly dies in her arms and she swiftly follows step after a tearful reunion with her husband. If the ending of the play seems decidedly out of character, as the faultless heroine and innocent child still suffer death, there is some compensation offered in that eternal bliss is promised. As Isobel tells her husband, 'We shall meet again in another world, and live together for ever and ever. Our little William awaits us now.'[24]

East Lynne contains what is surely the most famous line in melodrama, 'Dead! Dead! And never called me mother', and it, like many of the other plays mentioned here, is reproduced in Kilgarriff's *The Golden Age of Melodrama.*[25] However, I have chosen to analyse two fit-up plays which, though extremely popular, remain unpublished. Thus let us now turn to examine an Irish Political fit-up drama and a domestic one.

The Wearing of the Green

Cheryl Herr's essay introducing her selection of Irish political melodramas, explores why late nineteenth-century and earlier twentieth-century writers addressing a popular audience 'took upon themselves the task of promoting Irish Nationalism from the stage'. The question of politics and history portrayed in melodrama is particularly interesting when we recall that the origins of melodrama are placed within the context of the French revolution. However, Herr holds that, in Dublin, a theatregoer knew little of events such as the 1798 revolution except through theatrical representation, and that it was the blending of the melodramatic tradition with folklore, history, economic demands and contemporary events that created the Irish political melodrama. Political meaning, she concludes, 'came to a focus in the endless melodramatic replaying, from various angles, of the events of 1798'.[26] If, as she suggests, the plays created by the likes of Whitbread and Bourke for the Queen's Royal Theatre were fundamental to Irish audiences refusing to accept the 'truth' of historical events such as 1798, then it is particularly interesting to examine a play written about this revolution and performed by Irish fit-up companies until the early 1960s: *The Wearing of the Green.*

The Wearing of the Green, also known as *The Croppy Boy,* a patriotic play written for Irish fit-up audiences, was one of the more popular plays touring Ireland in the first half of the twentieth century. Though many versions of this play existed, it was originally written by the English playwright Walter Howard in 1898 and adapted for the Irish fit-up stage by M.F. Waldron from Ballyhaunis, Co. Mayo. First performed on the Irish fit-up circuit in Athlone in 1910, *The Wearing of the Green* probably has its origins, like Boucicault's 1864 melodrama *Arrah-na-Pogue,* in Lover's novel *Rory O'Moore.* The plot of *Rory O'Moore* is constructed around the historical 1798 rebellion, and included in this novel are some verses of the then popular rebel ballad, 'The Wearing of the Green.'

The Wearing of the Green thus borrows from literary sources and draws its theme from history, its hero being Miles Byrne (1780–1862), the Wexford-born United Irishman who fought at Vinegar Hill in 1798, and who was later sent to France by Robert Emmet, to enlist the aid of Napoleon for another rising. However, the mood of the play is very much derived from the anonymous rebel song, with its images of defeat and triumph, sacrifice, resistance and action. Boucicault re-wrote the song, making it even more revolutionary, and included it in *Arrah-na-Pogue*. The following version is taken from that play and was so strong in its attack on British 'tyranny' that after the play was performed in London, an official government edict banned it being sung in future performances in Britain.[27]

O Paddy dear, and did you hear the news that's going round?
The shamrock is forbid by law to grow on Irish ground;
St Patrick's Day no more we'll keep, his colours can't be seen,
For there's a bloody law again the wearing of the green.
I met with Napper Tandy, and he took me by the hand,
And he said, 'How's poor old Ireland, and how does she stand?'
She's the most distressful country that ever yet was seen,
They are hanging men and women for the wearing of the green.

Then since the colour we must wear is England's cruel red,
Sure Ireland's sons will ne'er forget the blood that they have shed,
You may take the shamrock from your hat and cast it on the sod,
But 'twill root and flourish there, though under foot 'tis trod.
When law can stop the blades of grass from growing as they grow,
And when the leaves in summer-time their verdure dare not show,
Then I will change the colour that I wear in my caubeen,
But till that day, please God, I'll stick to the wearing of the green.

But if at last our colour should be torn from Ireland's heart,
Her sons with shame and sorrow from the dear old isle will part;
I've heard a whisper of a country that lies beyond the sea
Where rich and poor stand equal in the light of freedom's day.
O Erin, must we leave you, driven by a tyrant's hand?
Must we ask a mother's blessing from a strange and distant land?
Where the cruel cross of England shall never more be seen,
And where, please God, we'll live and die still wearing of the green.

The play *The Wearing of the Green* re-works and channels these sensibilities in as rudimentary a fashion as the poem, through its inexorable nationalism and patriotism and its unyielding emphasis on heroism rather than on fact. The plot of this play, which is very much dependent on action, lacks any psychological motivation embracing instead the fundamentals of melodrama, farce, sentiment and burlesque. Herr points out that the heroes of Ireland's 1798 rebellion were 'almost immediately assimilated into the cultural standard of the martyred saviour',[28] so it follows that a melodramatic representation of such men would further inflate their qualities.

In this play, Miles Byrne is the typical brave hero, in love with the virtuous and pure Kathleen McGrath. The play opens with a scene where Miles' mother and Kathleen fret about the safety and whereabouts of Miles during the battle of Vinegar Hill. They look for information to the young stableboy Andy McGuire, too young to join the rebels, but eagerly patriotic and supportive of the rebel cause nonetheless. It is he who provides much of the action of the play and his role is a typical one in melodrama – to overhear and frustrate the villain's plots, to revere the hero and protect the heroine in the hero's absence, and to provide much of the comic relief of the play by courageously defying and relentlessly insulting the villain. Throughout the play, as in this scene, Andy supplies the two women, and thus the audience, with news on the rebellion and on Miles. Thus, the first we learn of the gallant Miles is through Andy, that he was 'foremost in the fight, and when he saw the day was goin' against us, he stemmed the tide, and turned the flood to Victory'.[29]

The tone of the play is thus quickly established. Miles is the gallant and talented hero, fighting for a cause supported by all the 'good' characters in the play. However, for each 'good' character, there has to be a 'bad' one so that the clear-cut ideas of right and wrong can be fully exemplified. In this play, the 'good' fall neatly into supporters of the revolution, and the 'bad' into the English or the Anglo-Irish, although two possible exceptions prevent the play from falling into blatant nationalism and stereotype. The first exception is Major Fitzgerald, an Englishman who is presented as having sympathies for our Irish rebel and for the cause, and the second, Jacob Daly, an Irish informer. Daly provides much of the comedy and farce in the play. His character is as two dimensional as his motives – love of money and lust for Kathleen – and though he is not excused in any way in the play, his cowardice and stupidity make him an almost pitiful character. For instance, in his first scene we are clearly shown that the women of the play do not fear him, and that even the young Andy has more wit and guile than he has:

> *Kathleen*: You'd be far better off fighting for your country instead of selling your soul for gold.

Daly: That's treason Miss. I'll be putting that down in my little book against you.
Andy: What is it you're trying to write Jacob? Is it your death warrant?
Daly: No, but maybe yours.
Andy: Faith! The day you'll be writing mine down, it's the white blackbirds with yellow tails you'll be seeing. Give me the pencil, and I'll write it myself.
Daly: No thank you. If there's any writing to be done, I'll write it down myself.
Mother: Leave us Daly.
Daly: Very good, I'm going, but if I hear one of you saying one wrong word against the red coats, I'll...
Andy: Put it down in my little book against you. (6–7)

However, behind the weak and gullible Daly lies a much more dangerous and hateful character – Captain Huntergown, the Irish-hating English man, and though he may no longer be the shifty, moustached, elegantly dressed, black-caped villain of nineteenth-century melodrama, he is nonetheless strongly stereotyped in this play and easily recognizable to Irish audiences as the wicked villain. Indeed, he is made all the more heinous because he is a distant cousin of Mrs Byrne, and thus of our hero, Miles. It is Huntergown who kills MrsByrne cold-bloodedly at the end of the first act: Miles has returned home, heroically putting his life at risk 'for the sake of a wounded comrade' (16); Daly has, true to form, informed, and Huntergown has found out that Miles is hiding in the barn. It is at this point that Mrs Byrne speaks to protect her son, in a tear-jerking sentimental scene designed to appeal to the many Irish mothers in the audience:

Mrs Byrne: Miles Byrne is my son. It is my duty to protect him.
Huntergown: Come! Speak you old hag, or by God, I'll transfix you to you own door-post.
Mrs Byrne: If you take Miles Byrne captain, it will be over my dead body.
Huntergown: Over your dead body let it be then.
(Sword through Mrs Byrne who falls) (20–21)

At this point Miles runs out of the barn, and is arrested and tied up by Huntergown, but suddenly Major Fitzgerald enters, and allows Miles pray over the body of his mother as long as he promises not to attempt escape. Once again, the audience is in no doubt about how to feel towards a character as Fitzgerald orders Huntergown to untie Miles saying, 'An Irishman's word is good enough for me.' (22) And as Huntergown is damned, Fitzgerald is firmly established as an honourable man. The first act thus draws to a suitable melodramatic close, with Miles kneeling beside his mother, grieving:

> *Miles*: Mother! Speak to me! No! She will never speak again. Laid low by the foul hand of the Sasanach. This is your work Huntergown, and I swear over the dead body of my mother, if I ever meet you alone, face to face, I'll take your murdering life. I'll have an eye for an eye, a tooth for a tooth, and a life for my mother's life. (22–23)

The second act, similar to many political melodramas, takes place in the courtroom where, predictably, the lying, cowering Daly provides most of the comic relief in his concern not to incriminate himself, blaming Huntergown for his deeds. Miles, on the other hand, remains the undaunted and gallant hero, and when asked if he is a rebel, replies, in a spirited speech surely written to promote nationalist feeling in the audiences, and one so popular with Irish audiences that it was often performed as a 'scena', a short piece performed during the variety part of a fit-up show:

> *Miles*: You ask me if I am a rebel? My only reply to that is, I am not a rebel. But, if to take up arms in defence of all one holds sacred, to right the wrongs practised on my country by yours, for the past five hundred years, so as to prevent loot, pillage, murder – if any of these things constitute a rebel, then I am a rebel, and am proud to be one. (29)

However, Miles is sentenced to death, although the Major does allow him a soldier's death and consents to his marrying Kathleen before the execution. The act ends with Miles professing his eternal love to Kathleen telling her, 'when I face the muskets of my comrades at dawn, it will be with one thought – of you, my own dear wife Kathleen, with one wish in my heart, may God love Ireland.' (33)

The final act of the play borrows broadly from Boucicault but though the denouement is similar, the action is different. In *Arrah-na-Pogue*, Shaun escapes from prison by dislodging the stone cell window, and rather spectacularly climbs the tower in which he is imprisoned. Like many other Boucicault plays, this sensational scene required elaborate stage machinery:

> The scene changes to the exterior of the same tower; the outside of the cell is seen, and the window by which he has just escaped. Shaun

is seen clinging to the face of the wall; he climbs the ivy. The tower sinks as he climbs.[30]

However, sinking towers were far beyond the financial reach of fit-up companies, so a different mode of escape had to be thought of. Thus, in *The Wearing of the Green*, it is the ever-resourceful Andy who concocts an escape plan for his master and, in a soliloquy, he informs the audience that he will tamper with the guns to be fired in the execution: 'Take out the shot, ram back the powder, and all that's left is powder and smoke that never killed a man yet.' (37) The execution goes ahead as planned, but not before the Major is once again given the chance to earn the audience's respect and, more importantly, to show up the English Government in the process:

> *Major*: I'm sorry Miles, but my Government would not allow me to take the hand of a rebel … but there is no law on earth which can prevent me taking the hand of a very gallant gentleman. (*Shakes hands*) (45)

Miles is fired at, but the plan has worked, and the final two scenes of the play deal with Miles' escape to France. Not surprisingly, Huntergown, almost manages to foil this and in a fast-paced penultimate scene, Andy allows Huntergown to mistake him for Miles, and in so doing sacrifices his life for him.

Andy's character thus shows itself as possessing the two fundamental traits of a melodramatic hero, virtue and innocence, and as such he is ready to die, the necessary pathos having been firmly aroused in the audience. However, there is another reason why Andy has to depart so stoically, namely that history has dictated the plot of the play, albeit loosely, and as Miles cannot transcend the historical process (as he survived the rebellion), it is up to Andy to fulfil the time-honoured role of martyr. Suitably, his final speech is the most sentimental of all, before his lifeless body is carried off the stage with the Irish flag draped over it:[31]

> *Andy*: Before you go will you bury me on the hill of Corrigan's Cove, and when you're over there in France, come down to the water's edge sometimes, and say one Hail Mary for me. I'll know you've said it for me Sir, for the waves will whisper it back to me. Mine was a young heart, but it beat true didn't it Sir, it beat true… (*Dies*) (61)

The final scene takes place at Corrigan's Cove. Daly, in an unexplained move, lures Huntergown into a trap where Miles can avenge the murders of his mother and Andy, the suggestion being that Andy's death has made Daly change heart and alliance:

> *Huntergown*: What's that bright object shining in the moonlight?
> *Daly*: That's the moon, shining down on the grave of little Andy McGuire. (62)

Miles fights Huntergown and kills him, and the play ends with the sudden appearance of the Major who confesses to witnessing the duel and to not wanting to save Huntergown. The Major and Miles part as friends, and Miles and Kathleen are left on stage as Miles speaks the final words:

> *Miles*: Very soon, Kathleen, we will be on our way to France, but let us hope that we can one day return to Ireland, and when we do, let us hope it will be an Ireland free, a people undivided, where we can walk without any fear of the wearing of the green. (66)

Given that audiences would have known that Miles Byrne never did manage to return to Ireland, these lines would have been particularly poignant. However, the fact that the audience knew the basic history behind the play, and were used to this sort of melodrama (either through fit-up productions or on a grander level, through the Queen's melodramas), where evil would eventually fall and good inevitably rise, they merely had to concentrate on enjoying the play. And as amusement was the aim of the fit-ups, both parties were happy. Though *The Wearing of the Green* does not, not surprisingly, survive in modern dramatic repertoire, and its success was certainly more theatrical than literary, *The Wearing of the Green* ends as the audience would have wanted it to, with all the wrongs righted, and with justice and bonhomie prevailing.

Pal o' My Cradle Days

Pal o' My Cradle Days, one of the most popular fit-up plays to tour Ireland, fits neatly into the category of 'domestic melodrama', and can be best described as a lachrymose sentimental play, aimed specifically at rural fit-up audiences.[32] It is believed that Mark Wynne wrote the original version when he toured Ireland in the 1920s and 1930s with his Celebrated Repertoire company, and although this version of the play is undated, references to electricity, and some borrowings from speeches from *Juno and the Paycock* would suggest that this version was written no earlier than 1928. *Pal o' My Cradle Days* focuses on a self-sacrificing Irish mother, Mary Cassedy, and her attempts to hold together a rather dysfunctional family in the face of poverty and corruption. Like all melodramas, moral appellations are recurrent from the start, and the characters in the play instantly fall into one of two groups: excessively good or overwhelmingly bad, the mother's unconditional love managing to conquer all adversity in the end.

The first act is set in a small cottage, the family home, which is about to be lost. Mr Cassedy, the head of the family, sits on stage at the beginning of the play and, addressing the audience, fills us in on the background:

> *Father*: Since I was discharged from Gallagher's, everything has gone wrong with us. Yes, discharged after twenty five years of service, and can't get a job since. Too old they tell me. Michael Anthony too, out of work, and my wife having to scrub floors and take in washing… This morning I got this letter from Peter Gallagher, the last appeal for his rent he says, and if not paid, out we go on the roadside. I was Gallagher's right hand man for twenty five years. I helped him build his business, and this is my thanks.[33]

With this, Cassedy informs us how a friend of his had suggested he steal what's rightfully his and, knowing the combination of the safe, he suddenly decides to take his friend's advice, and exits to commit the crime. Mary Cassedy and her daughter Moll now take their place on the stage, and immediately, the contrast between the anguished mother and the selfish daughter is set up, as Moll demands her dinner: 'For God's sake, Mother, get a move on it.' (3) Moll is engaged to be married to a pawnbroker, Frank, and insists on spending money on all the latest fashions, saying: 'Men are very scarce these days, and when a girl is lucky enough to catch one, she must cling tight, and not let go until he is hers for life.' (10)

The audience is naturally shocked by this behaviour especially as it has just been revealed Mary has not enough money to buy food for the dinner, but Moll is not the only problem – Mary's son Lar is just as selfish, and has just spent all his wages on an engagement ring for his girlfriend, Pat. We are no sooner told this than Pat enters, and as Lar introduces her to his mother and sister, she interrupts with a speech designed to appal the audience even more:

> *Pat*: No need to introduce me Larry. I can see for myself. Is this your fine home? And your darling grey-haired old mother? And your sister Molly – a lady you called her … Well Larry, my friends were right. They told me I was a fool to throw myself away on you. If you think I'm going to attach myself to a band of tinkers, you are

> very much mistaken. Here's your ring, and just remember that after tonight our engagement is broken, oh, very definitely broken. (*Exit*) (8)

Seconds later, Lar decides that he is 'wasting his time' (9) living at home, and leaves. Mary is distraught: 'He is a big loss. What am I going to do without his money coming in' (9), but Moll is unsympathetic and announces that she is also going to leave home. It is at this point that Mary's other son, Mark Anthony, makes his entrance and the audience can breathe a sigh of relief that all is not bad as he tells his mother, 'It's grand to come home after a hard day's tramp. I often think, Mam, that God knew what he was doing when he gave his man a mother.' (11)

However, this relief is short-lived, as the audience learns that not only has Mark Anthony not succeeded in finding a job, but that Mary has lost her job to 'swifter feet and stronger arms': 'Ah, sure it's a cruel, hard world when no one wants you when you grow old.' (12) With this, Cassedy re-enters, followed by a guard who accuses him of stealing Gallagher's money. Mark Anthony, the ever-dutiful son, steps in to take the blame for the crime, and is arrested. The act closes with Mark Anthony addressing his father:

> *Mark Anthony*: Come on now Father, hold your head up, look every man straight in the face, for no one can say a word against you now. (15)

The second act opens with Mary sitting at the kitchen table. She tells the audience that three years have passed since Mark Anthony went to jail, but that he is due to return home that day. As she looks out the window, awaiting his return, she sees a large car come down the street, and it transpires that the car belongs to Moll who had left home two years previously when she married Frank. The Moll we see in this act is even more monstrous than the audience earlier thought. She has not been in touch with her mother for all this time and is now a wealthy pawn-broker's wife who drives a daffodil yellow car, has a holiday home in Bray, and lives in a beautiful house where 'everything is run by electricity'. (16) Worse still (and incredible that an audience would be naïve enough to accept such an exaggeration) is her answer to her mother's enquiry whether her baby is a boy or a girl: 'Oh for heaven's sake, I don't know. I have a nurse to look after it. I'm far too busy.' (14–15) And when Mary tells Moll that her father is dangerously ill, Moll merely comments, 'He may as well go today as die tomorrow,' (17) and callously tells her mother not to pawn blankets in her husband's shop:

> *Moll*: It looks so bad in front of my friends. And another thing, please, please don't send any more letters to me asking for half-crowns. If I have any to spare I'll send them to you, and if you don't receive any, you'll know I haven't any. (17–18)

Moll proceeds to disclose that the only reason she is visiting home is to inform her family to stay away from her as she doesn't want anyone to know that her brother is a jail bird. As her role as a martyr dictates that Mary is acted *upon*, it is only after Moll's departure that Mary speaks to the audience saying, 'Poor Molly, how little she knows ... When her own selfish heart is broken with suffering, she will ... like many more, repent, when it is too late.' (19)

The latter part of the act sets the scene for this to happen as it deals with Mark Anthony's long-awaited homecoming. He tells the audience, 'it is only the exile who knows the true meaning of the word' (19), and informs his shocked mother it wasn't he who stole the money, but as everyone believes it was, he has no future in the village. Luckily, Mary had previously written to a relation in the States who is willing to house him, and so he leaves that evening to start a new life promising to keep in touch with his mother and to send her as much money as he can.

The third act takes place five and a half years later. By this stage, Mark Anthony's father has died, while Mary has lost the house and is now living with Lar and his wife, Pat. Pat is as odious as she was in the first act, and the only reason Mary is living with them is that she is cheaper to keep than a servant. Indeed, this is how she is treated by Pat, and throughout this scene, the audience shocked to hear Mary calling Pat 'Madam', as she has to. And when Moll calls to the house, Mary has to introduce her as 'Mrs Frank Freedman.'

The act continues in this vein, Mary's maternal sacrifice emphasized to extremes so that the audience can sympathize wholeheartedly with her. Unknown to Mary, Mark Anthony has been writing to her over the years, but Pat and Lar have been intercepting the mail and their lavish lifestyle is a direct result of the money Mark Anthony has been sending his mother in his letters. If there is any dramatic justice at this stage, it is that Lar and Pat are not happy in their marriage and Pat is scheming to run off with another man, but for Mary, life has become intolerable. She finally decides to leave, and in a speech which obviously found its inspiration in O'Casey's *Juno and the Paycock*, she makes her exit:

> *Mary*: Larry, my son, remember it was this old form of mine that gave you life, this heart that beat that you might live, these hands of

> mine that rocked your cradle in infancy, and taught you your first steps. And now I'm going to the only place my children have left for me.
>
> *Lar*: Where are you going Mother?
>
> *Mary*: Over the Hill to the Workhouse. (30)

However, seconds after Mary's exit, Mark Anthony returns back from the States and, in a front scene, rescues his mother just as she nears the Workhouse. This, as expected, is an emotional reunion, and ends with Mark Anthony telling the audience:

> *Mark Anthony*: A man may have many friends, a true and devoted wife, but he has only one mother, and to me she means the whole wide world. (34)

He ends the scene by singing the following verse:

> *Mark Anthony*: What a friend, what a pal. Only now I can see,
> How you've planned, and you've toiled so for me.
> I never knew what a mother goes through,
> There's nothing that she wouldn't do. (34)

The final scene is a happy denouement where previously unrecognized virtue is finally acknowledged. Mark Anthony has re-purchased the family home for his mother and Lar and Moll return home, transformed with belated remorse, asking Mary for forgiveness which she offers without question, though Mark Anthony thinks they should 'get down on [their] knees and thank God for having such a mother.' (37) Mary tells of how happy she is to have her children back around her, and the play ends with a direct emotional appeal to the audience:

> *Mary*: To you who are mothers, young and old, to you do I speak. You will know sorrow too perhaps – the parting of your loved ones for distant shores. Some of you here tonight have no mothers. Still, love her and cherish her. Remember she is the only one you will meet in this life who will love you with an unselfish love, forgive you no matter what you do. And remember too that no home, no fire side, can ever be complete without that friend, the pal of your cradle days. (39)

Pal o' My Cradle Days thus follows melodramatic dictates precisely, whereby virtue and innocence for the greater part of the play are enveloped by evil but, as the audience would have expected, the moral universe is eventually restored and all ends well.

It seems incredible that Irish audiences as late as the nineteen-fifties and early 1960s would welcome such poor drama, but the pathos created through the idealization of the village home and the Irish family in plays like *Pal o' My Cradle Days*, particularly the self-sacrificing, all forgiving Irish mother, was specifically designed to bring tears of recognition or lament to rural Irish audiences. As fit-up actor, Lawrence Hayes notes, 'We never played *Pal* without bringing tears to their eyes.'[34] We must also remember that audiences were not versed to investigate the psychology of the characters or plot; and domestic melodrama, like all other forms of melodrama, provided a world of escapism where obstacles could be overcome and dreams fulfilled. Melodrama portrayed a world of certainties and Irish audiences were happy with this.

Boucicault pointed out in 1877 that popular melodrama was a manifestation of the period he wrote in, but much of what he said can just as easily apply to twentieth-century Irish fit-up drama:

> There are three constituent factors in the drama: the author who writes, the actor who performs, and the public that perceives. Of these three, the public is the most important, for it calls into existence the other two as infallibly as demand creates supply. When our people shall demand the highest class of dramatic entertainment, a Shakespeare and a Garrick will appear. Until then, my dear friend, the world will rest contented with such poor things as you and me.[35]

The modern audience is now so far removed from melodrama that it seems farcical – extravagant, unsubtle and superficial. However, in its heyday fit-up melodrama provided audiences with what they wanted – escapism and entertainment – although the time soon came when audiences were offered many other forms of entertainment, especially with the advent of cinema and, later, television. These new forms of distraction caused the dissolution of fit-up drama; after all, setting, spectacle and sensationalism could be much more realistically and lavishly communicated through the medium of film, and provincial fit-up theatre simply could not contend with cinematic techniques.

So, as other forms of entertainment became more accessible to the provinces, fit-up companies began to decline. By the time television was available in the 1960s, audiences were finally drawn away from already emptying booths, tents and stages, and many of the most popular fit-up actors began to play roles in television dramas. Indeed, as early as May 1962, just five months after the inauguration of Ireland's domestic television service, when the first Television Audience Measurement (TAM) ratings were issued, the *Main Evening News* and Paddy Crosbie's *School around the Corner* were the only home-produced programmes; otherwise, it was canned-American imports that occupied the top ratings. Indeed, Fergal Tobin argues that *The Fugitive* 'had the whole country by the ears in the second half of the 60s, and there were remarkably few people out of doors on the night when the final episode was broadcast'[36] Quite simply, people no longer had to rely on the travelling showman to alleviate much of the banality of rural living. They now had choice, and so chose new, exciting televised plots rather than the old, well-known popular fit-up dramas.

In their time, however, travelling fit-up companies changed many lives, even temporarily, by offering provincial communities entertainment. At its height, the power of the fit-up company lay in its ability to transform a sleepy village into a hive of activity and excitement for the few days it visited. But as fit-up actor, Bob Bickerdike lamented, 'It would seem that we had the power to make the changes but not the power to resist the change'.[37]

CHAPTER FOUR

Experiment by all means[1]

The extent to which D'Alton's works were shaped and influenced by popular melodramatic stage conventions cannot be underestimated, but equally his representations of life and character went much further than this. Even his two novels transcend the melodrama they are laced with to reveal a complexity of character and theme where melodramatic elements are juxtaposed with a strong undercurrent of realism. Here D'Alton clearly delineates the dangers of romanticism through depicting protagonists who find it difficult to separate reality from idealism. These novels prepare us for his plays which explore the destructiveness of the de Valerian ideals that were engulfing Ireland.

The main tenets of melodrama dictate that its characters are eventually moved to recognition, that the villain is exposed for what he is, and that the victim's virtue is eventually realized and rewarded; however, we see a different sort of recognition in D'Alton's dramas. Only a select few of his characters achieve self-recognition, as Mangan does in *The Man in the Cloak* or Lar Broderick does in *To-Morrow Never Comes*, while many of them learn nothing, like Jane in *Lovers' Meeting* or the Hartnett parents in *The Mousetrap*. Correspondingly, the victims in these dramas – the daughters – die at the end of the plays, and thus assume the place that is normally appropriated to melodrama's villains. D'Alton's reason for inverting these practices, and for moving away from these tenets of melodrama, was to achieve a new form of recognition – audience recognition. He hoped that by showing his characters as products of society, and by exposing the wrongs of this society, he would bring his audience to recognize their faults. Unfortunately, his audiences were neither ready nor willing to face up to this.

Undoubtedly, D'Alton's theatrical experiences of melodrama influenced his playwriting insofar as this was the only form of theatre he knew intimately. However, because melodrama was instantly recognizable to his contemporary theatregoers, he could deliberately exploit its tenets to lull his audiences into believing they were watching a world they were familiar with. Many of his plays follow the typical popular nineteenth-century theatre dramatic personae of male lead/female lead, juvenile male and female, and a comic character. Also, the first act of his plays generally show a world at ease with itself, where the audiences can expect that the typical questions they ask will be satisfactorily answered: Will the young lovers marry? Will the families' financial problems be solved? Will the young woman resist temptation? However, just when his audience feels comfortable, D'Alton invariably thrusts it into a new world where there is little shelter.

D'Alton deliberately inverts his audience's expectations, although his methods of doing so vary. He can achieve this reversal through changing the setting of the play from a realistic one to a fantastic one, as he does in *The Man in the Cloak* and in *To-Morrow Never Comes*, or through unexpected events which propel the characters in the play into a new world, events such as Mary's pregnancy in *The Mousetrap* or the realization that Mary is in love with her half brother in *Lovers' Meeting*. Similarly, while his characters initially seem to resemble the heroes, heroines, villains and stage-Irish comic figures of Irish melodrama, on closer inspection these stereotypes disintegrate. The audience soon realizes there are no characters to protect the innocent, no male heroes to restore status quo, and thus no heroic Irish mothers to guide and form them. Even the comic characters prove to be largely 'irrelevant'[2] as comic reconciliation is not forthcoming, open-endedness usurping its place. Indeed, reconciliation of any kind is lacking in these plays, though time and again D'Alton lures his audiences into believing that they are standing on solid foundations.

By seeming to uphold popular theatrical conventions, and then undermining the very conventions he has appropriated, it is fair to say that D'Alton deliberately sends his audiences misleading signals at the beginning of these dramas to draw them into expecting a play based on popular conventions and beliefs. But, as we will see, this method often failed as his audiences chose not to acknowledge his social messages, preferring to cling stubbornly to the popular and the comic instead. We shall see how his fantasies, couched in realistic settings, perplexed his audiences (*The Man in the Cloak, To-Morrow Never Comes*); how the lack of clear generic resolution at the end of plays like *Lovers' Meeting, The Mousetrap* and *The Spanish Soldier*, allowed audiences to blame the character who was intended to be the victim; and how his subtle explorations of the effects of repression were either ignored (in the case of Hessy or Jane) or overturned (in the case of Hannie). Ultimately, we shall see how D'Alton tried but failed to reconcile popular myth with a modern view of Ireland.

D'Alton's first published work, the 1937 novel *Death Is So Fair*, though set in the revolutionary years in Ireland, deals less with the politics of the time than with the effect the revolution has on one man, clerical student, Marcus Considine.[3] In many ways Considine could be viewed as a 'holy gunman', yet this is not the image Louis wanted to present of him. Irish readers would have been quick to justify the actions of a clerical student activist, but D'Alton wanted us to see Considine as flawed. We do not meet him until the third chapter, and interestingly the description afforded us by the narrator is not one we would normally associate with a novel's protagonist. Rather, Marcus is presented to the reader as vapid and monotonous, lacking 'almost entirely a sense of humour',[4] someone who 'would never be able to laugh at his own vicissitudes though he would endure them with fortitude' (39–40). More telling, however, is the fact that he is described by the narrator as 'fanatical, loyal and extremely religious' (40).

Marcus is an idealist, someone who reverences the poet leaders of his country and who dreams of an Ireland that will be the apostle of the world. It is this enthusiasm that inspires him to sacrifice everything, even his priesthood, so that he might help his country and fulfil his dream:

> Ireland is the indestructible nation which God has miraculously preserved for the ultimate salvation of the world … I see in the future Ireland great and powerful, with spiritual power, honoured and regenerated. A country no longer drained of men, but teeming, flourishing in her former beauty, and for the one unworthy priest the church loses to-day, I see a thousand going out to lead the nations back to the one true Church, as Ireland's saints did before. (58)

In comparison, the other main character in the novel, Kilfoyle, is a ruthless, unrelenting leader who actively encourages Considine not to join the revolution. Self-described as a 'professional revolutionist' (62), competent yet brutal, he feels the leaders of the 1916 revolution 'deserved to be shot for their inefficiency' (42), that 'they would be alive and writing bad poetry fifty years hence if they had the wit to mind their own affairs' (42). Thus, whereas Marcus is a romantic, Kilfoyle views the revolution as 'a splendid game'. He tells Marcus, 'I warn you, you cannot achieve glory merely by failing as others have done before you. And the martyrdom you will no doubt attain will not be the martyrdom you would desire – there will be no glory to gild it, but ignominy in plenty.' (67) Too absorbed in his own thoughts, we are told that Marcus does not even hear Kilfoyle's prophetic words.

Marcus joins the revolutionary movement but steadily becomes disillusioned with it. He sees a policeman shot, not because he was a spy but because he knew too much about a bank robbery which a revolutionary had orchestrated. Further, he rightly suspects that most of the money stolen in the same robbery is kept for personal gain rather than being channelled into revolutionary funds. Worse than this, however, is the part he himself plays in the shooting of a friend he suspects to be a spy when, while knowing that there is no proof, he allows his compatriots execute him. Next Sergeant Mullaney of the Constabulary is gunned down and, though racked with guilt, Marcus does not prevent this either. This shooting leads to Marcus' brother's violent death by the Black and Tans and indirectly to his mother's death, seemingly of a broken heart. By this point Marcus has sacrificed everything, and only now does he realize that the revolution is no longer the crusade, the holy war he saw it as being. The final irony is that he does indeed become a martyr, as Kilfoyle predicted, but it is in a cause he has finally renounced.

The *Dublin Magazine* reviewer of *Death Is So Fair* noted that in this novel D'Alton is, 'in effect declar[ing] that patriotism even for Dark Rosaleen isn't enough'.[5] Indeed, in this sense *Death Is So Fair* is very different from the romantic songs and melodramas that would have graced fit-up halls at the time. Marcus' character is far from heroic, and Kilfoyle's prophecy that there would be no glory in failing, inverts melodrama's typical tableaux of heightening nationalists' deaths. In fact Kilfoyle emerges as a sort of anti-hero; his actions would have been elevated and revered in nineteenth-century historical drama, but D'Alton instead presents him in grim realism as a ruthless individual.

The question we must pose then is where D'Alton got his inspiration and why he decided to write such a bleak account of a revolution that was so idealized on the stages he performed on? He was an atheist so it is unlikely that he wanted his audiences merely to side with and forgive a misled priest – indeed, the novel suggests that Marcus Considine only has himself and his ideals to blame. We also know the backdrop to the first two chapters of the novel, that they were directly inspired by D'Alton's own experience at the time of the rebellion. Though just a teenager, the young Louis experienced the rebellion, was sniped at, and saw with his own eyes the death and destruction it caused. Yet, like most Irish men of the time, he was a Republican and, according to his sister, even carried dispatches during the war of independence.[6] Thus, we can assume that while he was not writing against a cause he believed in, neither was he willing to glorify its negative aspects.

What seems most likely then is that D'Alton decided to tell a story as a realist and, as such, deliberately went against the romantic pictures of revolution depicted in the fit-up dramas he both produced and acted in. However, there remain parts of *Death Is So Fair* which are still very much influenced by melodrama, albeit unconsciously. I refer in particular to the novel's characterization which, though strong, is lacking in psychological complexity, and where the minor characters in particular are tinged with melodrama: Kilfoyle is ruthlessly cruel, Mrs Considine passive and virtuous, John Considine simple and one-dimensional, and Norah beguiling and intransigent. In fact, the only character that is developed to any extent or that shows any psychological conflict is Marcus Considine; the other characters, like their melodramatic stage counterparts, are mere emblematic representations of simple truths, and to the modern reader seem motiveless and superficial. Their actions neither demand nor receive any justification and, true to melodramatic tenets, evil and good simply co-exist.

However, D'Alton's depiction of the peasant girl, Norah, deviates somewhat from the melodrama's template of the virtuous heroine, constantly pursued by the villain and continually in danger of losing her innocence. On the contrary, Norah is the pursuer in *Death Is So Fair* and thus is identified more with the villain than the heroine. Norah's role in the novel is to seduce Marcus: Her 'striking physical beauty' and the 'wild, remote, startled look in her violet eyes' like 'a panic-ridden, rushing foal' (87) are all weapons she uses to entice him. Indeed, it is she who constantly 'contrives' (87) to visit Manus despite his lack of interest and his mother's disapproval of her.[7] In the seduction scene, it is interesting to note the struggle between right and wrong and the polarisation of good and bad, so typical of melodrama. Norah, as persecutor, possesses almost super-human powers and is certainly distanced from more traditional portrayals of womanhood. We are told it is she who succeeded in 'drawing' Manus 'to the shadow of the hedge' and who 'clung to him with frantic violence' (171) when he tried to disengage himself. We note her strength and almost animalistic characteristics – she moves 'noiselessly', her eyes like 'a haunted animal', her lips 'very pale' (170), and when Manus 'endeavoured to disengage *gently* her *strong* hand from its grip on his coat … she *clung* to him with *desperate strength*, looking up at him imploringly with her *dilating eyes*' (171; my italics). Almost manlike, it is she who is 'driven headlong by the violence of her passion', and finally it is *her* 'wild and irregular' breathing, and *her* 'glazed' eyes that render Manus 'as powerless as an infant' (172). Lacking morals, she makes baneful decisions with ease, and though passionate and strongly characterized by D'Alton in some senses, her polarization is heavily influenced by melodrama.

It would be wrong, however, to assume that the content of the novel has its origins in melodrama, even if most of its characters do. In fact, it is here that D'Alton makes a clean break with this tradition. As we have seen, *Death Is So Fair* is not the patriotic, idealistic, coloured account of Ireland's revolutionary days that fit-up audiences were so used to. Indeed, the ending of the novel is far from a melodramatic closure where virtue is recognized, evil expunged, good reinstated and order restored. On the contrary, in *Death Is So Fair*, our hero gives up his cause and his life, disabused but strangely indifferent. Thus, rather than looking back to the age of melodrama, D'Alton seems here to be looking more to modernism, albeit tentatively. Manus has lost any heroic status and order is far from re-instated. The open-endedness of the novel is also problematic. Perhaps as a realist D'Alton could not write a solution where no solution existed. However, written and published in the 1930s, when de Valera's vision of an Irish idyll was being strongly advocated, D'Alton, a staunch realist, would have seen the irony in this new Utopian vision which, though glorified, was hugely flawed. Therefore the ending of *Death Is So Fair,* when Manus is incited to escape by the Black and Tans so they can shoot him rather than send him for trial, is morose yet caustic. The final scene where the Black and Tan lorry proceeds down the road dragging Manus' dead body behind it;

> bump[ing] horribly from side to side, slowly at first and then more quickly as the tender gained speed, performing an inanimate puppet-like jumping and hopping over the broken, slimy road (271)

is highly visual but also cruelly derisory, as the body jolts in unison with the 'roaring chorus' of the triumphant Black and Tans:

> Ta-ta, ta-ta, ta-ta, ta-ta we're going away
> Ta-ta, ta-ta, ta-ta, ta-ta we're on our holiday (271)

The novel's conclusion thus eradicates the popular tradition that preceded it, and prepares us for the unpleasant endings D'Alton would arrive at in many of his plays where the equally futile dreams of de Valera's Ireland are shown to be both ridiculous and destructive.

However, before he would broach such hard-hitting, critical themes D'Alton decided to explore the lifestyle he knew well, the world of the fit-ups. What resulted was second novel, *Rags and Sticks,* which follows a small family-run fit-up company, 'The Superlative Repertory Players', managed by the cunning but likeable Barney MacTansey. Known as 'a notorious dry-up shop', a company that 'does not pay and strands its artistes',[8] the players somehow manage to keep the company going despite its huge financial problems, largely accumulated through its members' over-consumption of alcohol. Financial backing and artistic merit both distinctly lacking, the only reason the company manages to keep on the road is through Barney's persistence:

> He was utterly improvident; in adversity his resource was magnificent; success was fatal to him. The end of a successful week found him in straits more dire than the termination of consecutive months

> of bad business. When half drunk he was generous, genial and audacious; this was his normal condition, for he could rarely afford to consume enough liquor to attain total inebriation. (18)

The novel however, is built around Mac Tansey's step-daughter, Ellie, and her search for happiness in a lifestyle she despises. Ellie sees herself as incompatible to the other members of the company and thus views herself as living in an alien community:

> She was caught in a trap within a trap … A round steel revolving trap with animals of the same breed running around inside it; and within that again a smaller trap revolving in the opposite direction and occupied by a solitary animal – herself. When the other animals did not ignore her altogether they regarded her with antagonism. In her effort to become independent of and indifferent to the others she withdrew herself more and more, completing thus the process of isolation. (42)

However, in a sense everyone is enslaved in the novel – Barney and Mrs MacTansey by their dependence on alcohol, Galbraith by his religion of fear, and Shotten by vanity and ambition. And like the other characters in the novel, Ellie finds it difficult to separate reality from drama, choosing instead to live out the melodramas she acts in. Romantic and idealistic, she pins her hopes of escape on a new man who joins the company, charlatan Donald Shotten, despite the fact that Mick Fannon, another company member, is hopelessly in love with her.

Shotten has joined the company from London, and unbeknown to the other cast members, is using the company and the alias Eugene Forden as a hide out from the police. At first he upsets fit-up convention acting in a naturalistic style, insisting on playing Marcus Superbus in his bare knees, asserting that tights were unknown in Ancient Rome. But his arrival gives the whole company a financial boost as he is greatly admired and attracts full houses wherever they travel. Ellie sees in him the solution to her loneliness and plays out her melodrama with him to the full; when he leaves her she is suitably despondent. With Shotten gone, the company hits financial difficulties once more. Ellie, in a bid to escape the fit-up lifestyle once and for all marries a small town hotel owner, Reardon, who turns out to be a secret drinker. But instead of allowing Ellie her wish to run a household, he insists that they take to the road with the Superlative Company. Trapped even more than before, Ellie inadvertently spurs Reardon to commit suicide, and a few months later bears his baby who dies at two months old. The novel ends with the disintegration of the company. Barney, having passed a false cheque is put in jail, the other members join other companies, Mrs MacTansey goes to live with her sister, and Ellie finally accepts the love of Mick Fannon.

In many ways the plot of *Rags and Sticks* echoes the melodramas performed by the Superlative Company. Like a tragi-comedy, the novel is fast-paced, at first largely humorous then suddenly tragic, before ending on a suitable romantic note. But while D'Alton's depiction is a lively, humorous one, it also has a very serious side – the travelling lifestyle is far from romantically depicted and its grim and even sordid side is equally represented by D'Alton along with all its other facets.[9] Indeed, it is this sordidness, coupled with the non-judgmental attitude D'Alton afforded the 'fallen' heroine of his novel, that led the censors to ban all editions of the novel in Ireland.[10]

The characters in the novel are a likeable lot. Their childlike hopes, that each new town visited will see a change in fortune, endear the reader and, despite their many quarrels, D'Alton makes it clear that they care for and depend on each other. But there is also an obvious desire on his part to present a less attractive side to his characters as noted by the review in the *Birmingham Post*:

> There is a feeling that however skillfully he draws his people, the author dislikes them and makes their drunkenness, the grossness, far more important than their decent qualities.[11]

Though he may hide his characters' less favourable qualities, D'Alton's portrayal is far from a simple 'disliking' of them; more that he was attempting to paint a realistic picture through honest character depiction. As the *Manchester Guardian* noted:

> Mr D'Alton succeeds remarkably well in suggesting the kind of people who drift into a 'fit-up' theatrical company, the peculiarities of the histrionic temperament, and the basic loyalties under the superficial hostilities and jealousies of the different members of the company both to each other and to the job. (8 February 1938)

In *Rags and Sticks* comedy, farce, drama and melodrama all intermingle, an apt melange of forms mirroring the irresolute fit-up lifestyle with its periods of fluctuating fortune and penury. Yet while the content of *Rags and Sticks* is primarily melodramatic, there is also an undercurrent of realism that cannot be missed. For example, while the end of the novel is romantic in some ways, it is also highly ironic. Ellie accepts the faithful Mick only as a last resort and though she finally achieves freedom, she has learnt that it is relative, that escape is an illusion. It seems clear then that D'Alton was trying to present a credible picture of life on the road, but encased in its realistic setting is a story that is often at odds with this depiction. Like *Death Is So Fair,* he juxtaposes melodrama and realism despite their poor blend. And just like his characters who find it difficult to escape from the melodramatic roles they play, talking and acting as if on stage all the time, D'Alton never really finds the balance between these two modes.

While *Rags and Sticks* is admittedly of little intrinsic literary merit, it is undoubtedly of great value in its depiction of the fit-up lifestyle. The *Times Literary Supplement* declared in 1938, 'As a picture of strolling players in the Ireland of to-day, this has a special theatrical interest',[12] but surely the novel is of even more interest now given the demise of the fit-up lifestyle. And considering that this tradition has been neglected to such an extent by theatre historians, *Rags and Sticks* is certainly an important text.

As a novelist, Louis D'Alton certainly showed flair. However, his true passion lay in playwriting. As a child, he had experimented with play writing, performing his creations for neighbours and friends. But it was not until he eventually set up his own company, having toured in many others, that he began to write his own plays. Written around the actors in his company and never published, there only remain a few scraps of his earliest plays. Among them is a play called *The O'Hagan,* where the parts of Robert Clanmoynagh and Sir Jonas Braithwaite are transcribed into a copybook owned by fit-up actor Kenneth Raymond.[13] Though it is hard to form a coherent picture of the plot of the play from two minor parts, it seems sure that *The O'Hagan* is influenced by, and fairly typical, of the type of fit-up dramas that were playing around provincial Ireland at that time. The play deals with the importance of inheritance and of one's name, and focuses on Clanmoynagh's attempts to marry a woman who refuses him as he was once an orphan. Eventually, Clanmoynagh is proved to be of good stock, and after a duel with Braithwaite, who questions his honour, he wins the hand of the maiden, Sheila.[14] The copy dates the first production of the play as having taken place at Rosslare on Sunday 16 June 1935, before being toured by D'Alton in his small fit-up company, where there were rarely enough actors to play all the roles. Not surprisingly, it was never published, but D'Alton had taken his first step towards becoming a fully-fledged playwright.

In its issue of 23 November 1937, the *Irish Times* concluded in a leading article 'The Changing Abbey' that the Abbey was continuing to function in the manner that it was founded, 'a playwright's theatre, a theatre in which the dramatist might make experiments for which the commercial theatre had neither time nor place'. Less than two years later Louis D'Alton had his first play produced at the Abbey, and it is precisely this relationship between experimentation and commercialism that he would try to reconcile throughout his initial years as a playwright. Analysing D'Alton's earlier plays from this perspective necessitates an examination of the notion of popular theatre, and of D'Alton as a 'popular playwright'. It is also important to analyse the context he lived and wrote in, as from this we can gauge the effects of Irish culture both on his writings, and on his audience. This in turn leads us to an investigation of his theatrical influences, in particular Irish melodrama which was the only theatre Louis had an intimate knowledge of when he began to write.

While D'Alton was very influenced by his experiences as a fit-up artist, and while his works were in many ways shaped by the melodramas he produced on the fit-up circuit, we shall see how he also tried to transcend melodrama in his initial plays. And while his primary aim was to expose in his dramas the faults inherent in the dominant ideologies of 1930s Ireland, D'Alton's audiences were unwilling to see these criticisms, demanding, albeit unwittingly, that he write plays that would gratify their tastes and desires. Frustrated by this, but also lured by commercial success, D'Alton would eventually give in.

The first of Louis D'Alton's plays to be published were *The Mousetrap* and *The Man in the Cloak.*[15] *The Mousetrap* has never been performed on the professional stage – D'Alton never submitted it to the Abbey Theatre to read and neither did he tour it on the fit-up circuit, more than likely because he knew his sympathetic treatment of the fallen girl and her seducer would not have been accepted by Irish audiences at that time. Set in the 1930s in the industrial town of Farraghnore, twenty five miles from Dublin, the play revolves around the Hartnett family, its entire action taking place within twenty-four hours, as the following events occur: *Act I:* Tressa Hartnett (daughter of Mary and Matthew) finds out that Marron, the man she is involved with, is married; Ned Hartnett (son of Mary and Matthew) is offered a much sought-after job at a new factory. *Act II:* Tressa tells her family that she is pregnant; Matthew suffers a stroke when he confronts Mary's lover; Ned attacks Marron and leaves him for dead; Tressa goes into labour. *Act III:* Marron dies from the injuries received in the affray with Ned; Ned is arrested; Tressa dies in childbirth.

It is clear that *The Mousetrap* is strongly influenced by the domestic melodramas that were so popular with provincial audiences. Yet despite this, D'Alton does attempt to raise contemporary issues and voices his politics through the character of Molly Whalen, Tressa's friend. The opening of the play centres around a conversation between Molly and Mrs Hartnett. To the modern reader Mrs Hartnett is highly conservative, but a large percentage of D'Alton's contemporaries would have held the same views as she does, and the issues that are raised in this scene, and then on throughout the play, are typical of those that were being debated in Ireland during the 1930s. The first opinion we hear is that Mrs Hartnett, like many of her time, is strongly against dance halls and thinks that something should be done 'to put a full stop to the scandalous carryin' on' (136) where 'the innocence of young an' tender girls' is being 'destroyed' (138). In an article written in *The Bell* entitled 'The Dance hall', Flann O'Brien quotes from the Public Dance Halls Act, stating that is was designed 'to wipe out abuses bearing on everything from sanitation to immorality.'[16] Undoubtedly, the latter problem was the real reason behind the Act, and with bishops and judges so opposed to the dance halls it was far from unusual to read comments such as the following from a bishop:

> There is one agency which Satan has set up here and there in recent years that does incalculably more harm than all the others we have mentioned. It deserves to be called after his name, for he seems to preside at some of the dark rites enacted there. We have in mind the rural dance hall.[17]

Energetic statements about the dangers of dance halls had been circulating since dance halls had first become fashionable. For example, in 1924, Bishop O'Doherty of Galway deplored the craze for dancing and advised fathers: 'If your girls do not obey you, if they are not in at the hours appointed, lay the lash upon their backs. That was the good old system, and that should be the system to-day.'[18] The debate about dance halls was also given ample coverage in the main newspapers of the day. In 1931, four years before the passing of the Public Dance Halls Act, the *Irish Times* printed the archbishop of Tuam's 'Public Warning to the Modern Girl' where it was declared, 'It was abominable to see girls of sixteen or seventeen doing just what they liked while the parents made no attempt to control them. Mothers, in this respect, were worse than fathers.' Speaking against dances, which the archbishop described as 'orgies of sensuality, held in devils' dens', he particularly chastised the girls who 'lend themselves for amusement' and who 'are keeping boys from getting married':

> Respectable men tell me that is why there are so many bachelors – they do not want to marry girls who go about 'gallivanting' at late

> hours, with painted faces. It will have to stop, or marriage will be reduced to a farce in this country.[19]

The same newspaper, the previous day, had published the bishop of Galway's plea to 'avoid occasions of sin' such as 'Company-keeping, dances and dance halls, mixed bathing and beauty contests'. He also warned against 'motor car abuses' where he pointed out that 'during dances, men and women go out in those motor cars and evil deeds are done there', lamenting that 'the next thing will be sun bathing, where people lie in groups practically naked ... Ask yourselves, in your hearts, are not these things that lead to foul thoughts, foul desires and foul acts?'[20]

The whole notion of illegitimacy was also widely discussed in Ireland at that time. Once again, public attitude was harsh, especially towards the unmarried mothers, although some, like M.P.R.H. in an article published in *The Bell*, took a more progressive view: 'Yet in this problem of illegitimacy three people are concerned, the unmarried mother and the father of the child, against the backdrop of a nation's life, the social amenities of town and country, or lack of them, the apathy of public opinion.'[21] Interestingly, the same article also makes reference to the Affiliation Orders Act, 1930 where the father of an illegitimate child could be ordered to pay contributions towards maintenance of the child, but points out that in reality 'only in two out of two hundred cases before the courts over a certain period was paternity successfully established – and the man solvent' (80). An even stronger indication of public attitude at this time can be seen in Section 14 of the same Act which states, 'Nothing in this Act shall operate to remove or diminish the liability of the mother of an illegitimate child to maintain such a child', which as M.P.R.H. points out 'fits in nicely with the "It's always the girl's fault any way" attitude' (80).

Mrs Hartnett, a product of her times, subscribes to this attitude. She reminds Molly of 'what happened to Lily Mansell' (137), and when Molly recants, 'Why the dances was held to blame for poor Lily's misfortune I never could see' (137), she is quick to answer her saying, 'Well your elders could, an' signs on it the place was closed down' (137). Lily Mansell had, in fact, committed infanticide, abetted by her father who buried the baby in the family garden. Here D'Alton temporarily raises another contentious issue which was an enormous social problem in Irish society in the 1920s and the 1930s – infanticide. Indeed, in the *Irish Times* between January 1930 and June 1931, no fewer than seven cases of infanticide were reported, and in one case it was even noted that the defendant was allowed out on bail to get married to the child's father.[22] Therefore, the reference by D'Alton to infanticide in *The*

Mousetrap is hardly coincidental, yet it is an issue he chooses not to explore fully. Mrs Hartnett's comment that, 'Lily in a penitentiary, himself in a prison an' the two sons gone out o' the place. That's your dance halls' (138), closes the subject.

However, the fact that D'Alton raises these issues at all is surely a first step. Further, it would be unfair to think that he was in any way advocating the type of attitude representative of Irish society at that time, the attitude offered by Mrs Hartnett. Indeed, the strong irony in her speeches and the fact that this woman's argument can be easily shown up by a young girl, advocates that D'Alton's own stance can be seen in the character of Molly. Also, everything that Mrs Hartnett denounces is followed by a statement which shows that she is merely parroting her husband, like when she condemns dances halls telling Molly, 'If me husband was to have his way he'd close up every dance hall in the country.' (136) Or when she castigates 'the pagan Sunday newspapers which should be kep' out o' the country like many more things, as my man often says' (137), proceeding to observe, 'A girl should grow up like a flower, full of sweetness an' vagrancy. That's my man's opinion an' I'll hold to it.' (37) Likewise, when Mrs Whalen comments that radios are 'grand, noisy company' (152), the only retort Mrs Hartnett can come up with is 'Me husband wouldn't let one into the house' (152); and even when she seems to be expressing her own opinion, like when she blames 'the pictures' for having 'all the young ones going round like hotcha queens' (144), we soon find out that Mr Hartnett feels the same when he tells his wife how annoyed he is that Molly had invited Tressa to the pictures: 'The same blasted picture-house should be closed down as ye often heard me say.' (169)

The Hartnetts are referred to as being 'too decent' (245) by Mrs Whalen, a pertinent comment. Indeed, Mr Hartnett objects so vehemently to the happy-go-lucky Whalen family – with their modern-thinking daughter and lazy son – that he sees fit to ban them from his house. Yet in spite of the Hartnett parent's blinkered conservatism, it is their daughter who falls pregnant, not as a result of the dance halls they denounce so readily, but under their roof and arguably as a result of their narrow-mindedness. Thus, Mrs Whalen's comment that the Hartnetts are 'too decent' is an apt admonition of a society that is too conservative for its own good. It may be obvious to the modern reader where D'Alton stands on these issues, but his attitudes are at best covertly projected, and in a play that is structured so traditionally and is so shaped by domestic melodrama, the subtlety of his arguments would surely have been lost to his contemporary audience. So, while D'Alton may be congratulated for opposing in *The Mousetrap* common reaction to issues like the disgrace of illegitimacy, and the supposed evils of modernism (dance halls, radios, and cinema), contemporary audiences largely would have viewed the play as being anti-modern. And while Mr Hartnett may have suffered a stroke, punished by D'Alton for being such a miserable, harsh and bigoted character, the contemporary viewer could just have easily have seen his illness as another consequence in a sequence of events directly set in motion by Tressa's immorality.

The ending of the play is equally problematic. D'Alton's own position is expressed through Molly, the voice of youth and reason. When Mrs Whalen expresses the view that ''tis all her [Tressa's] fault' (224), Molly is quick to reply, 'Ah! how does anyone know whose fault it is.' (224) She questions her contemporary's attitudes by asking, 'Why couldn't they have a little compassion in them? Why couldn't they have a little mercy on her, and on themselves? Is it bowels of iron is in the people or what?' (224); she even manages to be logic about an issue that was so emotive: 'We bein' the mo' prolific race in the world it's not altogether to be expected we wouldn't occasionally be getting prolific ... ah ... afther hours as ye might say.' (226)

Yet Molly stands alone in her liberalism. Mrs Hartnett is conspicuously absent from the final act, making only one appearance lamenting, 'Me poor Tressa ... me poor little girl. Where's Ned at all ... th'only one that's left to me' (245); the reference to Ned, who has just been led away on murder charges, only reinforcing to the audience the problems that Tressa has caused. Further, Mrs Whalen's comment when we find out that Tressa has died, that 'It's the will o' God' (241), and Ned's agreement, 'Maybe 'tis for the betther that way' (241) makes it far too easy for the audience to accept Tressa's death as an appropriate outcome, perhaps even a suitable punishment. Ned's remark that Tressa's face is 'lined and twisted with the pain' (242) to which Mrs Whalen replies 'It's the will o' God, Ned' (242), reinforces this. The play draws to a close with Molly questioning the Midwife as to whether Tressa's baby will live or not, to which the Midwife answers 'As nobody wants it, it probably will. That's usually the way at any rate.' (247) In reality, the mortality rate of illegitimate children at that time was as high as twenty-six percent, almost four times higher than that of parented children,[23] but if D'Alton knew this, he does not take the opportunity to make a point of it. The final image in the play is of Molly seated on the floor, her legs curled under her, tenderly addressing Tressa's premature baby. Her comment, 'Ah! and it's a queer world you're after comin' into' (247), is pertinent. The play may be set in an 'industrial town' where everyone is prepared to fight for jobs in the new factory and to welcome modernization for its financial benefits, but few are willing to modernize their attitudes – a queer world indeed.

The Mousetrap was the first of many D'Alton plays to explore the rift between modernization and traditionalism in Irish society. And if he does not go far enough in this play, it is likely that, without the aid of a seeming objective narrator (a tool he employed in his novels), he found it difficult to find a balance between writing a play that his audiences would have approved of, and impressing on that audience his own more liberal ideas. Unfortunately, *The Mousetrap* does not find that balance.

Published with *The Mousetrap,* was D'Alton's drama, *The Man in the Cloak,* a biographical play about the poet James Clarence Mangan. Unlike *The Mousetrap,* D'Alton decided to submit *The Man in the Cloak* to the Abbey theatre for consideration, and it was subsequently read and immediately approved by Hugh Hunt, Frank O'Connor and F.R. Higgins. Hunt's report was as follows:

> Wholeheartedly recommend this play for production. It is a heaven-sent opportunity to cover up weak acting by production. The expressionist treatment of Act 2 is what we badly need. In any case the play is a good one and the subject matter an important addition to the biographical play. I don't consider it a great play and it will require considerable cutting.
>
> Will the Directors kindly read this as soon as possible and I suggest we produce it on Sept. 20th; but it is a difficult play and I must be allowed to start work on it in a few days time.[24]

Frank O'Connor added to Hunt's remarks, 'Entirely agree. The second act must be cut to hell', while F.R. Higgins noted the plays 'Remarkably fine dialogue', called it a 'good pictorial play' and even added that he 'strongly favour production if possible also in America'.[25] Although *The Man in the Cloak* never did make it to America, it was produced in the Abbey Theatre just a week later than Hunt suggested on Monday 27 September 1937, and was a great success.

The Man in the Cloak is D'Alton's most experimental of all his plays and in many ways he took great risks by writing a rather fantastic second act to which Abbey Theatre audiences would not have been accustomed. It centres on the harsh realities of life in cholera-stricken Dublin in 1849, and from its tone to its tenement setting, it is obviously influenced by O'Casey. But D'Alton had his own issues to raise, his own problems to solve, primarily the same juxtaposition of opposites that plagued his protagonists in his novels: escapism and self-realization.

Why D'Alton chose to write about Mangan is unclear; however it is likely that he had recently read John Desmond Sheridan's biography on Mangan which was published in 1937;[26] indeed, the title of the play was the title given to the sixth chapter of Sheridan's biography.[27] In this play, Mangan has to confront the ghosts of his past before he can die peacefully, and it is through allowing his imagination take him back to his youth that he relives and finally understands his reasons for choosing the lifestyle he led. By employing the fantastic D'Alton allows the audience make that journey with Mangan.

Mangan is not present for most of the first act though we learn from other characters that he spends all his money on alcohol rather than paying his rent or even eating. Already then, the audience has a picture of the man, though of course, most of the audience would have known who Mangan was before attending the theatre. When we do meet him at the end of Act I, his first words firmly cement him as the tragic, pathetic character D'Alton wants to present him as being. Feverish and thirsty for alcohol he stammers:

> *Mangan*: What little dignity I have I must preserve ... and so ... even the most trifling sum would be ... greatly welcomed, and, for what it is worth, earn an artist's gratitude.[28]

The Man in the Cloak presents us with two views. On the one hand we see a man who is slowly losing the dignity he so cherished to a society and times which all but force people to beg an existence; however, D'Alton is also exhibiting a man who tries to shun reality through alcohol and drugs because he has never accepted his own limitations:

> *Mangan*: All other things I could have endured and triumphed over. Disease and privation and vicissitudes might have beset me and not daunted me could I but have felt that the glow of genius was constant. Could I have fashioned many songs of immortal substance I could have warmed myself at the fire of genius. My genius would have clothed my nakedness, it would have armoured me a hundred fold against the injurious blows that life has struck me. (29)

The second act of *The Man in the Cloak* transports Mangan back to his past where he has to confront his ghosts, and his failings. An interesting deviation takes place at the beginning of this act that is not recorded in D'Alton's published version of the play. In the script used for the Abbey production he has added a scene where the masked characters of Drunkenness and Melancholy appear on an almost dark stage so they are only 'dimly seen'.[29] In the conversation that takes place between these two characters we are told that Mangan's life has not been a success, that he hasn't long to live, that Drunkenness and Melancholy have 'followed him a long time', and that 'He might have been the genius he wished to be but for us.' Their appearance on stage is obviously constructed to give the Abbey audience some insight, however slight, into Mangan's despair, and to create audience sympathy for the melancholic, pathetic Mangan we will view in this act. However, on a practical level, the inclusion of Melancholy and Drunkenness also prepare the audience for the dream sequence that dominates Act II, as we are told very clearly by Melancholy, 'Yes, he's dreaming. He's reliving his life again.'[30]

In this working script D'Alton also emphasizes that the scenes in this act should have 'no definite background and should be shown against a black backing with the use of lights'. He also writes how the lighting should work and concludes that the first speeches should be 'spoken in a blackout, faintly and slowly'.[31] However, these directions are crossed out and the directions we read in the published version of the play are obviously those that D'Alton, Hugh Hunt and Tanya Moiseiwitsch finally decided upon.[32] It is worth quoting these stage directions in full here, as they serve to illustrate the atmosphere he wished to evoke in the play:

> There are three sets in this act. The centre set is behind back gauze. There is a table on a raised dais. Chairs at each end and one on each side centre. Interior backing. The set down R. behind front gauze shows stairs with banister set piece, occasional table and two chairs to represent a more luxurious dwelling. The set L. is a public house. A table, behind which is a form, at R. of table a barrel. This set is also backed by stairs and behind front gauze. The opposing stairs are used for the final scene in conjunction with centre set. When the characters assemble on stairs for the final scene they should appear only in silhouette and CATHERINE'S form passes down and up like a black moving shadow. In order to preserve the continuity, the dimming of lights in one scene should synchronize with their rising on the following scene in another part of the stage. Where this is possible, music should be used during each black-out and these made as short duration as possible. If it can be arranged that the intervals during each black-out are reduced to a negligible period, the characters should continue to speak the words of the next scene whilst they are taking up their positions in the dark. (47)

D'Alton's knowledge of staging and lighting had its origin in the fit-up world where, as we have seen, companies had to improvise special effects with very basic tools. It is also interesting to note the inclusion of music in the stage directions, music forming a central part of most of the melodramas played on the fit-up circuit. However, *The Man in the Cloak* is far from typical of those dramas performed by the fit-ups and in this play D'Alton largely avoids melodramatic conventions; indeed, in many ways he even moves beyond naturalism to a form of expressionism. This dream sequence was considered 'very daring' by the *Evening Herald* reviewer, and the *Irish Press* decided that in this act D'Alton did 'splendid work. Here he commands dramatic power'.[33] However, D'Alton's experimentation was not appreciated by everyone: Gabriel Fallon lamented that 'Act II revealed the measure of a dramatist's defeat', saying that the dream was 'really an old dodge' and that one 'cannot take to dreaming right in the middle of your play-writing',[34] and the *Irish Times* stated that 'the use of a pseudo-expressionist technique for the presentation of the second act does nothing to alter the realism of the play' (28 September 1937). However, surely the point of the act is not to transcend realism but to merge the different realities of Mangan's past and present. By doing this the audience can see the effect outside influences have on a person's psyche and can also be presented with a much more detailed representation of Mangan rather than just glimpsing the withered shell of a dying man. As the *Irish Independent* noted, 'The first and third acts give us the setting for Mangan's death, and the second act gives us his psychological history in six short scenes'. The reviewer goes on to comment that this is 'a rather crude device' but that it 'has the advantage of enabling the author to tell us unmistakable things about Mangan which a more subtle construction would leave to inference and deduction.' (28 September 1937)

D'Alton's journey into the fantastic thus acquaints the audience with the real Mangan and reveals to us parts of him realism alone could not have depicted. It must also be noted that his dream sequence and his inclusion of the many ghosts in this act, was a form deliberately chosen by him in order to best express Mangan's state of mind. The *Boston Evening Transcript*, 16 October 1937, notes that while Hunt was 'pre-eminently successful in getting the atmosphere of the cheap lodging house' in the dream sequence, 'the shadowy side was a little too substantial. The fault lay with bringing the phantoms up and down rather solid flights of steps and having them move across the stage in too much light. It tended to shatter the illusion of a dream.' However, *Dublin Opinion*, October 1937, states, 'The dream sequence was brilliantly produced, and here Mr Hunt must take his bow ... The way he made what looked like the shadow of Catherine's walk across the dark stage foreground after she was dead, was inspired.' However, the idea of presenting ghosts was not D'Alton's – Sheridan notes in his biography of Mangan that Mangan alleged that his dead father came back constantly to reproach him, a fact also alluded to by O'Donoghue in his biography of Mangan.[35] Sheridan also makes reference to what he terms Mangan's 'day-dreams' noting that they could have been caused by his opium addiction, his unhappy childhood, his mode of life, his genius or his drinking.[36] In a similar fashion, D'Alton's 'opium dream' also refers to all these possibilities.

In the first part of Act II, the audience is transported back to Mangan's youth, and here we meet Mangan's father, a drunk, conceited and bitter man who views himself as 'a man of exceptional intelligence' possessing 'great gifts, wonderful powers' (54). Mangan, according to his father, is 'a disappointed son of a disappointed father' (53) and indeed, despite their dislike for each other, father and son share many likenesses, and while this scene shows the struggle of a young boy against a domineering, self-pitying man, the audience can already see shades of the Mangan they met in Act I in his father in this scene. They share the same vision and use almost identical language to express it. Compare Mangan's first speech already quoted to the following utterance by his father:

> *James*: But I have a vision. I envisaged greater things and more ample fortune. I could not be satisfied with less. It is not in my nature to compromise. There is a kind of nobility in my nature ... There is a kind of nobility in me with which I am cursed. Mine are the failings of an aristocrat. (55–6)

Indeed, by the time we meet the second ghost of this act, Mangan's sweetheart, Catherine Hayes, Mangan is already beginning to sound like the ghost of his father – conceited and self-absorbed: 'Do not trouble yourself with my wretched condition, my dear Catherine. I make no doubt in time I shall rise superior to it' (61). Catherine represents hope but at the same time her ghost symbolizes unrealizable dreams because when Catherine dies, hope dies also. The poem Mangan translated for Catherine is suitably about hope and demise:

> I saw her once one little while and then no more;
> 'Twas Eden's light on earth a while and then no more.
> Amid the throng she passed along the meadow floor;
> Spring seemed to smile on earth a while and then no more;
> But whence she came, which way she went, what garb she wore
> I noted not; I gazed a while and then no more. (62)

Mangan describes the two hours a week he spent with Catherine as 'like being in a different world'. Yet so self-absorbed is he that he does not realize that she is dying. Like the girl in the poem, Catherine passes on, and the end of the poem serves only to predict Mangan's future, a future where winter will replace spring and where his only hope will be death:

Where shall I find rest, alas?
When first the winter's winds shall wave.
The pale wild flowers, the long dark grass
Above mine unremembered grave. (66)[37]

The next set of ghosts we meet in this act are that of Tighe and Blythe, representative of society, or more accurately how Mangan thinks society views him:

Tighe: He has written a lot that has very little merit. (67)

Tighe: It is thought strange by many that you let yourself down to the lower dregs of society. (70)

Tighe: Do you not think it degrades a great talent to put it to base uses? (73)

Blythe: [You are] a procrastinator, a pessimist and a punster, a prostitute poet and a procurer of illicit rhymes. (95)

Not only do we see the ghosts of Tighe and Blythe reiterate the charges Mangan made to his father, we also note that Mangan is continuing to sound more and more like his father and what is more, he is becoming a ghost himself. Indeed, the next time we see Mangan he has even taken on the physical appearance of a ghost, his hair 'bleached white', his eyes 'fixed and strange', his face 'expressionless' and his movements 'slower, less impulsive.'(78) Determined to 'make a song' of his 'misery', Mangan begins to write a poem ('The Nameless One', quoted in both Sheridan's and O'Donoghue's biographies):

Roll forth my song like the rushing river,
That sweeps along to the mighty sea;
God will inspire me while I deliver my soul of thee.' (96)

However, at this stage the lights dim and the voices of all the ghosts of this act are heard repeating the words and phrases that obviously haunt Mangan.[38] In a powerful conclusion to the opium dream and to the act, Mangan struggles to finish his poem:

Him grant a grave to ye pitying noble,
Deep in your bosoms, there let him dwell
He, too, had tears for all souls in trouble, here and in hell … (97)

but is interrupted by the voices which 'break out together, each one repeating the burden of their refrain in a confused irregular murmur becoming louder every moment. A stringent despairing cry' (97). Mangan repeats, 'Here and in hell', and the voices cease. The act closes with Mangan 'sitting with bowed head, wearily and quietly', once again uttering the words 'Here and in hell' (97).

In the third act the audience is once again transported back to a realistic time frame and setting. Mangan is finally at peace and welcomes death as a 'release from hell' (127). This is in stark contrast to the other characters in the play that are panic-stricken about the rapid advancement of cholera and its impending entry into the doss-house.[39] However, while the third act is certainly clever in its juxtaposition of moods, or as the *Irish Times* stated, 'masterly in its realization of the terror besetting an entire city',[40] it is undoubtedly the second act which showed D'Alton to be a writer of promise where his desire to see beyond the surface is coupled with a strong sense of theatre. The opium dream is as far from reality as it should be, yet ironically it is here that the audience begin to see the real Mangan. As Sheridan wrote in his biography of Mangan, 'The early misery of Mangan's … did not spring from anything in his circumstances or environment, but from the very texture of his mind.' (20) It is through the dream sequences of the second act that D'Alton shows the audience *his* Mangan, and offers a way of understanding him. And by going right back to Mangan's childhood to seek explanations for the adult Mangan's behaviour, he demonstrates a keen psychological curiosity, an interest he would explore more fully in his subsequent play *To-Morrow Never Comes.*

CHAPTER FIVE

Ready-made audiences

To-Morrow Never Comes, described by the *Irish Independent* as a 'psychological thriller'[1] premiered in the Abbey Theatre on 13 March 1939, a busy time for D'Alton who had not only written the play, but also produced it and stepped in to play the principal role when the actor F.J. McCormick became ill. D'Alton played the role of Lar Broderick, a miserable, selfish publican who talks himself into murdering James McEvelly in order to steal his money, which he supposedly keeps in a belt wrapped around his waist. The first act sets the scene for the murder, and takes place within a realistic framework.

The second is more experimental in its depiction of McEvelly's conscience. By bringing on to the stage the murdered McEvelly's ghost, *To-Morrow Never Comes* could have fallen into a type of melodramatic thriller where sensation and spectacle would have negated any intensity of theme or character. However, when it becomes clear that McEvelly's ghost is actually a product of Broderick's guilty conscience, the play begins to take on a new direction where the comedy and light-heartedness of much of the first act is replaced with the drama of a guilty man's dilemma.

In a deliberate move by D'Alton to accentuate the theme of the play (that one must accept the consequences of one's own actions), the ghost is actually more likeable than the living McEvelly was. Described by the *Irish Independent* as 'a genial, kind ghost who strains every effort to help his murderer'[2] we are told in the stage directions that the ghost 'smiles oftener' than McEvelly, that his voice is 'noticeably gentler' and that 'his character is now quite changed and the opposite of what it was'.[3] Having predicted in Act One that he would never forgive himself for murder, Broderick now faces the consequences of his actions. His words to McEvelly in Act One, 'You'd never forgive yourself for doin' a thing like that because ye'd be thinkin' of it an' it'd be on your mind at all times, an' you'd never forgive yourself', (28) shows his ability to rationalize; however, once he has committed murder, reason is soon engulfed by a guilty conscience.

When we first meet the ghost, the stage directions tell us that Broderick answers him 'as if he were answering his own thoughts' (65). Thus, McEvelly is no more than an extension of Broderick's thoughts, and Broderick even seeks clarification from him as to why he killed him: 'Tell me one thing if ye can. What was it put it into me head to kill ye? ... Why did I do it Jamesy?' (45) McEvelly's answer to Broderick is interesting: 'Ye did it because you're stupid, greedy an' callous, an' you've no imagination.' (45) By killing McEvelly, Broderick had turned his fantasy into a reality, but the money he imagined receiving does not materialize. So now he tries to reverse the process by bringing reality to fantasy. Thus, when McEvelly's ghost tells Broderick at the end of the second Act that the sight of him will send him mad when he returns and that his warning shall be the howling of the dog at dusk, Broderick thinks he can prevent McEvelly's return by killing the dog. He consequently kills the dog and although his ghost does not reappear, this action leads to his murdered corpse surfacing instead.

In the final act of the play, McEvelly's ghost is not seen again and only heard once 'speaking in a remote voice off stage' (80). In this act we witness Broderick's final struggle with his conscience and his ultimate confession. In Act II we heard Broderick describe his penance as like escaping from prison cell to prison cell, each cell being smaller than the last, and being unable to go back: 'An' I'm in dread o' the last tiny prison that won't leave me room to stretch or move. Me arms will be pressed tight an' I won't be able to breathe (Gasping) to breathe.' (48) However, it is not until the final act when the reality of his deed confronts him (in the form of McEvelly's corpse) that he finally admits to his crime.

The *Irish Times* remarked that this third act was necessary as *To-Morrow Never Comes* was 'not melodrama' – 'the third and final act fully justifies itself in the exposition of Lar's mental breakdown and weak confession of the crime.' It is interesting to note that this play was dissociated from melodrama, but we shall see that his experimental nature lessen as audiences began to demand entertainment rather than analytic exploration. *To-Morrow Never Comes,* however, was quite a novelty for Dublin audiences, the *Irish Times* review on 14 March 1939 headlining the words 'ORIGINAL TREATMENT', stating, 'So original is his [D'Alton's] treatment of the central idea that he has been led in some degree to sacrifice the technique of dramatic form.' D'Alton was thus firmly welcomed on the Dublin professional stage with this drama, his second successive success, and congratulated for his 'wholly new setting and treatment in the type of humanity he has chosen as the subject of psychological inquisition'.[4]

His subsequent play, *The Spanish Soldier,* turned out to be a turning point in his career. Here, the protagonist, Kevin McMorna, returns from Franco's war, crippled but in 'a state of religious ecstasy'.[5] Flowers in his room are moved mysteriously one night, and he wakes up somehow restored to full health.

Believing this to be a miracle, he decides to become a priest but must obtain permission from his wife to do so. At first she refuses, saying that it was she who moved the flowers, but she then withdraws this, leaving the end of the play open, with the audience given no answer as to which story is true.

At the outset, *The Spanish Soldier* seems to be a story about faith and spirituality; however, keeping in mind D'Alton's atheism and liberalism, it is more plausible that the play questions misplaced religious fervour, and encourages the audience to see that Kevin's actions and society's hero worship of him as being more irresponsible than honourable. General Franco's war was covered widely in both newspapers and journals in 1936, and it is likely that D'Alton read the many reports which were rather one-sided in their views. Take for example an article entitled 'Can Ireland Help Spain?' where Aodh de Blacam expressed his disapproval of those circles 'professing to be patriotic and Catholic', who showed 'ignorance' and 'indifference' at the situation in Spain. He declared that Ireland must, 'prevent the spreading of the fire to our own house, wherein there is more dry timber than we admit ... Modernism has gone further within us than we guessed'.[6] The same issue of the journal carries another article written by the Roman Secretariat of the Sodality of the Children of Mary, which gave numerous examples of young men willingly dying for the religious cause:

> A certain lad of 16 who was about to leave for the front as a volunteer said to his mother: 'Mother, please don't pray that I may return safe and sound, but pray rather that Communism may be utterly destroyed, and that God may no longer be offended in Spain'. Then he added: 'For this reason I willingly give my life'...
>
> Many are the cases that might be cited of families that have given, willingly and joyfully, as many as five sons to fight for the faith.[7]

It is probable that the sensationalism of articles like these sparked D'Alton to consider the consequences of such religious fervour in an Ireland he viewed as being already too conservative and righteous for its own good. As Davey Deasy tells Hugh in *The Spanish Soldier*, 'This is still holy Ireland, boy, don't forget, where a man's soul is his greatest possession.'[8] And as Kevin's wife, Hessy, speculates, it was probably the 'pictures showin' the corrupted bodies o' the dead religious that were tore out o' the graves to lie exposed in the public streets', (6) that prompted Kevin to leave Annakill for Spain.

The Spanish Soldier, despite its title, focuses primarily on Kevin's wife who lives with Kevin's mother, his Uncle and his brother Hugh. Twenty-five year old Hugh, who is in love with Hessy, is described by D'Alton as 'strong and active', 'intelligent' and 'rather sensitive'. (4) We are also told that his idealism has turned to cynicism, although D'Alton is quick to point out that this is 'not mere complacent cynicism for he has energy of mind and earnestness'. (4) As such Hugh can be viewed as being a spokesperson for D'Alton, for he is the only character in the play not awed by Kevin's religious experiences. In fact when Hugh's neighbour Davey Deasy exalts Kevin's for 'savin' the soul o' Catholic Spain from the anti-Christ Muscovites', (6) Hugh retorts, 'Savin' their souls. Bombin' an' blastin' them to paradise, gassin' them to glory, pushin' them into heaven at the point o' the bayonet. It's an oul game.' (6)

The relationship between Kevin and Hessy is questioned throughout *The Spanish Soldier*. We are told at the beginning of the play that Kevin and Hessy had only married a few months before he departed for Spain, a move Hugh disapproves of, believing it was 'none of his business to go': 'If he loved ye so much isn't it strange he'd leave ye without a word.' (6) Thus while we feel Hessy's excitement as she eagerly and nervously awaits Kevin's return, D'Alton hints in this first act that all is not well. We note Hessy's misery at hearing that the local townsfolk believe she drove Kevin away as she 'made a hard bed for him' (5) and see that despite her best attempts to be a loving wife, it is probable that she married Kevin when she really was in love with Hugh. When Hugh takes her in his arms before Kevin's return, 'for a moment she is limp and unresisting in his embrace' (17), and when he professes his love for her she angrily tells him that when she was free, he never spoke of this love.

When we meet Kevin in the second act we begin to sympathize even more with Hessy. We learn that Kevin has elected to sleep alone and when Hessy affectionately rests her hands on her husband's, the stage directions read, 'with a swift, involuntary movement he withdraws his hand and looks away', leaving Hessy trying 'to conceal that she is hurt' (II, 5). Hessy confides in Nano that Kevin has 'turned against' her and that he 'can't bear to have [her] near him' since his return, and when Father Conn tells her she must have patience her response is, 'I've had patience since I married an' little good it did me ... To be married an' not married, with a husband is no more to me than a black stranger.' (II, 26)

Our realization that the marriage between Hessy and Kevin has probably not been consummated reminds the audience of Kevin's mother's remark in the first act when she wondered if he should ever have married (I, 2). Even more worrying are the dreams Kevin is having of Hessy, dreams of him being in a forest and turning to stone below the waist, and Hessy 'smilin' an' tormentin' me; bendin' an' turnin' an' shapin' in a kind of dance ... beyond the reach o' me hands ... Bad images ... evil things ... tormentin' me' (II, 29). It is clear what D'Alton is suggesting here – the fact that he turns to the Virgin Mary to 'banish' these dreams leaves little doubt that is having problems balancing sexuality and spiritualism. However, when the flowers are mysteriously moved in his room and he walks again, believing it to be a miracle, his torments cease.

At the beginning of the third act we learn that Kevin has been on retreat for some weeks and Hessy once again is 'alive and eager with happiness' (III, 5), as she awaits his return. Yet her hopes are soon dashed as Kevin only returns to tell her he has decided to enter the priesthood, a wish she finally grants. The last scene appropriately focuses on Hugh and Hessy. Hugh, unable to woo Hessy from his 'weak and woolly'[9] brother whom he views as 'spirit mad, soul maddened', tells her she will have to 'grow old alone' and 'be chaste' so as to 'bring no shame' on her brother (III, 18). The scene concludes with Hugh leaving while Hessy kneels and prays silently, and thus, despite the images conjured up in one's mind by the play's title, there is no heroic action and no victory in this play. Hessy, so much more sensual and modern than the quiescent women in melodrama, ironically has appropriated their very fate by the close of the play, though it is sympathy not respect that we feel for what she has become – a despondent and passive martyr.

The Spanish Soldier was 'exceedingly well received' at the Abbey Theatre, both the acting and the suspense created by the play's structure, pleasing audiences and critics alike. The reviewer of the *Irish Independent* called the play 'brilliant, brilliant in its conception and execution and brilliantly played'. Both the *Irish Independent* and the *Irish Times* made specific reference to the 'rich comedy' in the play, primarily due to the character of Moses Furlong, played by F.J. McCormick, though both reviews noted that his part was 'irrelevant' to the play. However, such was McCormick's magnetism that the *Independent* commented that this irrelevance didn't matter as Furlong was 'such a joy to our hearts', and the *Irish Times* went as far as saying that McCormick's Moses Furlong 'will make largely for the success of *The Spanish Soldier*'.[10] However, audiences and reviewers alike chose to ignore D'Alton's obvious criticisms of Irish society in this play. From the mob who make money out of 'the miracle' selling weak tea at 'a shilling a cup', to the Church who are happy to accept subscriptions twice the amount needed for the Church Renovation Fund, to Kevin who is weak enough to marry when he is obviously not ready to, D'Alton is not slow in apportioning blame. He goes even further by depicting Hessy as being a sexually aware, and sexually frustrated woman, a particularly daring move. However, Irish audiences saw only what they wanted to see in the play, and this, along with many similar reprehensions, was conveniently ignored.

So successful was the play, that it was decided it should travel to America, a move which must have surely delighted D'Alton. And so in February 1941, *The Spanish Soldier* opened at the Little Theatre on Broadway under the title *Tanyard Street.* The première had been twice postponed but audiences eagerly awaited this production, sponsored by Jack Kirkland who had recruited such players as Barry Fitzgerald and Arthur Shields to act in it. However, its reception was disappointing. Once again, the reviews focused on the comic role of Moses Furlong and misread the play as being 'a modern miracle play', D'Alton himself being equally misrepresented as being 'interested in the religious aspects of healing'. The *New York Times* conceded that *Tanyard Street* was 'sincerely written' and had benefited from a 'sympathetic direction' from Arthur Shields, but it also noted 'Mr D'Alton has great difficulty in making his drama flow along the pathway of a theme. As if they were aware of some defect in the play, the actors are over-wrought, raising their voices to a sharp pitch, their faces tense with simulated emotion.'[11]

Once again, audiences had missed the serious intentions of D'Alton's play, and like their Irish counterparts, war-time American theatregoers wanted nothing more than amusement. The fact that Barry Fitzgerald was so 'pungently comic' in his role of Moses Furlong did not help matters. Indeed, the review in the *New York Times* largely concentrated on Fitzgerald's acting, seeing him as 'the incarnation of the comic spirit', though realizing that his role did not have 'anything to do with the main action.' It seems likely that the American audiences who attended the play had come to see Fitzgerald, the *New York Times* noting how people started to laugh 'the moment he poke[d] his squint face on the set', and that while he was on stage it was apparently 'difficult to think of anything else.' However, the review ends caustically remarking, 'nothing about *Tanyard Street* is more miraculous than the fact that Barry Fitzgerald is in it.' So D'Alton had failed to make an impression as a serious dramatist, his comic relief ending up the main focus of reviewers and audiences alike. When the play closed after just twenty-two performances, D'Alton, bitterly disappointed, vowed he would never again write a serious play[12] and, as we shall see, the plays he wrote after this experience were directed largely to the tastes of popular theatre audiences.

The Money Doesn't Matter was first performed in the Abbey Theatre on 11 March 1941, less than five weeks after *Taynard Street* had opened on Broadway. By this stage D'Alton was a well-known, popular playwright in Ireland, respected not just by Abbey audiences but also by the provincial audiences he knew so well being, more or less on continual tour around the provinces at this time. *The Money Doesn't Matter* was D'Alton's first attempt at pure comedy, and although it was pointed out by the *Irish Times* that the subject matter of the play could have shown the 'predicament' of the self-made man as 'a grim business' and even a 'tragedy', D'Alton very deliberately chose to see its lighter side.[13]

The play focuses on Tom Mannion and his efforts to overcome his humble beginnings by impressing all those in Annakill with his self-made wealth. Much of the comedy of the play lies in his endeavours to mould his children into being successful snobs – as Harvey points out, 'Father can't bear us not to be important.'[14] Unfortunately for Tom, none of his children reach his expectations: His eldest son Francis, whom Tom had elected to be his successor in his business, entered the church against his father's wishes and subsequently died in the foreign missions; Harvey, who had insisted on chasing his dreams of becoming a composer, ends up a drunk;[15] Veronica has married beneath her; and Norah, the only child living at home and thus Tom's last hope, wants to become a nun. Tom's other son, Harvey, who at the beginning of the play seems likely to fulfil his father's dreams by becoming a racing driver which according to Tom will be 'very good for business' as Harvey will 'meet some very important people' (14), is killed in an accident at the end of the first act. However, not even Harvey's premature and tragic death is allowed to stifle this comedy. In fact, his death serves no other purpose than to bring Veronica and Philip back to the family home where they do everything in their power to secure more money from their father.

Comparing this play to D'Alton's previous works, it seems peculiar that he so pointedly avoided allowing any tragic consequences to develop. Even the *Irish Times* noted that Tom's story 'has an immediate suggestion of tragedy' adding that the audience was 'prepared for the downfall which seems so certain to arise out of the pride of money that he has built around him'. Indeed, it is not just Tom who escapes a tragic end: Norah, who has the insight to know that her father will not even notice her absence from the house, is unaffected by his attempts to bribe a priest to prevent her following her vocation, or by his efforts to set up a match for her with a young man who is only interested in securing her dowry. On the contrary, these are amongst the funniest scenes in the play, and at no stage does D'Alton to lead the audience into contemplating the more serious aspects of this selfishness. The play ends happily – Harvey's death is quickly forgotten, Norah gets her wish to leave home and become a nun, and Veronica and Philip manage to return permanently to the family home. Indeed, there is a strong sense that Tom is rewarded at the end of the play, as Veronica replaces Norah in the family home and, in some ways, supersedes her by willingly assenting to Tom's plans to impress all around them.

The light-hearted nature of the play appealed to audiences and critics alike. Both the *Irish Times* and the *Irish Independent* comment on the quality of D'Alton's characterization, the *Irish Independent* noting that the play contained a 'rich and varied list of amusing characters', who 'kept us interested and amused throughout a most enjoyable performance'. The *Irish Times* similarly stressed that this was 'a most enjoyable play', which was 'warmly received', and *The Bell,* while admitting that the play did not 'profess great profundity', nonetheless declared it 'an amusing piece of foolery'.[16] What is evident here is that the audience responded well to being amused – as the *Irish Independent* concluded, the characters in the play were 'great fun, and that is what one wants in a comedy'. Indeed, this undemanding drama played for nine consecutively weeks, setting a new record for the Abbey.

Despite a decrease in the output of original plays, theatre audiences in Ireland increased during the 1940s. Hugh Hunt partly attributes this to 'the claustrophobic atmosphere of a city cut off from the rest of the world to which the theatre offered some form of escape'.[17] It is particularly interesting to view this comment in the light of fit-up drama that D'Alton was so involved in. We have already seen how fit-up companies offered provincial audiences (that is, those 'cut off' from city theatre) a form of escape from the drudgery of everyday rural life. In a sense then, we can view fit-up drama in provincial Ireland as being a microcosm of professional drama in a city that was correspondingly disconnected and isolated. And if anyone knew what audiences wanted at this time, D'Alton did. At the time of writing *The Money Doesn't Matter* he was touring the provinces, performing in and producing plays, and pleasing provincial audiences wherever he travelled. It was thus an easy adaptation to please city theatre audiences who demanded entertainment and escape form both the physical and emotional consequences of a world war.

What D'Alton offered, along with playwrights like Shiels, Robinson, and MacNamara was, according to Hunt, 'an evening's entertainment at which the average citizen could feel at home', thus leading the Abbey to 'become a theatre for the people'. Undoubtedly, D'Alton had seen what his audiences wanted and duly presented them with *The Money Doesn't Matter.* But while critics like Gabriel Fallon were able to see that D'Alton had found material for laughter in 'the worldly-wisdom of the covetous and the proud, a good healthy cathartic laughter,'[18] a scandal which not even Louis could have expected arose out of this play when Frank O'Connor wrote to *The Bell* in June 1941 criticising its vulgarity of theme and character, and its supposed caricature of Lennox Robinson as Philip.[19]

O'Connor did concede that the play was 'clearly the work of a dramatist who knows how to choose a dramatic theme and has the technical skill to handle it' (61), but he also raised some valid points. His criticisms that 'at no point do the characters in the play meet' (61), and that 'the father has nothing of the daughter in him, the daughter nothing of the father' (62), are both well-grounded. Indeed, the characters in the play are comparable to fit-up melodramatic representations of character in their stereotypical depiction, but D'Alton surely realized this and may even have been mocking himself when he has Tom remark at the end of *The Money Doesn't Matter*, 'The trouble with my children is that they are ayther too good or no good.' (73) However, O'Connor's view expressed in *The Bell* that 'the stage was entirely peopled by monsters' (62–3), is surely going too far. D'Alton was quick to reply to this stating, 'Five pages of splendid fol-de-rol to prove that the comic method employed in *The Money Doesn't Matter* does not conform to the tragic method of *Hamlet!* And I am supposed that this needs answering! Mr O'Connor doesn't need answering, what he needs in instruction.' (72)[20] What D'Alton was so irate about was that O'Connor had not seen the play for what it was – a comedy: 'The first lesson, dear children, is never to complain of rice pudding for not being jam roll, or roast beef. They are quite separate things.' (72) He further instructs O'Connor that 'the purpose of comedy is to produce only mitigated impressions and by no means to excite strong indignation at human frailty.' (74)

D'Alton also accused O'Connor of belonging to 'that highbrow school of lack of thought which supposes comedy to be an inferior art, and people that enjoy comedy, inferior people' (75). This comment relates back to D'Alton's decision to give his audience what they wanted. Further, when O'Connor wrote of meeting an English woman on her first visit to the Abbey Theatre who described the play as being 'a primitive delight in cruelty', and who 'was not aware of what the audience were laughing at' (63), he is unwittingly supporting D'Alton's decision – to write a play specifically for the audiences that chose to attend the Abbey Theatre at that time. We can refer back to Hunt's deduction that the Abbey had become 'a theatre for the people', and can deduce from this that 'the people' Hunt was referring to were Irish people, living in a very particular time and place.

In another letter written to *The Bell*,[21] Denis Ireland admitted that he 'got several good laughs in the course of the evening'(67) and that he did not 'blame Mr D'Alton for realizing what the Abbey audience wants and feeding them good and proper' (67). However, he went on to criticize the play asking, 'Has the State-supported Irish National Theatre become simply a kind of laboratory where experts in mass-observation can test their theories about the vacuity of the twentieth-century Irish mind, counting every manufactured laugh as a hit? If it has, then does this not amount to a complete reversal of Yeats' original policy, which was to go on giving us the best until we began to like it?' (68) It was Denis Johnston who answered this question saying that *The Money Doesn't Matter* 'is considerably better than what one normally expects'

(80)[22] and that the Abbey Theatre should not be become 'some sort of Shrine of National Endeavour' (80). Indeed, as Johnston pointed out, the Abbey Theatre was a publicly subsidized private company, 'who have been carefully selected, not to lead the Irish Drama into pastures new, but to provide entertainment for a ready-made audience' (80).

In the light of these arguments, it is particularly interesting to analyse the audience reaction to D'Alton's next dramatic offering, *Lovers' Meeting*, as ironically, when D'Alton presented a play that was wholly tragic, the Abbey audience insisted on laughing at it. *Lovers' Meeting* was submitted for reading to the Abbey in July 1941. Richard Hayes, medical doctor and film censor, read the script and was deeply impressed:

> The Abbey has rarely received for its consideration a more powerful and terrifying play than this one of D'Alton's. The sordid theme of the play is on the whole delicately treated, and yet it is certain I think to give rise to much adverse criticism of a liable on the national character, on Irish womanhood.[23]

Shocking the audience into recognition of the nation's faults was probably D'Alton's intention. Indeed, of all D'Alton's works, the theme and exposition of character, is strongest in this play. Yet, as we shall see, both D'Alton and Hayes underestimated the capacity of Dublin audiences at that time to discard the full horror of the play.

Lovers' Meeting, described by D'Alton as 'A Tragedy', focuses on the Sheridan family. The main plot of the play concerns the young Mary Sheridan, daughter of Jane and Tom. Mary is in love with Joe Hession, who turns out to be the son of a man Jane had been in love with many years previous. It unfolds that Mary is actually Jane's illegitimate daughter, the result of the love affair between Jane and Joe's father, and so Joe is actually Mary's half brother. The play ends in tragedy with Joe hanged for murder, and Mary committing suicide.

Phyllis Ryan, then an eighteen-year-old juvenile actress with the Abbey, played Mary. She remembers clearly the uproar the play caused even within the Abbey cast, the rather sordid subject matter of the play dividing the actors who played in it.[24] Further, the Abbey directors were adamant that Phyllis' character be played as insane but D'Alton, who attended all rehearsals, was unyielding in his belief that Mary was far from mad. Phyllis Ryan, caught in the middle, described the whole affair as 'a frightening ordeal', and writes of it in her autobiography, *The Company I Kept*:

> Louis took me aside one day and said that Mary, as written, was quite sane when she decided to take her life to be with her lover, rather than marry the repulsive old man forced on her by her unloving parents. He was of the opinion that the Abbey directors wanted her to go out of her mind so that her terrible end could be attributed to madness, and he was not having any of this. The whole point of suicide was to expose the lack of compassion and Christianity in rural society, particularly from an all-powerful church obsessed with sin and damnation. Louis argued that Mary had made a sane decision to die with Joe, rather than live in a sordid, loveless coupling.
>
> Frank Dermody was converted to this view, and rehearsals proceeded. But the clouds were gathering, and one day Dermody came down from the office and said that the board insisted that Mary should be played like Ophelia, driven mad with the shock of all the tragedy that had befallen her. Frank really agreed with Louis, but he was mortally terrified of authority, whether that of the board or of the Church. He pointed out to Louis that Joe was Mary's half-brother as well as her ex-fiancé, and that she had to be out of her mind if she expected to have an incestuous love-affair in the next world. Louis stuck obstinately to his argument. In the next world, if there was one, he declared, the two lovers would be spirits, and that transcended everything. Mary was sane; she was not a simpering idiot, and he would not have her made into one.[25]

D'Alton convinced Frank and Phyllis of his views, and after the opening performance he was, according to Ryan, 'ecstatic'. However, Frank Dermody was blamed by a 'furious' board who insisted that Mary change her playing of the final scene. D'Alton's battle was lost.

On the surface *Lovers' Meeting* could be described as a play written against the made match. But it goes much deeper than this, exposing the problems that result from repression, specifically sexual repression. In his opening stage directions, D'Alton gives a detailed picture of the set, the semiotics of which, at first glance, suggest a typical provincial Irish family home of that day (1941): the stone flagged kitchen, the wide, high fireplace in which a great bank of turf burns, the earthenware pans of milk, the three home-made loaves of brown bread and the broom near the fireplace, all suggest a homely atmosphere.[26] However, on closer inspection the semiotics also point to some less cosy images: 'The place conveys a sense of Spartan prosperity and is almost superhumanly clean' (7); the hearth of the fire is 'clean swept', the table 'scrubbed white', the curtains on the window 'stiff with starch', and the religious pictures of 'The Elopement' and 'The Reconciliation' hang on the 'white-washed walls' alongside an oleograph of the Blessed Virgin' (7). Thus, while the overall image is one of a spotless exterior, the audience should discover that this is, in fact, a deliberate shield established by Jane who endeavours to enshroud the darker secrets of her home and her soul, her attempts at scrubbing clean her surroundings being the outward manifestation of a need to eradicate her past 'sins'.

When the play opens, Jane is making sandwiches. Described in the stage directions as 'A resolute, self-disciplined woman, exteriorly cold and unimaginative' (7), Jane is immediately presented in stark contrast to her husband Tom who is 'a big, kindly man, domesticated, easy-going and instinctively generous natured'(7). The first action we see is Tom putting his arm around Jane's shoulder 'affectionately' and saying to her, 'D'ye know that I feel all the better for that bit of a nap? And how is my Gerrl?' (8) But Jane is cold and detached, and responds to Tom saying, 'Ye should slip on your coat, Tom, an' go as far as the end o' the boreen' (8). Thus, an immediate sense of non-communication and detachment on Jane's part is visible to the audience, a feature that augments as the play continues.

D'Alton makes it very clear in *Lovers' Meeting* that Jane's greatest fault is not that she loved, or felt and acted on passion, a passion which led to Mary's illegitimate birth, but that she subsequently allowed herself to expel any emotional feelings from her life. What is even more calamitous is the fact that she extends this resentment of love, this continual suppression of desire, to the person who has come to epitomize her 'sins', her daughter Mary, whom Jane views as the product of her misplaced passion. Indeed, in Jane's final conversation with Mary she tells her, 'Seein' ye grow up before me [was] like a livin' sin'. (60)

Jane does her utmost to deny Mary the opportunity to experience any of these emotions, above all sexual desire. This is why she tries to force Mary to marry the old, unattractive widower, Batt Seery. As far as Jane is concerned, 'Lovin' and marryin' has nothin' to do with each other' (11). However, Jane's expulsion of love is futile and her repressed emotions return despite herself when she comes face to face with Joe Hession. Throughout the play Jane has coldly maintained that Joe is 'no match' for Mary, but when Joe stands on her doorstep, all she can see is the ghost of her dead lover, his father Mick:

> (The effect of his presence on her is extraordinary. She looks at him in growing terror. When she speaks it is with a great effort in a ghostly whisper)
> *Jane:* Mick … Hession

> *Joe*: (cheerfully) Joe Hession, ma'am, me father was Mick Hession. 'Tis him you're thinking of. They say I've a terrible likeness of him.
> *Jane*: Yes ... a terrible likeness. You're voice even ... (33)

For the first time we see Jane portraying emotion, but she quickly gains control of herself:

> *Jane*: (recovering herself) The table is waiting to be cleared (33)

although she cannot help but recoil when Joe utters the word she dreads:

> *Joe*: But when we love ...
> *Jane*: (Sharply, almost in terror) Don't say that (shaking head). You're not to say that ... You're not to say that. (33)

However, this lapse in Jane's defences is only momentary. Even when the truth emerges about Joe, and he is sentenced to death for murdering his uncle the very day Mary is due to marry Batt, she refuses to alter the date. Instead, she compares Mary to herself saying, "Tis for the best. She'll not be looking back. 'Twould have been well for me there was no repentin' an' longin' an' lookin' back. 'Twould have been well for me now.' (57) And so she advises Mary is to act as she has done:

> *Jane*: By submittin' an' hardenin' yourself. Be strivin' day in an' day out alongside your husband an' welcomin' the least unwelcome touch, till you harden yourself against shrinkin' away. Strivin' to care up your family. 'Tis a short while only till the softness is gone out o' ye. (61)

The last conversation Mary has with her mother is a desperate attempt to make Jane fight for her husband, who is leaving her. When Mary tells her how her father loves her, all Jane can say is, 'I don't know what I could say that would keep him.' Mary's answer is clear: 'If ye could tell him that ye loved him, Ma', to which Jane replies, 'I can't understand that it should matter now.' (61) Ironically, it is this denial of emotion, this deliberate repression that has made Jane so untouchable, that spurs Mary to achieve through suicide what her mother would never allow herself – to choose love at all costs.

For D'Alton, Jane is the epitome of Ireland gone wrong and is representative of the dangers of the moral insistence so dominant in de Valera's Ireland. Her repression is that of Ireland's, the repercussions of which, though plain to see, were being continually denied by those who insisted on the moral correctness of the de Valera mentality. But however forceful D'Alton's characterization of Jane was, his intention was missed by the Dublin audiences. In fact, so mis-read was the character of Jane that the *Irish Times* declared, 'It was too hard to believe in [Jane's] dark passionate past', adding that the doom created by D'Alton 'seemed strangely unreal'. The fact is, Irish audiences at that time simply did not want to see doom, and so intent were they on enjoying the play that they insisted on seeing it as a comedy. The chief victim here was the character of Hannie who was laughed at throughout the whole play, much to D'Alton's dismay.

Unlike the other women in the play Hannie's marriage was a love marriage as opposed to a made match. However, her husband left her soon after the marriage and Hannie has seemingly convinced herself, and tried to convince everyone else, that he writes regularly to her and will be returning home soon. Her daily trips to the post office to collect the letters that never come, and her regular tidings of 'good news' to anyone who will listen, are signs that her whole existence is lived both through and for her fantasy. The reaction to Hannie from the other characters in the play shows a distinct lack of understanding. Frances' deduction that 'she's half cracked' (19) is typical of society's response to fantasy. Because fantasy lies outside the realm of reality, and because there is no language capable of crossing the divide from reality to fantasy, the whole concept of fantasy is nullified, and the broad, linguistically viable concept of 'madness' takes over. Hence Frances' attempt to explain Hannie's desire to escape from the restrictions of reality: 'She's a kind of an oddity an' cracked in her way o' going on. She's quare an' doesn't act sensible.' (19)

Even the theatre critic of the *Irish Times* referred to Hannie as being 'half-witted',[27] yet she is the only female of her generation in *Lovers' Meeting* who does not suppress desire, the only person who refuses to allow society oppress her, and thus the only person who can express unhidden emotions. Hannie knows that other people laugh at her, that they see her as insane, but she refuses to allow the stigma of this social diagnosis to subjugate her reality, a reality that though grounded in fantasy, is a reality nonetheless. In fact, Hannie points out to Mary that the other characters in the play are in many ways the same as she is:

> *Hannie*: Sometimes I'd see them give a sly grin at me out o' the corner o' me eye when they wouldn't think I'd be noticin' them. Oh, yes, indeed. Even a blind man would feel the cold. An' do you know what they'd be laughin' at?
>
> *Mary*: Their own foolishness.

> *Hannie*: Nothin' but my foolishness, because they seen me smilin' an' chattin' away to meself. And they'd notice it and then they'd smile to themselves an' say she's out o' her mind the oh'oul fool – doin' the very same I was doin', smilin' to themselves an' talkin' to themselves! God help her they'd be sayin' an' I delighted with meself. (21)

The main difference between Hannie and her contemporaries quite simple: Hannie is happy. She says, 'Oh, yes, yes, I'm a bit queer in meself betimes. (*Brightly*) But d'ye ever see me frowning?' (21) Indeed Hannie is happy because she allows herself to express her desires, and because there is no place for these desires in the world she lives in, she uses fantasy to escape this reality and finds happiness beyond its restrictions. In the world D'Alton portrays, reality is cruel; it is a world where marriages are nothing more than bargains and where love seems futile, being either repressed (in Jane's case), opposed (in Mary's case) or unrequited (in Hannie's case). In this world, one had only two choices – to remain within the bounds of reality and suppress, or to escape to the freedom of fantasy and express.

Hannie's role in *Lovers' Meeting* is twofold: through her D'Alton wanted his audience to see the faults inherent in a society which forced its people to either accept its restrictions and be accepted, or to renounce its limitations and be exiled. However, her exile also served to show the audience that it was possible to repudiate the restrictions of reality and still be happier than by obediently accepting its thwarted rules. D'Alton, however, is not advocating her way of living as an ideal one; he does not profess to have any answers to this problem, and this is why *Lovers' Meeting* ends in tragedy. D'Alton knew that his contemporaries had to fight the fears that emanated from those in power, fears of an Ireland that was rapidly moving into a modern world, but he also realized that the process of alleviating the protectionism imposed on his nation's people was going to be far from simple.

For Mary however, Hannie is a figure of hope and it is natural, albeit tragic, that she follows her advice:

> *Hannie*: An' whenever it is ye should ask God one favour an' one favour only ... 'Dear God', ye must say, 'let me die now; now let me die'. That way ye could escape that one sorrow is in the world. There is only one sorrow, ye know ... It's the sorrow of knowing such great happiness couldn't come to ye again, an' that nothin' else is worth livin' for. (22–23)

For Hannie, life without happiness is not worth enduring, so by clinging on to her fantasies she keeps the hope of happiness alive. In Hannie's eyes death is pleasant in that it offers relief from reality; her comment 'I went through it an' I know' (23) shows us that she has already suffered a death. This death is spiritual, but she has achieved a certain resurrection through fantasy, as fantasy offers what reality denies her – hope.

In Act II we see just how far Hannie can revert into her fantasies and how fantasy can transcend time. Hannie believes Joe's late night tapping on the window to be Martin, her estranged husband, and the next time we see her she is wearing a very short skirt, silk stockings and a blouse: 'Her eyes glitter excitedly, her high cheek bones are heavily rouged. Her lips carmined.' (46) Believing that Martin is on his way home, Hannie has reverted back to her youth. In the following scene Hannie and Jane stand face to face, the former personifying fantasy, the latter reality:

> (Jane enters, going to the fireplace. She looks at Hannie disapprovingly).
> *Jane*: Where'd you think you're goin', Hannie? Got up like that.
> *Hannie*: (Brightly) I thought I'd tidy meself up a bit. I might take a stroll for meself later on. 'Twould do me good – might blow the cobwebs off me.
> *Jane*: Ye'd have a right to go upstairs and blow that skirt off yourself first.
> *Hannie*: Ye wouldn't think it too youthful, would ye? 'tis the fashion anyway.
> *Jane*: Gettin' yourself up like a little gerrl is no fashion for a woman o' your years.
> *Hannie*: Why not when I have the figure for it.
> *Jane*: Ye haven't the legs for it. What are ye doin' to your face?
> *Hannie*: I done nothin' at all to me face. Havin' a high colour is natural to me. Oh! Yes, yes, indeed. It's a wonder now ye never noticed that before, isn't it.
> *Jane*: (dryly) A great wonder indeed. Ye'd better try lowerin' it a bit. 'Tis far *too* high. (*Exit*) (47)

Here we see two sisters, the one happy and hopeful, the other cold and sardonic. And we see the inherent tragedy in both sisters as they both know what desire is yet neither can communicate this shared experience. Instead both rely on their own different methods of delusion and suppression in order to cope with life.

Through this delusion and suppression, both sisters lose their innate identities. In fact, Hannie tries to take on Mary's identity at the end of the play, becoming the bride to be:

> She comes centre, her arms close to her sides, her hands sticking out, her fingers outspread affectedly. She smiles brightly and puts her head to one side. She turns completely round standing in one place, looking back over her shoulder and murmuring to herself. She runs to the mirror and looks into it, patting her hair. She hums the air of 'I know where I'm going' and looks down the length of her outstretched arms to her fingers. (Murmuring): I will is what I have to say, I will. (She plucks out her dress at the sides). An' I must walk this way. (She walks with great stateliness) And then I must stop. I will, I must say, I will. (63)

At this point Hannie sees Mary reading a letter from Joe, and presumes it to be from Martin. When Mary tells her it is not, Hannie, momentarily, cannot sustain the fantasy and '*Quite suddenly she breaks down and cries*' (63). However, when Mary 'touches her shoulder compassionately' and goes upstairs, Hannie immediately returns to her cocooned world of fantasy, 'dries her eyes and sits smiling brightly, her feet tapping' (63). By the end of the play we see Hannie 'smiling more brightly than usual' (69) when she says of Mary, 'I looked down the length of her. I saw her feet weren't touching the floor'. Hannie is happy once again because she has seen Mary 'shining' and because she has once again managed to escape the horrors of reality.

D'Alton's characterization of Hannie is an obvious exploration of the notions of fantasy and escape. Yet the drama reviewer of the *Irish Times* commented that her role was 'wholly unnecessary', saying

> It really did nothing for the play beyond confusing it between tragedy and comedy. It took the audience too long to realise that this half-witted creature was not there for the purpose of being laughed at, and when it was seen that the part might have some tragic meaning, be something in the nature of a chorus, it was too late.[28]

It is interesting that by insisting on laughing at Hannie, the audience blocked out 'reality' in the same way that D'Alton's characters did. Using laughter as a defence mechanism, the audience followed Frances' recognition that 'There's no one cryin' then but a good share breakin' their hearts laughin' at her.' (20) The full tragedy of the play was thus deliberately missed by its first audience. As its reviewer said:

> The existence of an unknown relationship between certain characters in this version of the story should have had the effect of plunging it

> into deepest tragedy, but this is not what exactly what happened in the play as it was seen last night.
>
> One wonders what really happened in a production to a work where what was apparently intended as comic relief from the pressures of tragic relationships and the distress of poignant situations becomes almost the whole play. Surely that cannot have been the intention, nor completely the aim of all the players. It must then have been the will of the audience driving hard towards an evening's enjoyment.[29]

Lovers' Meeting does not deliberately set out to be comic; any comic relief was designed to amuse and settle the audience, to provide brief relief from the ensuing tragic events. So intent, however, were its audiences on distancing themselves from the tragedy that they refused to recognize its onset.

Christopher Murray's deduction that 'Times were so bad in Dublin in 1941 that no audience was prepared to undergo tragic experience in a theatre',[30] helps the modern reader understand the audience's reaction. Indeed, Dublin was in the midst of a depression, a result of the 'inevitable consequence of inhabiting a small underdeveloped island in a hostile world'. Rationing was commonplace as commodities ran in and out of supply, so even the basics such as sugar, tea, bread, butter and fuel were often scarce and very expensive. In fact the *Irish Times* reported on the same day that *Lovers' Meeting* was reviewed that Sean Lemass, Minister for Supplies, was debating the feasibility of requiring the early closing of businesses and offices during the winter months 'as a means of conserving fuel and power supplies'.[31]

Furthermore, it was predicted by de Valera on the very day that *Lovers' Meeting* opened in the Abbey that Ireland would soon become involved in the war; it is thus hardly surprising that the Abbey audience refused to absorb the full tragedy of the play. However, the fact was that Ireland was becoming increasingly isolated. As F.S.L. Lyons points out:

> At the very moment [Ireland] has achieved stability and full independence, and was ready to take her place in the society of nations, that society dissolved and she was thrown back upon her own meagre resources. The tensions and liberations – of war, the shared experience, the comradeship in suffering, the new thinking about the future, all these things had passed her by. It was as if an entire people had been condemned to live in Plato's cave, with their backs to the fire of life and deriving their only knowledge of what went on outside from the flickering shadows thrown on the wall before their eyes by the men and women who passed to and fro behind them.[32]

Lovers' Meeting was an attempt by D'Alton to entice those people to turn around and face the fire of life. Unfortunately, the people were not ready to do this.

We have seen how D'Alton's audiences unequivocally rejected any didactic proclivities embedded in his plays, especially his aspirations to convince his theatregoers of the necessity that Ireland move into the modern world. And as a commercial dramatist, D'Alton eventually decided to conform to his audiences' dictates. 'Money can hire the best artists to provide careful productions of the best plays', writes Tyrone Guthrie in *Theatre Prospect*: 'Money can hire the best artists to provide careful productions of the best plays. Money can buy advertisement [sic] to persuade a gullible public to go and see these productions, but no amount of money can persuade an audience sincerely to enjoy what is not to its taste.'[33]

But even when D'Alton did succumb to popular will in the ironically-titled *The Money Doesn't Matter*, he still couldn't please everyone and paradoxically, it was this play, intended to be a harmless comedy, which caused an outrage. Greed portrayed on stage, even in a comic matter, was seemingly too much to handle. When we compare this to the many important issues D'Alton was trying to alert his audiences to in his serious plays (religious hypocrisy, intolerance, repression etc.), genuine concerns which were conveniently ignored, we realize that this was precisely the old Ireland Louis was writing against. We can thus conclude that Gabriel Fallon's invitation in 1937 to 'Experiment by all means. The theatre is the place for it', was prematurely made, and while playwrights like D'Alton were eager to bid farewell to the old Ireland, Irish audiences were unwilling to bury it.

CHAPTER SIX

Greasepaint wars and welcome welcomes

The advent of the second-world war and its accompanying economic repercussions should have meant that fit-up tours were less financially viable than ever, and indeed life on the road during this time was no easy task. However, juxtaposed with this was a social consequence of war, that being a desire on the part of the public to escape the horrors of the times. Consequently, entertainment was demanded more than ever, and fit-up theatre ended up playing a large and important role during these years. D'Alton's involvement in wartime touring theatre was substantial, but this time also served him well in his quest to temporarily escape the demands of city theatre. Having become firmly established at the Abbey with the success of his first plays, and been delegated a responsible position as producer in the Abbey Theatre in 1939, within six months he had resigned from this position and instead spent the next six years carving out an existence as a fit-up manager and producer.

When Hugh Hunt resigned from his position as producer in the Abbey Theatre in November 1938, he was replaced by D'Alton in January 1939. However, two months after D'Alton produced his second play *To-Morrow Never Comes* in the Abbey, he also resigned from this position and was succeeded by Frank Dermody. The fact that D'Alton produced at the Abbey for a mere six months is puzzling. It is possible that he gave up this position in order to concentrate wholly on achieving his ambitions of becoming a successful playwright. But if this was the case, it is surprising that he took up this position in the first place. Another possible reason for his resignation could have been due to a strained relationship that existed between him and Ernest Blythe. Indeed, just over a year after his resignation, a dispute arose during the rehearsal period for *Lovers' Meeting* between D'Alton and Blythe, and not only did D'Alton have his subsequent play, *You Can't Be Too Careful,* produced at the Olympia Theatre, but he did not submit another play to the Abbey for over six years. And while he did work with Blythe in 1939 managing the Abbey Player's tour, it was away from the theatre and Blythe's assertive reach, so creative differences were less likely to develop. Whatever D'Alton's reasons for returning to a touring life, this break from city theatre and his immersion back into provincial life served its purpose as the plays he wrote after this period secured his position among his contemporaries as a popular and highly-regarded playwright.

D'Alton's first steps back on the road were with the Abbey's second company's tour of the Provinces, a tour he had helped to initiate, along with Ernest Blythe and F.R. Higgins. The first written record of this proposed tour can be seen in the Abbey Theatre's minute books where on 1 September 1939 it is documented that a provincial tour for the Abbey's second company was proposed. It was suggested that the tour take place in the spring of 1940 with the intention 'to visit various country towns, both large and small. To travel, if possible, with small sets specially made to suit limited stage accommodation, and to use portable lighting.'[1] On 24 November 1939, the same minute book records that F.R. Higgins had requested permission to fix up contracts for the tour, suggesting that the tour should occupy three months. The board agreed that Higgins should 'make enquiries as to the expenses likely to be incurred and that he should communicate with local managers with a view to finding those who would be interested in the proposal'. By the New Year plans for the proposed tour were making headway. On 5 January 1940, Higgins reported to the Abbey board that he had requested a report from Dermot Kelly of Longford Productions outlining the arrangements that could be made with towns visited by their company. Interestingly, Higgins also noted that Louis D'Alton had provided 'valuable verbal information' and had offered his services as Manager of the tour.

D'Alton was obviously the primary adviser to the directors of the Abbey in relation to this tour, his experience as a fit-up artist certainly serviceable to Blythe who had come to the Abbey from a political background. Both he and Dermot Kelly submitted reports to Blythe about the proposed tour, but it is D'Alton's ideas that Blythe quotes throughout his final report, 'Report on Prospective Provincial Tour.' This report is divided into eight sections (Introduction; Fit-up; Sets; Transport; Players and Staff; Lighting; Publicity; and Box Office and Booking Office), and six of these sections credit D'Alton's ideas and advice.[2]

On 25 January 1940, Higgins reported to the Abbey board that he had sent letters to 24 towns to local managers of the halls offering one third of the gross box office takings; as favourable replies were received from 15 managers, it was decided at this point that the tour should go ahead. D'Alton's knowledge of fit-up theatre led directly to his suggestion that bookings be made on a seven-day week, and that Saturdays be used for travelling, as this day attracted the worst houses, while Sundays traditionally drew the largest audiences. Admission prices for the shows were to be based upon the experience of the

Longford Company, ranging from a limited number of reserved seats at 3*s.* 6*d.* each, to seats of 3*s.*, 2*s.* and 1*s.*. Blythe also drew on the fit-up practice of having the best seats nearer the stage, 'instead of the usual arrangements in the Cinema Halls where the cheap seats are near to the Screen'. It is also interesting to note that in typical fit-up fashion, Blythe was advised to make sure that competition from elsewhere was minimal, although in this case it seems that other fit-up companies were not the main worry: 'Powers to cancel Contracts in the event of a local Mission colliding with our week's visit, should be made a condition of all arrangements with Proprietors.'[3]

Of course, travelling from town to town would require a fit-up, and the traditional fit-up of a light portable frame, portable proscenium, wings and tableau curtains was decided upon: 'Mr D'Alton would be prepared to supervise the making of the fit-up, and in his opinion all the incidentals and accessories for the fit-up would not cost more than TEN POUNDS, including curtain and frame.'[4] The repertoire would include three plays, George Shiels' *Professor Tim* and *The Jailbird,* and Lennox Robinson's *The Far-Off Hills,* where a kitchen and a sitting room would be the only sets needed apart from a bedroom which 'could be created from curtains'. D'Alton also assured Blythe that another well-known fit-up trick – that of borrowing any furniture needed for the plays from local families – would cut down on costs, and at the same time create space when travelling. Transport itself was an important consideration. Blythe noted in his report that Longford in a recent tour had used a very large lorry and trailer for the sets and props, and five cars for the players and staff. However, he decided that D'Alton's suggestion was more practical: 'Mr D'Alton thinks that Railway transport is more economical and particularly at the present time during petrol restrictions.'

D'Alton also stressed the need for an advance manager to travel one week ahead of the tour. His duties would be to find a suitable shop to act as a booking office, to inspect billing, to do publicity work with local newspapers, to arrange advertising, to organize train travel, and to secure suitable accommodation for the players. Also, D'Alton would supply two men to act as scene shifters, one of whom had a sufficient knowledge of scenery, at salaries of £2 5*s.* per week. As far as lighting was concerned, a small lighting set was all that was needed as D'Alton would loan the tour a switchboard and an overhead lighting box. It was also decided that a touring manager should accompany the twelve players (five women and seven men) who would be one of the seven male players and play small parts: 'Mr Louis D'Alton offers his services in that capacity at a salary of £5 per week, plus £2 living expenses.' Indeed, D'Alton negotiated a bonus for himself, 'a commission of 5% which if granted, should only be paid when our gross takings exceed £150 per week'.

It is recorded in the Abbey Theatre minute book that D'Alton accepted this package on 2 February 1940. On this date it was also decided that there would be a nine-week rehearsal period for the tour under Michael J. Dolan, and that D'Alton should start work in the office one month before taking the company out.

The actors who would tour were also selected on 2 February 1940 and were as follows: Fred Johnson, Gerard Healy, Dermot Kelly, Harry Brogan, T. Wilson, T. Ryan, Louis D'Alton, Maureen Delaney, Phyllis Ryan, Bonnie Fagan, Eithne Dunne and Shela Ward. Blythe was keen to send out a 'second class company of players' so that salaries and living expenses could be kept below £90 per week, 'main' Abbey players being used only 'in important towns like Galway and Sligo'. A few weeks later and, the projected venues for the tour were listed as follows: Drogheda, Dundalk, Monaghan, Clones, Cavan, Longford, Boyle, Sligo, Ballina, Castlebar, Tuam, Roscommon, Ballinasloe, Galway, Ennis, Tipperary, Clonmel, Fermoy, Dungarvan, Wexford, New Ross, Kilkenny, Carlow, Tullamore, Mullingar, Athlone, Birr, Roscrea, Nenagh, Thurles and Maryborough.[5]

For Blythe, the tour would only be successful if it made a profit but he seemed confident that this would be the case as, 'according to all indications, we would meet with a very fine reception in the country and I feel convinced that under capable management there is no reason why we could not get out of such tour a handsome profit'.[6] The Irish Provincial Tour travelled from April to August 1940, but unfortunately resulted in a loss of £242 3*s.* 9*d.* Indeed, even before the tour began, the Abbey Theatre accounts recorded deferred expenses for the Irish Provincial Tour of £210 6*s.* 5*d.*, and by late August this figure had risen to £307 2*s.* 6*d.*. Why exactly the tour made a loss is unspecified, but obviously the expenses of sending the second Abbey Company on tour outweighed the remuneration made on the door. Whether D'Alton was directly to blame for this loss is also unclear; however, as manager of the tour, he was responsible for both its financial and artistic success. Whether or not the tour attracted sufficient audiences, or was an artistic, if not a financial, success is hard to gauge. Newspaper reports on the tour are scant, and though the venues were well advertised in local newspapers, there are no reviews of this tour.

The Abbey Theatre Players began their provincial tour in Dundalk on 15 April 1940, the venue being the Town Hall Cinema. On 15 April George Shiels' *Professor Tim* was performed; on 16 April O'Casey's *The Shadow of a Gunman*, preceded by Martin McHugh's *A Minute's Wait*; and on 17 April Lennox Robinson's *The Far-Off Hills.* Admission prices, the same for each venue of the tour, were as follows: Reserved: 3*s.* 6*d.*, 3*s.* and 2*s.* Limited: 1*s.* From Dundalk the tour moved

1 Louis D'Alton on his confirmation day, aged 15.

N.B.—To avoid long waits, when changing scenery, songs will be introduced between the acts.

48th Year of Uninterrupted Tour.

48th Year of Uninterrupted Tour

THE CELEBRATED

La Comedie Irlandaise Co.

So well-known as a fully responsible, solvent and enterprising Touring Management, specially organised to support the well-known popular Actor. . . .

Mr. WM. L. DOBELL

— ON TOUR —

**" From North to South the cry they swell
Our favourite actor is Dobell."**

All intoxicating liquors strictly prohibited on the premises during business hours. No intoxicated or disorderly persons are admitted, and very strict silence and order are maintained during the performances.

PROGRAMMES, ONE PENNY.

The Attendants will supply Opinions of the Press and Photographs if requested

Licensed to play the Pieces of the Society of Dramatic Authors when required.

Note—An Efficient Actor is Retained as Understudy to Mr. Dobell.

Secretary and Treasurer—**Miss Madge Merryweather**, to whom please present all accounts and they will be promptly paid

2 Advertisement for William Dobell's La Comedia Irlandaise Company.

3 William Dobell's fit-up transport.

4 Fit-up artist James Holland, in villian costume.

5 Louis D'Alton, *c.*1920.

6 Louis in costume for one of his early melodramas, *c.*1930.

7 Noel D'Alton, *c.*1924.

8 Louis, Anne and Sheila D'Alton.

9 Babs D'Alton and Louis D'Alton's daughter, Sheila.

10 *They Got What They Wanted*, Westend Production, Embassy Theatre, 1950.

11 Louis, Anne and Sheila D'Alton.

12 Noel D'Alton (on the left) with the Killarney Players.

13 Louis and Anne D'Alton.

14 Eithne Mulhall.

15 Fred Johnson and F.J. McCormick in *The Spanish Soldier*, 1940.

16 Louis and his second wife, Eithne Mulhall.

17 Sinead Cusack and Ingrid Craig in the Druid Theatre Company's revival of *Lovers' Meeting*, 1990.

to the Diamond Cinema in Monaghan, this time playing for four days (18 April to 21 April), the extra performance being an Edward McNulty play, *The Courting of Mary Doyle.* The tour progressed to Clones on 22 April for three nights, then to Cootehill, Co. Cavan on 25 April for a further three nights, before crossing the border to Newry for six nights, followed by Armagh, Tyrone and Fermanagh, playing three or four nights in each venue.

The Company then crossed back over the border and the Western section of the provincial tour began on 16 May 1940 in the Abbey Cinema in Boyle, Co. Roscommon, where it performed for four nights. On 21 May it moved to St Joseph's Temperance Hotel in Longford for six nights, then on 27 May to the Savoy Cinema in Sligo where F.J. McCormick was sent to play with the company for seven nights. On 3 June the company played a week in Ballina, Co. Mayo; on 10 June, a week in Galway; and on 17 June, a week in the Gaiety Cinema, Ennis. When the company played in a town for seven days, *The Shadow of a Gunman* was performed on two successive nights, followed by *The Far-Off Hills* and *Professor Tim,* while *The Courting of Mary Doyle* made up the seventh night, sometimes preceded by Lady Gregory's *The Rising of the Moon* or *Workhouse Ward.*

From here, the tour's trail becomes more difficult to follow. The Company played four nights in the Oxmantown Hall, Birr, Co. Offaly from 4 to 7 July, an interesting venue because Robinson's *Drama at Inish* was added to the repertoire, and because Anne D'Alton stepped in to take the place of Bonnie Fagan who had become ill. On 8 and 9 July *Drama at Inish, The Shadow of a Gunman, The Rising of the Moon* and *The Far-Off Hills* were performed in the Abbey Hall, Roscrea, Tipperary, and the tour was then meant to visit Maryborough, Tipperary Town, Clonmel and Thurles before moving to the Southern section of the tour. However, I have been unable to locate any advertisements for the tour from this point on. The final section of the tour was due to start in Charleville, Cork at the end of July, and then move on to Killarney, Tralee, Fermoy, Dungarvan, Waterford, Wexford, New Ross, Kilkenny, Carlow, Portarlington, Mullingar and then Cavan once again.

It is likely that financial problems were at this stage beginning to affect the tour, and perhaps its advertising suffered. In any case, the Company had returned to Dublin by 9 August 1940, and as it would have been impossible to visit all the above mentioned venues in such a short space of time, we can conclude that the tour ended sooner than was originally planned. Interestingly, the Abbey Theatre Players visited Kilkenny in September 1940. The *Kilkenny Journal* advertised that the Abbey Theatre Plays, presented by the National Theatre Society, would be performed at the Kilkenny Theatre on 9, 10 and 11 September 1940. Shiels' *The Jailbird,* O'Casey's *The Shadow of a Gunman,*

Lady Gregory's *The Rising of the Moon,* and Lennox Robinson's *Drama at Inish* made up the chosen repertoire, the seat prices starting at 9*d.* for the pits, rising to three shillings for the balcony. However, although the plays received good publicity in the *Kilkenny Journal,* they were not reviewed, and it was not until D'Alton returned to Kilkenny with his own company in October 1941 that we read: 'On a visit of the Abbey Players on tour last year, Mr D'Alton was the producer, and the audience on that occasion were so pleased with the entertainment provided that a return visit of the players was eagerly awaited.'[7] It seems likely, however, that this venue was not part of the 1940 provincial tour, but rather a one-off visit.

It is difficult to determine whether or not the audiences who attended the performances of the Abbey Theatre Company on their tour were as satisfied as the Kilkenny theatregoers, given the lack of reviews; however, what we can be certain of is that some of the players touring were less happy. The group of junior and senior players who toured as the Abbey second company was chosen by Blythe, and included Fred Johnson, Gerard Healy, Eithne Dunne, Brian O'Higgins, Maureen Delaney and Phyllis Ryan. Ryan remembers Maureen Delaney 'in shock' that she had been chosen to tour:

> Being parted from most of her contemporary acting friends was bad enough, but travelling with a fit-up repertoire, for a period of months under less than ideal conditions, was a serious ordeal for a lady in her middle years. I went to her dressing-room when the news was announced, and found her in tears. Although I could see that a big name was needed to sell the Abbey wares in the provinces, she was the only one of the top four – the others were F.J. McCormick, May Craig and Eileen Crowe – to be sent out. She was aware that refusal to go might finish her with the new managing director, just as those left behind were conscious of some loss of identity in the influx of new Gaelic-speaking performers.[8]

Touring during wartime, and having to cope with wartime restrictions, was no easy task, and the newspapers that advertised the tour provide an interesting accompanying cultural and historical datum, the main focus naturally being on the war. For example, when the tour visited Monaghan in April 1940, a full page of the newspaper that advertised the tour was allotted to a day-to-day record of the war in diary form entitled, 'How the War Goes On'[9], and when the tour reached Fermanagh, the headlines of the *Fermanagh Times* on 2 May 1940 read, 'Twelve Setbacks for Hitler and the Norwegian Blitzkrieg Plan.' Two weeks later the same newspaper quoted from de Valera's statement made on 11 May confirming Ireland's neutrality, and reported that within the previous week the scenes of action on the war front had shifted from France and Norway to Holland, Belgium and Luxembourg, and that Chamberlain had resigned as prime minister and had been replaced by Winston Churchill.

By the time the Abbey Players visited Omagh in May, newspapers were reporting how the Norwegians were 'Resisting Germans Gallantly',[10] and when the tour reached the Free State, the ongoing war continued to dominate the headlines of provincial papers. For example, when the Abbey Tour was advertised in the *Sligo Champion* on 25 May 1940, 'German Landing in Eire' headlined, the edition also reporting on questions in the Dáil about the possibilities of a German invasion of Ireland. A week later, on 1 June 1940, the same newspaper headlined the 'Fierce Fighting for Dunkirk', and noted how the German advance had been checked; and when the company were performing in Ennis two weeks later, de Valera was also there calling for men to join the regular army. Under the headline 'Is Liberty Worth Fighting For?' the *Clare Champion* quotes de Valera's speech given in Ennis where he analysed the situation for Ireland: 'We will have to bear all these sacrifices in the future like the small nations of Europe had to bear them if we are to maintain our liberties.'[11] Indeed, the sacrifices ordinary Irish people had to make were many. As F.S.L. Lyons points out in *Ireland since the Famine,* the war made itself felt very clearly in Ireland for those who stayed at home as commodities ran out of supply and rationing had to be imposed.[12] Lyons notes that private motoring all but ceased in 1943 and that long-distance travel became increasingly difficult, even by public transport, a fact that would have affected fit-up companies greatly. Gas and electricity consumption was also cut substantially, and coal was almost unobtainable at times. Rationing was common, notably on clothes and food, which created much hardship, especially amongst the poor. But another factor posited by Lyons was the psychological consequence of war on a country that was so isolated: Ireland had been finally 'ready to take her place in the society of nations' as war broke out, but the shared comradeship, the tensions and liberations of war had all passed her by. Consequently, six years later she emerged dazed and unable to take her place in the much-changed world.

However, that the tour continued is an indication that everyday life in provincial Ireland still prevailed, and the same newspapers that reported on the war also continued to write about day-to-day local happenings. For example, the day the *Fermanagh Times* reported the Norwegian Blitzkreig Plan, a front page article saw fit to relate the story of an Ulster girl who was 'jilted at the altar'. Similarly the *Tyrone Constitution* reported a ten pound fine which was imposed on two Londonderry men who pleaded guilty to importing into Northern Ireland (in contravention of the customs regulations) twenty-seven and a half pounds of butter, twelve dozen boxes of twenty-five matches, and four stones of oats.[13] And in the Republic of Ireland, on the same page that the *Sligo Champion* reported the 'Fierce Fighting for Dunkirk' on 1 June 1940, a 'Successful Whist Drive' also received a headline.

Undoubtedly, the war and wartime restrictions, especially troublesome in their effect on a touring company, added to the many other exasperations that made up the daily existence of a touring manager like D'Alton. When he had proffered his services as touring manager, he willingly put aside his writing for six months, obviously welcoming the opportunity to manage a tour of this size and quality, though the financial backing to do so would also have been very alluring to someone who was more accustomed to struggling with the financial insecurities of the fit-up existence. D'Alton now had the opportunity to make a success of a provincial tour that he had jointly formulated, and as touring manager and producer he would have known he was instrumental to its success. However, everything from rationing to travelling restrictions, not to mention the necessity of dragging sets and costumes back and forward across the border, must have made the tour virtually impracticable. And the fact that half the company were comparatively untried actors and actresses, and that some of the more experienced actors and actresses were decidedly unhappy about having been sent on tour, must have made D'Alton's job as manager even more arduous. Nonetheless, as far as he was concerned, the benefits that arose from the tour were worth the hardships, and if the Irish Provincial Tour was not a financial success for the Abbey Theatre, it certainly heightened D'Alton's reputation in the provinces as a fit-up producer of first-class quality, albeit at the expense of the Abbey. This tour, his life back on the road, his position as manager and producer, and the opportunity he had to act once again, induced D'Alton to form his own touring company which was initiated in 1942.

By this stage five of D'Alton's plays had been successfully staged in the Abbey (*The Man in the Cloak, To-morrow Never Comes, The Spanish Soldier, The Money Doesn't Matter* and *Lovers' Meeting*) and his next offering, *You Can't Be Too Careful,* would be staged in the Olympia in May of that year. He was thus beginning to achieve success as a playwright and the timing could not have been better for him to undertake a countrywide tour that would promote his plays to audiences, the majority of whom would not have seen them performed in the Abbey Theatre. The 1942 repertoire consisted of the following plays: D'Alton's *You Can't Be Too Careful, To-Morrow Never Comes, The Money Doesn't Matter,* and *Lovers' Meeting;* O'Casey's *Juno and the Paycock,* and *The Plough and the Stars*; St John Ervine's *Boyd's Shop*; Paul Vincent Carroll's *Shadow and Substance,* and *The Wise Have Not Spoken*; Shaw's *Arms and the Man*; and Edward Paulton's *Her Temporary Husband.* The players who accompanied Louis on the tour were Anne D'Alton, Shela Ward, Tom Ryan, Brian O'Higgins, Arthur O'Sullivan, Tessie O'Neill, Charles Carey, Mollie Hall, Terry Wilson, Joe MacColum, Sean Colleary, Sheila Manahan and John McMahon.

On 17 February 1942, the *Cork Examiner* reviewed *To-Morrow Never Comes* which had played the previous night at the Cork Opera House. The play was received enthusiastically, the reviewer commenting that 'were it not so rich in natural drama, *To-Morrow Never Comes* ... might truly be described as one of the best Irish comedies seen in Cork for ages. Indeed, the play is unique in its wonderful blend of comedy, tragedy and stark drama.' D'Alton received special mention as 'the author-producer-leader' and was complimented on 'doing much to raise the standard of theatre in Ireland when he conceives and presents such plays of this clever blend of varied types of entertainment'. The audience were equally delighted with the play 'hovering between permanently frozen spines and gales of laughter'. Interestingly, the psychological complexity of *To-Morrow Never Comes,* as noted by the city papers when it had premiered at the Abbey Theatre, was obviously lost on the Cork audience who preferred instead to be entertained by 'the humour of the Irish public house', and the 'creepy scenes'. Nonetheless, the review concluded, '*To-Morrow Never Comes* is a play that once seen will rank in the memory with the outstanding plays of to-day.'[14]

In October 1941, D'Alton brought his tour to Kilkenny where *To-Morrow Never Comes, The Money Doesn't Matter* and *Juno and the Paycock* were performed to the Kilkenny theatregoers who flocked to see the plays, the *Kilkenny Journal* noting on 4 October 1941, 'The success of Mr D'Alton's visit can be measured by the increased attendance each night.' By July of the same year, D'Alton's tour had reached the south east and on 18 July 1942, readers of the *Free Press* in Wexford were informed that Louis D'Alton's plays would be staged the following week noting, 'the playgoers of Wexford are in for a treat during the coming week in the visit of Louis D'Alton and his company to the theatre Royal.' *To-Morrow Never Comes,* described by the paper as his 'most absorbing play of thrills and suspense' was included in the programme along with *You Can't Be Too Careful* which had been produced at the Olympia Theatre in Dublin the preceding May, and *Lovers' Meeting.* In fact, the only non-D'Alton play to be performed was O'Casey's *Juno and the Paycock.*[15]

During this time D'Alton was in touch with Sean O'Casey by letter, a correspondence that had grown over the period he was sending O'Casey money orders for royalties due to him. It is obvious, from the these letters, that D'Alton was pleased with the tour's success: O'Casey wrote to D'Alton on 20 August 1942 saying, 'I am glad you are able to say that, so far, everything has gone well; and I hope the same story can be told till the end of the tour.' Indeed, O'Casey makes specific reference to the Wexford dates telling D'Alton, 'I'm glad the boys of Wexford gave you a good reception.'[16] Interestingly, O'Casey also makes reference to the effects the war was having in Ireland. He tells D'Alton, 'I hope the transport difficulty wont [*sic*] imprison you in Dublin', a pertinent comment since at that time Ireland was suffering as commodities ran in and out of supply. Indeed, a few months later private motoring would almost cease and long-distance transport by public means would become increasingly difficult as many of the steam trains and coaches were very old, and it was not economical to keep them in repair.

For O'Casey, the problems of travel in Devon, where he was living, were also setting in: 'Here it is getting very difficult, too; and soon only those engaged on war work will be allowed to travel', but for him the effects of this were minor. He informed D'Alton that the impossibilities of travelling did not trouble him: 'What with playing with the children, using shears and billhook on the hedges, and doing a bit of digging, I'm fairly ill occupied.' For O'Casey, the main 'inconvenience' was 'the scarcity of paper and typing-ribbon'.[17] However, O'Casey was quick to realize how such difficulties would affect travelling producers and fit-up artists like D'Alton whose job it was to bring drama to the provinces – indeed, art would have been one of the first things to suffer had organizations like ENSA and CEMA not been set up. As O'Casey wrote to D'Alton, 'I'm afraid all Art is non-essential; wasnt it Oscar Wilde who said "all Art is useless". And Oscar knew something, with all his faults; anyway, none of his imitators have reached his level yet. We can live without art, though life wouldnt, couldnt be a very high one. But it would be life.'[18]

Meanwhile D'Alton's tour continued to bring drama to the provinces. From Wexford, the tour went to Waterford, then to Thurles in August 1942, from there making its way up the east coast to Drogheda where it played from the 3rd to the 6th September 1942. The tour was a success wherever it played, its repertoire welcomed, and the acting abilities of the cast applauded and praised throughout. By October 1942, the company had once again returned to Kilkenny, its arrival coinciding with the day local newspapers notified householders that tea was being rationed. From Thursday 2 October to Sunday 4 October, *Lovers' Meeting, You Can't Be Too Careful, Shadow and Substance* and *The Plough and the Stars* were performed, the plays advertised a week in advance in the *Kilkenny Journal* where it was reported in an obvious puff, 'Theatregoers and especially those who enjoy a first rate play, will welcome the return visit to Kilkenny of Louis D'Alton's Company in the Abbey Theatre Plays. Mr D'Alton paid a very welcome visit to Kilkenny last year and those who had the pleasure of witnessing the plays were loud in their praise and acclamation.' The report ended equally favourably noting that 'Patrons who pay a visit to the Theatre next weekend will have the great pleasure of seeing a first rate company in a series of first rate plays' (26 September 1942).

Less than a month later O'Casey wrote to D'Alton saying he was 'glad Kilkenny did well for the *Plough*'. However, his more general comments in the same letter about theatre at this time are also worth quoting:

> It's hard times that we have to depend on the country folk. It's the same with the theatre here – if the stalls dont fill, the play comes off, no matther how the cheaper seats may be packed nightly. It is a bad way of doing business. A bad way of doing anything; so I've thought for more than forty years, and I'm more convinced than ever now[19]

The following month O'Casey again wrote to D'Alton. By this stage D'Alton was reaching the end of his tour, but judging from O'Casey's reaction, things were beginning to go wrong:

> I'm sorry that you got into a bad patch in Castlebar and Claremorris. It must be pretty trying to play in these freezing halls. It's an experience I shouldnt like to go through, almost as bad, I imagine as a Russian winter, for it can be damned cold in Ireland of the pleasant streams. I've often sat shivering in fireless rooms in Dublin when I was a kid, and once again when I was a grown man, and it wasnt an experience that would make one sing 'Praise God from whom all blessings flow!'[20]

O'Casey rightly comments to D'Alton, 'You seem to do very well, indeed, considering the smallness of the Irish towns.' D'Alton however, must have welcomed the fact that the tour was drawing to a close. As manager it would have been difficult for him to organize a lengthy tour of this size at this time, and although D'Alton did continue to bring plays to the provinces in 1943, it was on a smaller scale. Nonetheless, he had become a household name now and was still receiving, to quote O'Casey, 'welcome welcome[s]' wherever he travelled.[21]

1941 and 1942 had been fruitful years for D'Alton. His tour had been a great success, two of his new plays were produced at the Abbey (*The Money Doesn't Matter* and *Lovers' Meeting*), another at the Olympia (*You Can't be Too Careful*), and a previous play was taken to Broadway (*The Spanish Soldier*, retitled *Tanyard Street*). However, 1943 would bring difficulties in D'Alton's personal life that would eventually bring his marriage to Anne to an end. While on the Abbey Provincial Tour, Louis had embarked upon an affair with the actress Eithne Dunne, and though this ended after a few months, by all accounts, Anne 'never forgave him'.[22] John Cowley remembered joining D'Alton's Company in December 1943 at Fethard, Co. Tipperary, and played with them until 1944. However, soon after he joined the company he began an affair with Anne: 'She had no qualms about it. Because Louis had had a very serious affair with the late Eithne Dunne. This still rankled with Anne. I didn't know what I was walking into.' When this affair became public in 1944 Cowley left the company, accompanied by Anne: 'When Louis' very loyal stage manager told him that I was having an affair with his wife, he put a fortnight's notice up immediately. End of tour, Anne and Louis went into Mullingar to start separation proceedings.'[23]

It was probably the break-up of his marriage that prompted D'Alton's next action, his move to England with his actor brother Noel to work with ENSA. When exactly the D'Alton brothers travelled to England is unclear and there are no records to confirm when exactly they played with ENSA. However, Louis met his second wife, Eithne Mulhall, while working with ENSA, and his sister Babs remembers that he worked for some time with Ian Priestly Mitchell, the broadcaster who had been asked to direct some plays for ENSA. We only know that D'Alton travelled to England no earlier than 1944 and had returned by spring 1946.

ENSA could be said to have its origins in the first world war where the Entertainment Branch of the Navy and Army Canteen Board, under the direction of Basil Dean, organized companies to perform drama, musical comedy, revues and melodramas. Each company had its own cast and repertoires, and toured the camps, fit-up like, boosting the morale and entertaining the troops. On 24 June 1939 the *Daily Telegraph* carried a report that Basil Dean had met with Godfrey Tearle, Owen Nares and Leslie Henson to evaluate what role the theatre could play should war break out. Previous to this Equity was preparing a registrar of actors who would not be fit enough to fight, and who could instead be used for wartime entertainment, and by June 1939 five hundred actresses and actors had offered their services to entertain troops and evacuees. After more consultations with entertainment bodies, the Entertainments National Service Association (ENSA) was devised where actors, singers, musicians and playwrights would be employed to provide entertainment for the armed forces and munitions workers during wartime. An actors' exemption list was drawn up whereby key actors could remain at their posts and be exempt from the Services, and in March 1942 it was agreed that all actors should offer six weeks' work a year to ENSA or any other national service entertainment.[24]

MRS. LOUIS D'ALTON

PRESENTS

THE IRISH PLAYERS in A REPERTOIR OF ABBEY THEATRE AND WEST-END PLAYS.

— IN —

ABBEY HALL, ROSCREA

SIX Nights Commencing

SUNDAY, 25th MAY 1952

MONDAY: THE WISE HAVE NOT SPOKEN

(By Paul Vincent Carroll)

TUESDAY: THE JAIL BIRD

(By George Shiels)

WEDNESDAY: MICHAELMAS EVE

(By T. C. Murray)

Thursday: JUNO AND THE PAYCOCK

(By Sean O'Casey)

FRIDAY: First Production in Ireland:

A Priest in the Family

(By Kieron Tunney and John Synge)

Saturday: REBECCA By Daphine Du Maurier.

SUNDAY: By Popular Demand:

PEG O' MY HEART

(By J. Hartley Manners)

Doors Open 8 p.m. Curtain 8-30.

ADMISSION 3/- (BOOKABLE), 2/- and 1/-

Seats may be BOOKED at Theatre from 11-30 a.m. to 1-30 p.m.

ALL PLAYS UNDER THE DIRECTION OF MRS. LOUIS D'ALTON.

A 1952 poster for the Irish Players in Roscrea

With the outbreak of war, the Theatre Royal, Drury Lane, became the headquarters for ENSA, a good choice as its large size allowed stage equipment to be built and constructed, including standardized fit-ups. The Drama section of ENSA was controlled by actor-producer Henry Oscar, who organized plays, producers, and casts into home and overseas tours. By the close of 1944 more than a dozen of these companies were touring England, two covered Northern Ireland, six more toured the shifting fronts in France, Belgium and Holland, four toured Egypt and a permanent ENSA Repertory Company was in operation in India.[25] Travelling, either on home or foreign fronts, closely resembled fit-up travelling conditions, and such noted actors and actresses as Ivor Novello, Diana and Margaret Rutherford toured Normandy and Belgium for four months in 'barns, sheds and bombed buildings'.[26] An ENSA actor who played in France describes these conditions:

> Since last December I have been on tour with an ENSA Company. We have now covered all parts of the country, entertaining all three branches of the Services. For the first seven months we were on what is known as Category A tour, playing in big garrison theatres up and down the country ... Now we are on Category B, touring as a self-contained unit in a motor coach with a portable fit-up stage and curtains, lighting, furniture, props and costumes, and we play in every type of hall or hut imaginable in the most out of the way places... In this way we feel the Stage is doing a little to cheer the leisure of those who are doing so much for their country.[27]

London's Imperial War Museum houses many private accounts of life touring with ENSA. One such collection is the memoirs of C.M. Lowry which details, among other things, her work and participation in the naval concert parties organized by ENSA. She quotes a dancer with the company who details typical conditions of a concert tour in France and Belgium:

> We toured the French and Belgian ports for four weeks, entertaining all allied Servicemen, who were waiting to move up into Germany. The opera houses were barely habitable. No window, no heating, and rubble and abandoned German vehicles, tanks and barbed wire were everywhere outside. Our lorries had to drive carefully, as the countryside was mined. The show sparkled, music, laughter and dance. I used to change (at the last possible moment) from duffel coat, seamen's oiled sweater and seaboots into the briefest of dance costumes, and rush down by torchlight, using interminable iron stairs from dressing-room to stage.[28]

Gracie Fields, who wrote to her family during her tour of the Pacific from May to September 1945, captures both the good and the bad aspects of touring. In a letter written on 27 August 1945 from Tarakan Island she describes a concert where ten thousand soldiers attended, and how a 'lovely stage and dressing room' had been built for them 'dolled up with flowers'. One soldier presented her with a corsage of orchids that he had gathered in the bush, and at the end of the show she received a heart-shaped brooch with the words 'To Gracie from the boys of Tarakan' engraved on it. However, the company's previous stop in Balikpapan was much different:

> What a mess the place is! All the oil tanks blown to bits and all the tiny villages – you can hardly tell where they are. In fact, there's absolutely nothing for miles, only burned out and shattered shacks ... It was our worst place for food ... We had a couple of shows on top of a truck to the patients in Hospital and last night was our biggest crowd ever ... nearly 25,000. You could see cigarettes being lighted for miles.[29]

Thus, while conditions were far from perfect, both ENSA participants and the audiences they entertained seemed happy with their lot. For ENSA artists, there was satisfaction in knowing they were helping the war effort, and the vast majority of the audiences entertained by ENSA companies were more than happy with the concerts and light entertainment provided. Some, however, were decidedly against some of the shows performed as can be seen in Lieutenant Commander Hughes' diary. His Naval party was based in Ceylon, and in November 1944 was treated to an ENSA concert performance:

> I have just left what purported to be entertainment. An ENSA show called 'Fantasia'. Three women loaded with sex appeal and dirty songs. That isn't entertainment and I'm sure it isn't what the men want. Here we seem to have some hundred odd completely sex-starved Marines – to judge by their comments, groans etc.[30]

Commander Hughes ends his account by saying that when he came out of the show he played the Piano Concerto No.1 'and felt a little better'. However, his resolve to set up a 'discussion group' for 'adult education' to replace ENSA performances unsurprisingly fell on deaf ears. His judgement that this wasn't what 'men want' may have been emphatic, but it was certainly misguided, as was realized by B.M. Holdbrook who organized for an ENSA company to visit the Pay Corps at Bournemouth (sometime between 1945 and 1947). In her memoirs she remembers being somewhat 'shook' by the first item, a hula hula dance 'with the girls decked out in straw skirts and undulating in a very sexy way'. However, she admitted that the concert was 'a riot especially with our men', and remarks that after the show she and the other women 'waved them [the company] good-bye and tried not to show our jealousy'.[31]

Even more enlightening is Brian Rix's account of taking *Twelfth Night* on tour:

> It is true that our audiences were grateful to be entertained but it was the pretty young pages (our fairies from the *Dream*), pushing Ernst Stern's reversible screens about, who received the greatest attention. Whistles and whoops accompanied every appearance, while groans and raspberries provided the general background to the actors struggling through William Shakespeare's somewhat tenuous plot.

Indeed, Rix goes on to describe playing to some American troops at Tidworth where within five minutes of their first performance (one of five) only the officers were left. Donald Wolfit, who was part of the company, was furious with the Officer Commanding and as a result, the following evening was a complete contrast:

> Not a murmur was heard – no restless feet, no applause or even laughter. It was as if we were playing behind thick plate glass. We were nonplussed and commented on it to the officer in charge afterwards … 'I just had a talk to the men this morning', he said, 'and in case there was any further trouble tonight I had the military police parading the aisles with their revolvers out of their holsters.'[32]

Ultimately, audiences wanted to be entertained, and while ENSA tours of Shakespeare, Ibsen, Strindberg and Shaw saw little opposition in camps and garrisons, it was light drama, comedies, farces, thrillers and melodramas that were the most popular. Coupled with the fact that theatre would have been an unknown quantity before the war to many of these soldiers, the preference for light entertainment was also a reflection of the sombre times during which ENSA was operating. We have already seen how even Irish audiences, albeit indirectly affected by the war, expressed their preferences for comic plays to be performed in theatres at this time. And indeed, most of the long runs on the London stage in the war years were witty comedies. It can thus be concluded that ENSA coped remarkably well with the enormity of its task, and while some were quick to snub its accomplishments[33], it is clear that ENSA succeeded in its goals to entertain, and did so in the most difficult of conditions. It must also be remembered that the achievements of ENSA stretched further than wartime entertainment as it also played a large part in creating a post-war audience which appreciated drama and demanded good nation-wide theatre in times of peace.

Another organization which had a similar brief and function to ENSA was the Council for the Encouragement of Music and the Arts (CEMA), the forerunner of the Arts Council. CEMA was formed in December 1939 under the harsh social and economic conditions of wartime England, its belief being that promotion of the arts to the public could function as both a morale booster and an educational exercise. CEMA's initial income came from a private philanthropic source, the American Pilgrim Trust, but in April 1942 the scheme became entirely government financed. Peter Noble describes the immediate aims of CEMA as being (1) to provide music and drama to meet the conditions of blackout; (2) to entertain the large concentration of workers in new centres; and (3) to rebuild the collapse of existing sources of theatre and music.[34]

By 1941 CEMA was supporting an increasing number of professional companies to tour Great Britain, its most important activity being to bring drama to factories and hostels all over England. As many audiences had 'never seen a play before in their lives',[35] the work CEMA did was groundbreaking; in fact, between 1942 and the end of the war, CEMA had sent three hundred actors in thirty-three touring companies, nine of which were specially formed for the factory and hostel tours. For the D'Alton brothers, the move from ENSA to CEMA was an understandable one. Not only had they experience of bringing drama to the masses during the war with ENSA, but they were both long-standing fit-up artists. To obtain government funding for a tour would have been very enticing indeed – despite the fact that CEMA companies were non-profit making, and any reserves accumulated had to be put back into CEMA to be used to further their cause of bringing good quality theatre to the public it served. However, the tour would be well funded, well organized, and relatively stress free as financial considerations were not the artists' or producer's concern.

The D'Alton brothers would have applied for permission to produce a tour in CEMA's Northern Ireland headquarters. They would have been issued the necessary funds, and D'Alton's company would have been made exempt from Entertainment Tax since it was now officially non-profit-making. Above all, the company would have had complete artistic freedom once its plans were accepted. Nonetheless touring conditions would not have been any more glamorous than those fit-up companies like the D'Alton brothers were used to. John Casson, the son of Sybil Thorndike and Lewis Casson, describes how his parents toured South Wales with *Macbeth.* Though state funded, travelling conditions varied little from the humble fit-up company:

> They had a lorry for the bits of scenery, the props and two hampers for the 'acting clothes'. The company travelled in a small bus. Each afternoon they would arrive at the new place, find their billets and then set up the very simple set and lighting in what was usually the scout or parish hall. The scenery consisted of a couple of screens, a bench, two 'throne' chairs and perhaps a drape or two at the side.[36]

The 1946–1947 CEMA annual report details Louis D'Alton's tour of Northern Ireland. The report reminds us of the aims of CEMA, 'In order to meet the needs of the country, the Council continued its policy of providing good drama in country towns', and details D'Alton's tour in two paragraphs headed 'The D'Alton Company' which I shall cite in full:

> In April, 1946, Mr Louis D'Alton, the well-known Irish playwright and actor, was asked to form a company to present three plays:– A.A. Milne's comedy *Mr Pimm Passes By*; John Millington Synge's classic, *The Playboy of the Western World*; and *Shadow and Substance*, by Paul Vincent Carroll.
>
> The Milne comedy was performed mainly in schools and the other two plays were presented in towns and village halls throughout the Province. Taking it all over, the tour, which visited the following fifteen towns was an artistic, if not a financial, success:– Carrickfergus, Portadown, Newtownards, Ballycarry, Ballyclare, Limavady, Londonderry, Omagh, Strabane, Irvinestown, Portadown [*sic*], Portrush, Coleraine, Armoy, and Ballycastle.[37]

The Louis D'Alton Company consisted of nine players: Louis and Noel D'Alton; Phyllis Ryan of the Abbey Theatre; Coralie Carmichael of the Gate; a young Belfast actress, Mary James; Eithne Mulhall (who would later become D'Alton's second wife); John Cassin; Hugo Pomoroy; William Crean and John Colin. Louis D'Alton produced the three plays, Shiela O'Reilly acted as stage manager, and the stage electrician was George Fitzpatrick. As we shall see, the chosen plays were not terribly well received by their audiences; however, the acting abilities of the company were, on the other hand, applauded by critics and theatregoers alike.

C.E.M.A. NORTHERN IRELAND

presents

The

Louis D'Alton Company

in

SHADOW & SUBSTANCE

by PAUL VINCENT CARROLL

Mr. PIM PASSES BY

by A. A. MILNE

and

THE PLAYBOY OF THE WESTERN WORLD

by J. M. SYNGE

For further details see local announcements

A page from a CEMA flyer for a Louis D'Alton Company performance.

On 1 May 1946 the *Derry Standard* reviewed *Shadow and Substance* which had 'delight[ed]' the Derry Guild Hall audience the previous evening, the reviewer opening his article saying, 'If the remainder of the plays produced by Louis D'Alton, under the auspices of CEMA, are as enjoyable as *Shadow and Substance* ... then dramatic lovers would be well advised to book their seats immediately'. Cannon Skerrit, played by Louis D'Alton merited special mention as the part was 'played with assurance and interpreted by an actor who has the essential flair and the necessary imagination to reveal this complex ecclesiastical luminary as envisaged by the dramatist'. Louis D'Alton's portrayal was 'completely satisfying', and 'the impeccable way the witticisms flowed off his tongue', was noted along with his 'studied gesture' of the clergyman, and his 'finesse that never paled', which was all in all 'acting at its highest'. Noel D'Alton received praise being 'the possessor of a resonant voice that is a joy to hear', and Phyllis Ryan who played Brigid was also complimented as 'the ideal, winsome and mystical maid'.[38]

The *Derry Journal* was not quite so impressed with the production, its main complaint being with the play itself which, 'could only have emanated from a mind tormented with a good deal more shadow than substance'. The reviewer felt that 'talent, capable of a high achievement was wasted in an attempt to build drama on a cheap, trashy theme'. However, once again, Louis D'Alton and Phyllis Ryan were praised for their histrionic abilities, their parts 'filled so capably by Louis D'Alton himself as "Canon Skerritt", and Phyllis Ryan as "Brigid" that one felt oneself wishing that the play was as good as their acting' (1 May 1946).

The second play offered, *Mr Pimm Passes By*, was reviewed favourably by the *Londonderry Sentinel* on 2 May 1946. Noel D'Alton, who played the role of George Marsden, was 'at his best in the second and third acts in which he had more scope'. Special praise, however, was reserved for the nineteen-year-old Mary James, who played Dinah, and was 'quite convincing and kept up a youthful sparkle in her voice', for Brian Strange which was 'one of the best cast parts in the play', and for John Cassin whose 'proof of his growing capabilities was evident from the way in which he handled the part of the fiery-tempered school teacher'.

The final performance in Derry was *The Playboy of the Western World*. The *Londonderry Sentinel* had predicted that this would be, 'one of the best plays of the tour', but it was in fact poorly received by Derry audiences. Once again, it was the play that was blamed by the Press and by audiences alike. The *Derry Standard* reported, 'while the acting was magnificent, the audience who went to the Londonderry Guildhall last night went away disappointed'. The play, quite simply, was not what the audience had expected, and while the *Derry*

Journal assumed that this was a play 'which Dublin regarded as a reflection on the Dublin character', it argued that Derry audiences found its story 'unreal':

> It is true, to a certain extent, that some women become hero-worshippers of criminals but in the play one is faced with the difficulty of believing that four women in the play could fall under the spell of the vagabond playboy because of his boast that he hit his father with a loy on the 'ridge of his skull'.[39]

The *Derry Standard* also made reference to the lack of credibility of the plot:

> Making full allowances for the almost abnormal mode of life in some of these isolated, self-contained communities in the West of Eire, it would be difficult to accept the behaviour of the characters as typical of life anywhere in Eire.[40]

Indeed, this elevated view of the national character was what led to the Abbey riots when *The Playboy of The Western World* was first performed. Interestingly, both the *Derry Journal* and the *Derry Standard* commented that while Ulster audiences could sympathize with the man 'on the run', the theme of *The Playboy* was not credible. As the *Derry Standard* reported, 'The hero is not a political fugitive, but a common murderer.' The language of the play also shocked the Derry audience because it introduced frequently the Deity, a fact that both newspapers reported.[41]

However, despite these objections and the fact that 'there was neither message nor moral purpose in the play'[42] the quality of acting was given much coverage in the reviews. The *Derry Standard* described the acting as 'a rare treat', predicting that 'the people of Londonderry will certainly turn up in far larger numbers when this brilliant company next comes to the city and presents plays of a more acceptable (to Ulster audiences) type.' It remarked that John Cassin (as Christopher Mahon) 'played his part flawlessly', that Noel D'Alton 'gave a very fine interpretation of his part of the publican', and that Phyllis Ryan's study of Pegeen Mike was 'a marvellous piece of acting. She rose to great emotional heights in a most convincing manner.'[43] Similarly the *Derry Journal* commented that Cassin 'displayed quite a degree of versatility' in his character, that Phyllis Ryan 'made full use of every line', that Noel D'Alton 'gave his best performance of the tour and gave his part a personality in itself', and that Louis D'Alton as Jimmy Farrell 'also made his character live'. Thus, while the play itself left Derry audiences cold, D'Alton's company received much praise.

Barry Cassin (then John Cassin) who formed part of this tour, remembers how the company would travel at night to their next destination, so tight was the schedule. This was the only time Cassin worked with D'Alton, but his memories of D'Alton are interesting 'I don't think I had any particularly strong feelings towards Louis. I certainly didn't feel any fear of him as a junior, but he wasn't a man I particularly warmed to. I found him rather distant.' But what Cassin remembers most about D'Alton was the relationship they had as actor/director:

> I found him very very helpful as a director to a young actor, immensely so. I was very surprised at him in rehearsal – he might sit for two or three rehearsals and say absolutely nothing at all, and then take one aside and say just a few words and that was enough.[44]

Clearly, D'Alton had learned much during these touring years and it is unlikely that he ever regretted his decision to resign as producer in the Abbey Theatre. However, when the war ended and a sense of stability began to slowly percolate Ireland, he began to think once again about returning to Dublin where he could re-commence writing for the theatre. He had yielded to his desire to return to what he was used to, life on the road, but after six years of travelling and managing other people's day-to-day lives, as well as his own, it was now time to settle.

Undoubtedly, the previous six years had been exciting for D'Alton; he had managed, produced and acted in touring companies, both his own and others, and this diversity of tasks enhanced his knowledge of all aspects of theatre. But equally important for him was the opportunity to study the provincial lifestyle, as it was this way of life and these people that he would write about in his subsequent plays. Six years on the road, performing in small towns and villages, and working so closely in a team of people, gave him ample material and ideas from which he would draw when he resumed his writing. It was thus time for him to begin concentrating once again on his play-writing, and so it was that 1947 heralded his return to the Abbey, this time purely as a playwright. Tragically though, Louis D'Alton's writing days were numbered and four years later his theatrical career was cut short by his untimely death. However, by then he had written four new plays for the Abbey theatre, plays which were written specifically to attract large audiences and which, though cynical at heart, were undoubtedly tailored to suit the tastes of the Irish theatregoers D'Alton had observed, judged and successfully performed to during his touring years.

CHAPTER SEVEN

Giving them what they wanted

You Can't Be Too Careful, written and produced by Louis D'Alton opened at Dublin's Olympia theatre on 15 May 1942, and although the play was never published, we can gauge its plot from its reviews. Fonsy Duncan, the play's protagonist, writes a book loosely set around Coelavin, supposedly a village in the Midlands. He calls the book *O Cursed Spite,* its title alone asking for trouble, which prompts his neighbours to see themselves as characters in the story. Considering that this play was performed almost a year after the controversy that exploded in *The Bell* about *The Money Doesn't Matter,* it is clear where Louis got his inspiration to write *You Can't Be Too Careful.* Described as a 'Satirical Comedy', even the very title of the play can be read as a reflection of D'Alton's reaction to the scandal where he was blamed for deliberately parodying Lennox Robinson as an alcoholic. 'O Cursed Spite' is thus a fitting title for the fictive book in this play.

You Can't Be Too Careful received good reviews. The *Irish Independent* on 18 May 1942 headed its review 'Brilliant New Comedy', and described the play as 'a first-rate comedy idea and has the great virtue so rare in comedy, an unexpected twist at the end that makes the last act better than the first'. Two days previously, the *Irish Times* had noted how the play 'kept a receptive Olympia audience fully amused for almost the whole of its first performance', and how it 'has in it the elements of popularity', though it did criticize the play's theme as being 'a little complicated', stating that it did not require the lengths of 'explanation that it is given here and there, at the expense of what should have been its own swift and natural action right through'. Similarly, Gabriel Fallon referred to *You Can't Be Too Careful* in *The Standard* on 29 May 1942 as, 'a large slice of first-class entertainment' which 'entertains from curtain-rise to curtain -fall'. Though Fallon noted that the play was, 'rather over subtle in parts and over-wordy on the whole', he nonetheless decided that it was 'a dexterous manipulation of the life and literature equation (the most dexterous I've seen), full of witty, clever dialogue and interesting characterization'.

You Can't Be Too Careful, seen in this light, and rich in satire, marks an apt beginning for the new cynical D'Alton that was to emerge over the next eight years where, lured by his success as a 'popular' playwright and disappointed by his audience's failure to respond to the more serious nature of his previous plays, he would set out to write comedies that would please his audiences. In one sense this plan worked well – his plays attracted large audiences and he became even more popular as a playwright. But he also became a victim rather than a champion of popular taste, as this decision meant he had to repress the many social and political grievances he had written about and explored overtly in his earlier plays. However, we should by no means view D'Alton's latter plays as failures, but rather consider them from the viewpoint of popular drama. In fact, one of his final plays, *This Other Eden* is undoubtedly his finest work, and while his other four comedies are less scathing in their attack on the Irish hierarchies of power than his previous plays, his clever use of satire and comedy makes many trenchant comments on Irish fickleness and hypocrisy.

1947 was an important year for D'Alton. Not only had he returned to the national theatre after having toured with ENSA and CEMA, but he also married again, this time to Eithne Mulhall whom he had met during his work with ENSA. They were wed on 29 September 1949 at Kensington's Registry Office in London, his friend Charles Fitzsimons acting as best man. Eithne and Louis subsequently lived at 55 Kensington Court in London, although Louis returned to Ireland regularly where he would stay in his aunt's home in Drumcondra, Dublin, where his mother also lived.

The year 1947 began well when *They Got What They Wanted,*[1] staged in the Abbey Theatre on 18 February 1947, proved quickly to be one of D'Alton's most popular comedies. It is set in a small Irish town, and centres on Bartley Murnaghan, the cultured yet indolent head of a household where financial problems are at the fore. Bartley does not work, nor does he want to, and he continually ignores his wife's concerns about this. However, when an American lawyer arrives in the town, seeking heirs to a substantial fortune, Bartley goes to see the lawyer, and within hours the news that the Murnaghan family have inherited the wealth has spread throughout the town. This immediately increases the Murnaghan's credit rating and their reputation among the community who had previously snubbed them. Determined to make the most of the rumour, Bartley does nothing to prevent the news from spreading, and with his newfound entrepreneurial skills becomes a business tycoon securing deals for all his children. The rest of the play concentrates on Bartley's ingenuity, and the family's newfound status in this small midland town, and by the time the news comes that the Murnaghan family has not inherited the fortune, the good work is done.

They Got What They Wanted is a fast-moving comedy designed specifically for the popular theatre. Bartley Murnaghan is the typical stage Irishman full of blarney, wit and charm, and much of the play's appeal lies in his ingenious moneymaking schemes and his determination to get the better of the hypocritical townsfolk. The play is obviously designed to entertain, the *Irish Independent* on 19 February 1947 calling it 'a delightful piece of entertainment', its reviewer commenting, 'personally I enjoyed every moment of the fun'. This was the final Abbey play F.J. McCormick would act in before his death, and his depiction of Bartley Murnaghan was not surprisingly the cause of much of this fun, the *Irish Times* noting his 'assurance and poise' in the role which 'made it seen deceptively easy', while the *Irish Independent* declaring it one of his best comic roles.[2] It seems that D'Alton had finally submitted to writing a comic role that would be the core of his play, a move that was hardly unexpected given his audience's reaction to the secondary comic characters that D'Alton had previously limited himself to depicting. Productions of his previous two plays, *Lovers' Meeting* and *The Spanish Soldier* had shown Louis that his audiences saw his characters the way they wanted to see them, focusing solely on those who gave entertainment value. The character of Bartley Murnaghan emanates from D'Alton's acceptance of this fact.

They Got What They Wanted can thus be best described as a benign comedy. Undoubtedly, D'Alton is satirising the greed and hypocrisy inherent in small-town Ireland as well as ridiculing how financial tycoons can be made. However, his satire is never biting and his audiences are not encouraged to laugh at the satire itself, but at the more benevolent content it envelops. For the post-war audiences who flocked to see the play, *They Got What They Wanted,* with its undemanding plot and characterization, fitted neatly into a comic convention where audiences could take it for granted that all would live happily after. Indeed, D'Alton even reproduces the familiar ending of a comedy, a wedding, in this play. If we apply Allardyce Nicoll's attestation that 'laughter is indeed pre-dominantly social'[3] to the time that this play was first performed, then *They Got What They Wanted* can be viewed as a play which captured the post-war desire to laugh as a community, a community that had finally been released from the repercussions of the Second World War.

The play ran for twelve weeks at the Abbey and made a substantial profit over its run. It also became D'Alton's most produced play, receiving numerous revivals in the Abbey over the following ten years and was even produced at the Embassy Theatre in London in 1950 where it was described as a 'cheerful farce'.[4] The play also received great success on the fit-up circuit and was often performed by amateur dramatic societies. Interestingly, in the *Irish Times* review of its Abbey premiere, it was noted that D'Alton, who knew 'both his theatre and his small town from A to Z', had written the play, 'with more care for the theatre-minded provincial towns than for the pseudo-sophisticated suburban play-tasters of Dublin'.

Undoubtedly, D'Alton's experience on the road, both as a fit-up artist and a director with ENSA and CEMA, had shaped his dramatic writings to which he had returned after a two-year break. He had seen at first hand what his audiences demanded, but was also clever enough to realize that there was not as great a chasm between provincial and city audiences as the above review would suggest. Indeed, if these 'pseudo-sophisticated suburban play-tasters of Dublin' did not appreciate his newest drama, then their absence went unnoticed as Dublin audiences flocked to the Abbey to view this popular comedy.

However, the popularity of *They Got What They Wanted* did have somewhat of an adverse effect on the play's 1950 revival at the Abbey where it drew very small audiences. The Abbey board had chosen the play as a 'filler-up', one that could be 'got ready in a few days',[5] and be performed while the next Abbey offering, Seamus Byrne's *Design for a Headstone* was being rehearsed. There are a range of reasons why audiences were poor: one factor was the Clontarf bus strike that kept many of the Abbey patrons away. The second can be attributed to the timing of the play, that it had been produced directly after Yeats' *The Countess Cathleen.* As Blythe realized: 'There seems to be some foundation to the theory that any run of a poetic play tends to drive away our ordinary audience … we should arrange as far as possible always to have a poetic play followed by a new play, which will bring the ordinary audience back.[6] Another possible cause was that audiences may have become saturated with revivals of *They Got What They Wanted* – as Blythe noted, 'the play has been done much more widely and frequently by amateurs throughout the country than was realized in the Theatre'. Thus, the success of the play in provincial Ireland manifested by its numerous productions on the amateur circuit, could quite possible have checked its growth on the professional stage.

More successful than the Abbey revival of *They Got What They Wanted* was the film of the play that which was produced by Alex Boyd with the Associated British Picture Corporation and released in 1951. At first the film was to be called *Smiling Irish Eyes,* but eventually the title *Talk of a Million* was settled on in England and Ireland, while in America it was named *You Can't Beat the Irish.* The film was directed by the popular English film director John Paddy Carstairs (1910–70) and starred Jack Warner as Bartley and Barbara Mullen as his wife. Carstairs used this film to support less well-known actors giving leading roles to five then completely unknown players (Joan Kenny, Elizabeth Erskine, Ronan O'Casey, Vincent Ball and Paul Connell) saying, 'Somebody's got to do something before long about the famine in stars. We've got to get youngsters and build them up big. It's the only way.'[7]

The film begins with an inset which reads, 'The Irish Village of Clankeely where nothing ever happens and nobody has anything to do but talk about it',[8] and varies little from D'Alton's play, a fact that was noted in its reviews. *The Picturegoer* commented that 'although the script writing is quite competent, it hasn't been able to disguise entirely the story's stage origin',[9] but *To-day's Cinema* congratulated the producers who 'very sensibly under the circumstances, have made little attempt to disguise the production's theatrical origin'. As far as this review was concerned, 'the film's appeal ... lies almost entirely in its flow of airy dialogue and its carefree comic characterizations.'[10]

The comic appeal of the film was also emphasized in its reviews. *Variety* termed it 'a pleasantly entertaining bit of whimsy', a 'talky but mildly amusing yarn about an Irish family',[11] and *To-day's Cinema* stressed its 'amusing story', its 'entertainment', and its 'amusing, blarneying dialogue and comic, carefree characterizations'.[12]

Released in America by Stratford Pictures, *You Can't Beat the Irish* played at the Park Avenue Theatre from May 1952. However, while its American audience were enthralled by the Irish setting and its picture of small-town Irish life which provided 'much of its intrinsic charm', the combination of its lack of performers known to the U.S. public and the 'heavy Irish brogues' of the film 'in which the entire cast talks like Barry Fitzgerald', meant the picture did not pull in large audiences.[13] In England and Ireland, the film was more popular, welcomed as an 'unpretentious but efficient piece of work that should be warmly appreciated by popular audiences, especially with the stars many fans.'[14] So D'Alton had not only become a playwright of popular drama, but had also firmly established himself as a comic dramatist whose plays could be adapted for the screen under the 'enjoyable light entertainment of popular type' banner.[15]

D'Alton's next three plays, *The Devil a Saint Would Be, This Other Eden,* and *Cafflin' Johnny* were written after his marriage to Eithne, and in March 1951 he handed the first of these plays, *The Devil a Saint Would Be* to the Abbey for consideration. Blythe was quick to act. In a Manager's Report written on 7 March 1951 he wrote, 'Louis D'Alton ... has just handed in a new play which I have read hurriedly. It contains a good deal of rather well done theological argument – it is entitled *The Devil a Saint Would Be* – and is altogether unlike any other play we have had from him. It must certainly be seriously considered.'[16] The comedy was immediately given to Lennox Robinson, Robert Farren, and Richard Hayes to read. Hayes had submitted his Reader's Opinion within two days commenting, 'D'Alton breaks new ground in this play and I think with success. It is a delightful comedy and the central figure Stacy [sic] with her droll wisdom in repartee is well drawn.'[17] Next to comment was Robert Farren, who three days later submitted his report which noted 'a good deal of humour and a good deal of fancy in this, as well as nice shrewd bits of characterization.' However, Farren decided that the play be returned as 'despite its intermittent entertainment and cleverness', he found it 'tedious'.[18]

The final reader to submit a report was Lennox Robinson whose view was the exact opposite of Farren's. Robinson wrote, 'I like this play immensely and I think we should certainly do it', noting that while 'all the characters are well drawn, Stacey is a masterpiece'.[19] Blythe agreed with Robinson and although he was at first a 'little irritated that so much of it is in the form of duologues [sic]', he finished reading the play, 'with a definite feeling that it ought to be accepted'.[20] The play was accepted and on 10 April 1951 Blythe wrote to Louis in Drumcondra telling him that while a 'little cutting' was needed, *The Devil a Saint Would Be* would be performed by the Abbey.[21]

By the end of May 1951 the wheels were set in motion on *The Devil a Saint Would Be.* Blythe was happy with the reception the revival of *The Plough and the Stars* was receiving, and in his Manager's Report of 23 May 1951 predicted that this play would 'certainly run three or four weeks after the re-opening', which would enable the company to prepare *The Devil a Saint.* However, what Blythe could not predict was D'Alton's death, nor the fire in the Abbey Theatre, two events that stalled the production of this play.

D'Alton had been ill for some time with Hodgkin's disease, which was diagnosed in July 1950 when *They Got What They Wanted* was playing at the Embassy Theatre in London. He had been admitted to the Hospital of St John and Elizabeth's in Maidenvale, London, under the care of Dr Patrick Corridan. However, his long-term friend Charlie Fitzsimons, who visited him every day, told him about an American doctor who claimed he could cure Hodgkin's disease. Desperate to recover, D'Alton became a patient of this doctor, and spent much of his savings in the process, but after some months returned to Dr Corridan when he realized the treatment was not working.[22]

D'Alton's last visit to Dublin was in April 1951. Blythe reports having met him during this visit and that he was 'anxious to have an early decision on *The Devil a Saint Would Be*'.[23] D'Alton obviously knew his time was limited and, indeed, for most of his stay in Dublin he was confined to bed in the dining room of the family home, which had been temporarily turned into a bedroom for him. Before he returned to London, he took Babs aside and told her not to go to London when he returned there until she received a telegram from him. 'You'll know then', he told her.[24] D'Alton returned to London in May and three weeks later sent a telegram to his Babs telling her the time had come. Babs and her brother Noel left immediately, but when they arrived at the hospital on 15 June 1951, they were told that he had died a few hours previous. His wife Eithne had popped out to the shops, and Louis had died alone.

D'Alton had written his will on 16 December 1949, and in it he bequeathed all his real and personal estate to Eithne. Fifty pounds was left to his mother Catherine, and the same amount to his daughter Sheila, and to his friend Charles Fitzsimons. Babs and Noel were both left one hundred pounds. He bequeathed all his theatrical scenery and effects (which were then stored with J. Barnett of Adelaide Villas, Dargle Road, Bray) to his mother and to Noel in equal shares. Paragraph Five of his will requested that his body be cremated, as soon after his death as possible, at the nearest Crematorium under arrangement by Eithne, Babs and Fitzsimons. His ashes were to be given to Eithne for disposal.[25]

At the time of D'Alton's death, *The Devil a Saint Would Be* was in rehearsal for the Abbey. However, on 18 July 1951 at twenty-five minutes past midnight, a fire broke out in the dressing rooms of the Abbey and by the following morning all that was left of the theatre was a shell. Interestingly, Babs remembers that there was a copy of the working script of *The Devil a Saint Would Be* in the green room of the Abbey the night the fire broke out, and while everything around it was burned, the script itself remained untouched apart from its edges which were slightly charred. This script is now in the Abbey Theatre Archives, the char marks clearly visible.

The Devil a Saint Would Be received its premiere at the Rupert Guinness Memorial Theatre on 11 September 1951 where the Abbey Company was temporarily playing. It is a comedy that centres on the conversations of an elderly lady with a saint. Stacey, the lady in question, lives with her niece, Ellie, and Ellie's husband, Sean. When the play opens we hear from Sean and Ellie that money has once again gone missing from the till in their shop:

> *Ellie*: The Saint again, I suppose.
> *Sean*: The Saint how-are-ye: It's Stacey.
> *Ellie*: It's the one thing. Aren't the pair of them hand in glove.[26]

Thus, right from the beginning of the play it is inferred that the Saint is a figment of Stacey's imagination; a few moments later Ellie spots Stacey and remarks, 'God help her, she's away out o' the world entirely' (7). The implication that Stacey is mentally unstable intensifies throughout the play as she begins to give away all her money. As far as she is concerned, her actions are perfectly justifiable, as she believes a saint is counselling her to act so, but to her family she is insane, and they eventually arrange to put her in a mental institution.

There are many comic scenes in the play which entertained the audience during its run at the Rupert Guinness Hall, in particular the scenes with the tinker couple who con Stacey out of her money, and the scene with the guard who tries in vain to make her fill out the form to apply for her Old Age Pension. However, the comedy in this play is strongly satiric and we do not have to look too hard to see the criticisms that underlie it. The Law, the Church and the State are all rebuked, and once again greed, personified in Stacey's son-in-law Sean, is the butt of much of D'Alton's satire. Initially Sean is presented as a grateful but concerned son-in-law, grateful because Stacey has been so good to him over the years, but concerned because she is spending her money unwisely. However, when Stacey willingly turns over the shop/public house to Sean and his wife, he changes. As Ellie tells him, 'You've gone money mad, Sean', (41) and Sean himself admits, 'I'm after tastin' blood now and I like it. I'll make myself a big merchant yet, d'ye hear? I'll die leavin' plenty.' (42) He even considers accepting forged money from Cassidy the tinker and passing it on as real. Ironically, it is Sean's change of personality that makes Stacey accept that perhaps she is mad. Sean, wanting her out of the way, tries to get her admitted to a mental institution, a move that she surprisingly does not oppose: 'To be in my right mind I could never have been fooled the way I was. When I see the harm done an' the change made in poor Sean there all through me. I knew I should be less than sensible.' (72)

Sean receives no punishment in this play that ends with Stacey's death. Thus, while D'Alton satirizes and criticizes him, along with the institutions that go along with his plan, his aim was not to correct them, as melodrama would have dictated, but rather to entertain the audience for the duration of his play. Perhaps D'Alton hoped that the audience might reflect upon the play and see his criticisms in hindsight, but at no stage in the play are the ramifications of greed or hypocrisy portrayed. In fact, *The Bell* described *The Devil a Saint Would Be* as a 'peasant comedy' written for an audience 'who can afford to laugh at peasant speech and mannerisms, having safely escaped to the white collar and the big city'. The review further informs us that 'most of the fun is derived from the turns of speech of the characters', and from the author's 'acute' observations, and that it is 'tolerable entertainment if you … don't take the moralizing too seriously'.[27] However, D'Alton's 'moralizing' in this play is deliberately covert, the focus instead being satire. So while the characters in the play are quick to judge Stacey as being insane because she believes she is being counselled by a saint to give all her money away, they still refer to 'the Saint' as being something real. Guard Herrity admits, ''Tisn't every house that has a Saint round it', (19) and Sean and Father Johnny even go as far as to check out the Saint's credentials.

The *Irish Times* described the play as 'an excursion into theology'.[28] However, it would be more accurate to see the play as being one where the notion of theology is questioned through its satire. For example, Guard Herrity's problem with Stacey is that she chats to the Saint rather than prays to him, and that she does not call the Saint 'his Reverence' when she discusses the 'shockin' weather' with him. Similarly Father Johnny may well get annoyed when Stacey relates to him that the Saint has talked about other saints in heaven 'struttin' around, cockin' their halos' (34). However, his incredulity of Stacey's vision is founded on the inappropriate language the Saint uses. As he tells Stacey, 'I'm raging with you Stacey, to believe such nonsense. To imagine a true saint would talk the like of that instead of very grandiose utterances.' (34)

D'Alton plays with his audience in this play. The simple-minded naiveté of many of the characters is presented to us early on, and for those of us who quickly elevate ourselves above this foolery, our expectations are subverted when we actually see and hear the Saint:

> The Saint rises slowly from the ingly [sic] seat and moves into view. He goes towards the window and looks out. He is a fine burly man who looks as if he could take a fall with the best. There is nothing austere or ascetic about him, but his eyes have an air of candour and simplicity. He is dressed in a brown monk's habit. (37)

For the remainder of the play then, the audience is in the position of being able to see how society is at fault in its exiling of things it does not understand to the realm of the imagined, and in its judgement of those who experience the unfamiliar as being insane. We now begin to empathize with Stacey and to feel hostile towards the characters, especially Sean, intent on judging Stacey as mentally unstable. However, by the end of the second act, our judgement is once again questioned when the Saint turns out to be a demon. In a clever move by D'Alton, the audience is thus not only kept entertained in this second twist, but our beliefs are further questioned when the holy water Stacey throws at the Saint produces an 'agonised shriek' as he disappears in 'a burst of flame and smoke' (62). We too have been fooled by his monk's habit and his 'air of candour and simplicity' (37). By the time the Saint reappears in the third act the audience has been transported back to its initial instinct to mistrust and disbelief, and we congratulate ourselves for not being fooled by the 'gentler and humbler' (75) presence of the new Saint. It is not until Stacey once again flings her holy water and he simply dries himself off, that we realize that we have been fooled once again.

The final act of *The Devil a Saint Would Be* concentrates on the notion of madness when Sean, along with the lawyer, the doctor and the priest all sit in judgement on Stacey. Doctor Nolan diagnoses Stacey as suffering from 'acute obsessional neurosis', and Mowran the lawyer, who viewed Stacey as being 'odd' (23) in the first act, claims that 'most people are undoubtedly mad. If they weren't people like myself would never be able to get a living'(68). His reasoning behind her madness is simple: 'Handing away her property and money is proof enough she's mad. Such an act entirely lacks the rapacity … the avariciousness of the normal human being.' (68) Sean, who embodies this rapacity and avariciousness, unashamedly declares, 'Mad is what she is and I've no doubt of it' (69), while his wife is ineffective, her opinions of no consequence because, as Sean says, 'Ellie will say what I tell her to.' (69)

Interestingly, it is Father Johnny who tries in vain to persuade the others to be lenient on Stacey. He had originally disbelieved Stacy calling her simple-minded and saying, 'I believe you have this whole thing made up' (30), although his main reason for chiding Stacey was that he felt she had wanted a private saint of her own: 'And could you not find company as good in the great multitude of the saints appointed for your admiration by the Holy Church?' (31) However, in this final act Father Johnny reprimands Sean for his greed telling him sternly, ''Tis you that are mad. The greed of gain is entered into you till you don't know what you're doing.' (69) Nonetheless, it is decided that Stacey be institutionalized and the scene ends with Stacey's acceptance of her fate.

The final scene of the play is both charming and satiric. The good Saint has returned to Stacey, and she decides to accompany him to heaven's gate to plead for his re-entry there. Once again our views of the Saint at Heaven's gate (presumably St Peter though he is never named) are subverted, as rather than being a kindly, humble man, he is irksome and pompous. However, all ends well when the gates of heaven are left open and Stacey and her Saint enter together. The play ends with the '*sound of a distant silver throated fanfare*' as the '*small figure of Stacey stands humbly silhouetted in the increasing glow of a supernal light. As she moves forward into the light the fanfare becomes louder.*' (90)

The Devil a Saint Would Be was well received by critics and audiences alike. The *Irish Independent* noted, on 11 September 1951, 'a quality of inspiration' in its presentation, and both the *Irish Independent* and the *Irish Times* commented on the clever comedy of the scenes, in particular the scene where Guard Herrity wants Stacey to fill out her pension form, which the *Irish Times* described as 'one of the finest' pieces of dialogue that D'Alton ever wrote. The *Irish Independent*'s description of the same scene as, 'a lovely piece of fooling' is interesting as it alludes to the balance between the scene's impishness and pathos: 'the muted sword clash of temperaments, the philosophising delicately but surely balanced on the edge of foolery', an apt reading of D'Alton's aims in the play. The happy ending of the play, where there is no retribution, no price to be paid for greed and wrong-doing, shows that D'Alton deliberately chose to highlight the comic side of the play rather than focus on the satire that hides a more sinister aspect.

Blythe was very happy with the production of *The Devil a Saint Would Be* and wrote in his Manager's Report that it was 'extremely well received'. He also commented that the play 'plays better than it reads' and went as far as to predict that if 'D'Alton had had the health to amend it along the lines suggested to him, it might have been easily the best play he wrote.' However, Blythe admits, 'there are a number of tiresome patches in it, and quite a number of scenes that are far too like each other.'[29] This opinion is reflected by the *Irish Times* which noted that the exits and entrances were 'clumsily contrived', that there was 'a certain lack of economy in the dialogue', and that at times interest flagged. All reviews commented on Bríd Ní Loinsigh's portrayal of Stacey. The *Irish Times* described her acting as 'particularly convincing', *The Bell* as 'a technical feat of the highest order',[30] and the *Irish Independent* declared, 'It is Bríd Ní Loinsigh's play as Stacey.' Similarly, Blythe admitted, 'a great deal of the success attending its production is due to Bríd Ní Loinsigh's acting of the part of Stacey.'[31]

While Blythe was happy with the performance of *The Devil a Saint Would Be,* he was far from happy with its set design. This was a difficult time for the Abbey as most of the sets used in its plays had been destroyed in the fire. Moreover, as the Abbey company had to re-house itself, first in the Rupert Guinness Hall and then in the Queen's Theatre, there was enough to worry about without having to cope with disquiet about poor sets. Vere Dudgeon was the set designer for *The Devil a Saint Would Be,* and Blythe wrote about him in his Manager's Report criticising his sets for this play saying they were, 'shockingly bad and looked like the kind of thing an amateur company might set up with the aid of miscellaneous bits and scraps.' It seems Blythe was not alone in his criticism as his report continues, 'Various people complained to me that it was very far from evoking the atmosphere of the public house in which the action of the D'Alton play took place.' Blythe concluded that 'the Old Vic was not a good place to allow Vere Dudgeon to go for technical training,' and resolved to 'have a serious session with him about his designs'.[32] While Dudgeon's design's for the revival of O'Casey's *The Silver Tassie,* which followed this production, were equally disappointing, according to Blythe the whole production of this play left a lot to be desired. This was the play that was chosen to open the Queen's Theatre, but after the first night, Blythe realized a mistake had been made. The play did not fill the house after the first night, and while financial returns the first week were 'lamentable'[33] by the second week they were 'distressing'.[34]

Blythe had underestimated his audiences by choosing *The Silver Tassie,* and it is interesting to compare it to *The Devil a Saint Would Be* which had opened three weeks before the end of the Abbey period in the Rupert Guinness Hall, and despite 'the great doubt in the theatre as to how *The Devil a Saint Would Be* would run',[35] was very well received. O'Casey's more serious play, on the other hand, did not attract audiences. Blythe described this play as 'a very pretentious one', but also realized in hindsight that:

> a good deal of the interest it originally had because of its picture of certain reactions to happenings of the first World War has been completely wiped out by the intervention of the second World War, which was in so many ways more destructive and horrible and which largely eliminated the distinction felt so strongly in the 1914–18 period between the men in the trenches and those who remained at home.[36]

Put simply, this post-war audience did not want any reminders of the hardships of war, and a light comedy like D'Alton's *The Devil a Saint Would Be* proved to be much more enticing. And while D'Alton's play was taken off after two weeks to make way for *The Silver Tassie,* interest in it was, according to Blythe, 'not by any means exhausted and it could have run on another couple of weeks'.[37]

It was thus decided that D'Alton's play be transferred to the Queen's for a couple of weeks. However, Blythe's main concern, that the two-week respite while the play was being transferred to the Queen's would have been detrimental, was proved correct as *The Devil a Saint Would Be* only managed to pull the same number of patrons as *The Silver Tassie* had in its second week. We must also remember, however, that the Rupert Guinness Hall was considerably smaller than the Queen's, and that there had been a certain curiosity in this hall which had not been seen by the public before the Abbey went there. As Blythe noted, 'The trouble during the last fortnight is that we have been drawing houses which would not have been too bad at all in the Abbey, but which are hopelessly inadequate in view of the extra expense to be borne in the Queen's.'[38]

This period of transition for the Abbey was thus a difficult one. Not only did the Company have to try to fill this bigger space, but also smaller problems (like the leak in the roof that Blythe mentions in his reports or the watered-down whiskey that was allegedly being sold in the bar)[39] seemed to plague the board. Despite the fact that the government gave a supplementary grant of £85 to the Abbey to help cover the enormous expenses of this new theatre, Blythe decided, 'The financial aspect of the present period emphasizes still further how necessary it is that the new Abbey should be small and adapted for running with minimum staffs [*sic*], so that we shall not always have to concentrate on the Box Office.'[40]

The year 1952 saw two D'Alton plays revived at the Queen's: *The Money Doesn't Matter* (14–26 April 1952), and *They Got What They Wanted* (24 November–6 December 1952). Both plays made a loss, *The Money Doesn't Matter* resulting in an estimated loss of £396 and *They Got What They Wanted*, £973.[41] In a Manager's Report written after the opening week of *The Money Doesn't Matter*, Blythe blamed the sudden burst of good weather for the receipts not being better: 'The summeriness [sic] of the weather affected even last Friday night, and quite a number of seats which had been booked by 'phone were not taken up'.[42] Good weather aside, there were more pertinent reasons that even popular crowd-pulling plays like *The Money Doesn't Matter* and *They Got What They Wanted* were unsuccessful, although we must remember the sheer size of the Queen's – as a two-week run at the Queen's was equivalent to a four-week run at the Abbey, it is not always useful to compare productions of the two theatres for this reason.[43]

Blythe's reactions to the problems with the Queen's were dictated in a Manager's Report written directly after the 1952 revival of *The Money Doesn't Matter.* The report begins, 'I take our experience with *The Money Doesn't Matter* as proving conclusively that, in the Queen's, with an ordinary type of moderately successful play, we can only have a run of two weeks.' Given this, new strategies had to be adopted in order to increase theatre audiences. Blythe knew he had to widen the circle of supporters that normally attended the theatre and one way of doing this was to run 'popular new plays' that would attract new audiences. However, on the other hand, it was going to be difficult to fill the theatre for two weeks with a well-known popular playwright, let alone a playwright who did not have a reputation.[44] A shortage of good plays was a constant source of worry to Blythe. In a Manager's Report dated 12 December 1951, he writes,

> Two of our most prolific writers, Shiels and D'Alton, are dead. I do not think that we can expect to get anything from Brinsley Macnamara, Rutherford Mayne, or T.C. Murray, and I should say that it is certain that we shall get nothing further from O'Casey or Paul Vincent Carroll [...] In the circumstances, I am afraid that there

> is nothing we can do at the moment except to hope that some newcomer will give us, very soon, a play of high merit or of great drawing capacity.[45]

In order to overcome this dilemma, Blythe suggested that those new plays which had merit, but which were not such as to justify a fortnight's run in the Queen's, should only run a week, 'without authors feeling insulted or discouraged'. He also realized that it was important to encourage playwrights to keep writing for the theatre so that authors would not turn to film and radio writing. The report ended on a note of caution: 'The fact that it is so easy to lose large sums in the Queen's means that the production of each new play will be even more speculative than in the past.'

When the *Irish Times* reviewed *The Devil a Saint Would Be* in 1951 it observed the 'strongly Shavian note' in the arguments of the play.[46] D'Alton's next play to be produced at the Abbey, *This Other Eden*, written at the same time as *The Devil a Saint* is unmistakably a rewriting of the theme of Shaw's *John Bull's Other Island*. The play was handed to the Abbey in January 1953 by D'Alton's widow, Eithne, and was read by five readers: Lennox Robinson, Ernest Blythe, E. Patrick, Richard Hayes and Robert Farren. All but Hayes noted the link to *John Bull's Other Island* and all but Robinson recommended the play be accepted. Robert Hogan notes that *This Other Eden*, 'with typical Dublin snideness' was called 'a poor man's *John Bull's Other Island*':

> Using the discussion technique, the play is certainly a witty modern consideration of the issues Shaw had discussed. Like *John Bull's Other Island* and O'Casey's *Purple Dust*, D'Alton's play characterizes Ireland and the Irish character by opposing it to England and the English character.[47]

D'Alton's play, set in 1947, is indeed influenced by Shaw's drama, as can be seen in its humour, its plot, and the ultimate Shavian accord that is reached at the close of the play. Hogan remarks how D'Alton is 'Shavingly [*sic*] canny about holding the attention of the audience', and gives examples of the fact that the play has 'more than enough plot and such noisy incidents as the blowing up of the memorial hall and a village riot.' Indeed, he concludes that in this play 'D'Alton plays the Shavian game almost as well as the old master.'[48]

D'Alton's representation of England is Roger Crispin who arrives in the small town of Ballymorgan to buy an estate. At the same time that Crispin arrives, the town is preparing to unveil a statue to the memory of Commandant Carberry who was ambushed and killed during a Black and Tan assault. The first act of *This Other Eden* concentrates on the bewilderment Crispin instigates by his sympathy to Ireland's cause, and his expectations of being 'deservedly hated, detested [and] execrated'[49] by all because he is an Englishman. However, the plot soon thickens when we learn that the much worshipped Carberry had fathered an illegitimate son, Conor, who is now aspiring to become a priest, and although the community know this fact they have decided to hide the truth from Conor, seemingly to protect him but really because it would tarnish the memory of a man they insist on viewing as a hero. When Conor inevitably learns the truth about his birth he destroys the statue and the memorial hall built in memory of his father. Around the same time it becomes known that Crispin is the Captain whom Carberry was to meet the night he was murdered, and it is he who is at first blamed for the bombing of the stature and the burning of the Memorial Hall.

To make matters worse, Crispin has fallen in love with Maire McRoarty, the high-spirited daughter of the local 'gombeen man.' Throughout the play Maire has threatened to return to England, despite her father's wishes, to escape the small-mindedness of Ireland. McRoarty believes nothing could be worse than for Maire to return to England; however, when she agrees to marry Crispin, in spite of the fact that he has revealed himself to be illegitimate and proud of it, consternation breaks out. However, in typical Shavian fashion, all is resolved by the end of the play and harmony is restored in Ballymorgan.

Robinson wrote in his Reader's Opinion that he found the main theme of *This Other Eden* 'very hard to swallow', and focuses on the details of the play which he found unbelievable – the fact that Conor is ignorant of his birth, that he would set fire to the Memorial Hall, that he is dissuaded from becoming a priest because of his illegitimacy, and the community's reaction to the fact that the patriot died an unmarried father. Describing these singularities as 'entirely unnatural', he ends his report with an emphatic, 'I am against the play.'[50] Having read Robinson's opinion, Blythe re-read *This Other Eden* and submitted a Second Opinion which answered Robinson's remarks about the lack of credibility in the play stating that, 'if it were regarded as a realistic play and not as a satirical extravaganza' he might agree with him. As far as Blythe was concerned, the play was 'full of excellent up-to-date stuff which would be greatly enjoyed'.[51] Interestingly, in both reports Blythe stresses the importance of accepting, producing and billing *This Other Eden* as 'an up-to date study of the theme of *John Bull's Other Island.* Otherwise critics would announce the fact as a damning discovery'.[52]

This Other Eden is the most openly satiric of all D'Alton's works. Its wit is biting and cynical, and the laughter it produces of an intellectual type when compared to the ordinary amusing ridicule of his previous comedies. Richard Hayes noted that the play focused on the 'hypocrisies and lack of moral courage in contemporary Ireland', and while this is true, it is interesting to note the range and number of other contemporary issues it touched on, issues which included cultural differences, emigration, the power of the clergy, the wealth of nuns, censorship, sexual liberation, the Irish language, the made match, illegitimacy and violence. As Kevin Rockett points out, referring to the film version of the play, even modern art becomes an issue, as the statue erected to the memory of Carberry is 'a crude modern art sculpture which becomes an object of ridicule to the villagers.'[53] It is through the community's reactions to issues like the statue that D'Alton can begin to expose and deride the hypocrisies that he saw in contemporary Ireland.

Much of the comedy in *This Other Eden* comes from the humour inherent in these hypocrisies. The scenes between Clannery, the ardent anti-English nationalist who D'Alton describes as 'excitable ... fanatical, irascible' but 'good natured and well meaning', (9) and Crispin, the Englishman who speaks Oxford Irish and who is disappointed whenever the British Empire is not attacked, are particularly clever. It is scenes like these, where neither man fully understands the other, despite proclaiming to know all, that D'Alton's satire on English-Irish relationships is at its sharpest. Crispin's characterization is reminiscent of Broadbent's in *John Bull's Other Island,* although as Kevin Rockett points out, in *This Other Eden* it is not Crispin that cynically manipulates the Irish as 'this opportunity is reserved for the Irish themselves.'[54] Crispin is far from the stereotypical Englishman the community are expecting, and is in many ways more interested in Ireland than the majority of the play's other characters. Indeed, when he first speaks Irish to Maire Mc Roarty, whom he will eventually marry, she does not understand him. And when Tweedy, the hotel bar man, tells Crispin that the Irish will not even use their language to curse in, he is very disappointed. However, as Maire and Devereaux state, the fact that Irish is not spoken is because it is of no use in Birmingham.

Many of the themes and issues raised in *This Other Eden* are inter-linked. The theme of emigration is one such example, linked in with the broader theme of liberation. Net emigration for the years 1951–6 was 196,743, nearly three times the pre-war rates, and higher than any other equivalent period in the twentieth century.[55] Yet D'Alton decides to focus on reasons for emigration other than economic necessity, and shows Maire's reasons for emigrating to be a result of her feeling stifled in Ireland, especially as a woman. So, while she may laugh at the fact that no Englishman of forty has ever been able to resist what they term her 'intelligent conversation', (34) or that she would only have to 'plasther a brogue an inch thick on [her] tongue' and the English would want her to 'go on talking forever' (14), the fact remains that England can offer her the freedom that eludes her in Ireland.

As D'Alton makes very clear, this is a woman strong enough to drive ambulances in the blitz, but considered weak enough by the Irish state as to warrant protection from the evils of books. As Maire tells Crispin, one of the reasons she went to England was to read a book: 'I was tired of seeing lists of banned books, and wanted to see what it was the English were allowed to read that I wasn't.' (37) When Conor questions her as to whether or not books and plays are banned in England, she answers, 'Maybe. But since they're allowed to read stacks of things that I'm not, they must be freer than we are. And I object to being less free than others.' (37) Maire lists her reasons for emigrating to her father, reasons which include: to escape from the monotony of life in Ireland; to be able to cough aloud 'without being suspected of heresy, treason and immortality' (13); to be judged for what one is, not for what one pretends to be; and to be able to say in public that which one says readily in private. As she tells Devereaux, 'It was a nice change from Ballymorgan where you can't look sideways but someone has you down for committing the seven deadly sins.' (14) However, behind this anger is a melancholy that D'Alton is keen to explore, and while emigration is shown here to be a positive experience that advances open-mindedness, it is a not choice made without a price. As Maire tells Crispin, though she loathed Birmingham and ached to be back in Ballymorgan; even so 'the drab horror of Birmingham could never take the heart and soul out of me and make me despair like Ballymorgan' (35).

In many of D'Alton's works, the dichotomy between fantasy and reality undercuts the action. Of particular interest in *This Other Eden* are the notions of nationalism and heroism and their direct relationship with fantasy, as in many ways D'Alton has come full circle from his treatment of a similar theme in his very first novel *Death is so Fair.* In *This Other Eden* the majority of the community still worship the nationalist ideal and deliberately ignore the facts that contradict this. Only Devereaux, ironically the most direct link to the War of Independence in the community, can see beyond this game, and when the modern art sculpture commissioned to secure the heroic status of Carberry is denounced by all as not being like him, it is Devereaux who points out, 'Nothing anyone is saying about him is a bit like him, ayther' (7), and who protests that Carberry's memory has been 'embalmed in words' (8). The other characters in the play willingly banish the truth behind Carberry and readily espouse the fantasy they have created instead. McRoarty remarks that Carberry's death 'make[s] a lovely story with the Commandant dyin' a martyr's death', (20) and even Sergeant Crilly insists on seeing Carberry as 'a very romantic character with his escapin' from gaol, and fightin' a whole community single handed nearly.' (8) It is only Devereaux who promotes the reality of the situation: 'There was nothin' romantic about Carberry, Sergeant. If you put any man in gaol won't he do his best to break out of it; if you put him in danger of his life he'll run mad with a gun an' kill all before him.' (8) The nationalist dream for Devereaux has 'dwindled down to the story of a tall chimney here and there blackening the beauty that was' (79), a view that reminds us of Considine's frustrated idealism in *Death is so Fair. This Other Eden*, set thirty years after the 1916 events written of in *Death is so Fair* thus testifies to the fact that post-colonial Ireland still lived in its past and would not be able to embrace a bright future without facing its own hypocrisies. As Devereaux points out, 'What is it but a country for the old, stumbling to a fearful salvation.' (79)

The theme of dissimulation is also explored through the community's reaction to Conor's status in it. Not only are the inhabitants of Ballymorgan prepared to overlook the failures of Conor's father in order to promote his heroic image, but they also deliberately foster a dual attitude to Conor's situation. When Conor decides to stay in the town everyone is shocked because as McRoarty says, 'It's not a question at all of what you did but who you are! It's that you have to be ashamed of.' (66) Similarly, McNeely admits to Conor:

> *McNeely*: (*Quite sincerely*). In private none of us would think any the less of you, but in public we should have to show the strongest disapproval of your very existence, even. In private we should wish you every success. But if, in fact you did succeed, your success would constitute a grave scandal to everyone and be a moral outrage. (66)

Even the second generation can't escape this inbred conservatism, as we see when Maire admits that finding out Conor was illegitimate 'was the same as being told that he was a criminal, or a murderer ... I thought there must be something very wicked in my nature that I could still be so fond of him.' (15) She even tells Devereaux that it was her shame and embarrassment of Conor's illegitimacy that actuated her departure to England. Further, when Conor is told by the Dean of Studies that he should not even consider becoming a priest, Maire tells him that the Dean had 'good reason' for what he told him, and that perhaps it is 'the will of God' that Conor should stay away from his vocation (39). However, Maire's attitude changes by the end of the play and when Crispin proudly announces that he too is a bastard and that he intends to be fully open about this, she announces 'firmly and with unconcealed joy': 'I shall insist upon your telling the story as often as possible and in case you miss out any of the details I shall be there to remind you.' (77)

Indeed, the whole notion of morality is questioned in this play. Conor draws attention to the hypocrisies of the other characters when he tells them that it is they that ought to be ashamed and not him, and when he proclaims the real reasons behind their hopes that he leave the town:

> *Conor*: By staying I should become a sort of walking conscience in your midst, a living reproach to your shams, a constant reminder of your follies; a perpetual exposure of your public and private moralities. (66)

Thus, in *This Other Eden,* as in so many of D'Alton's writings, moral hypocrisy is a theme that is never far from the surface. But in this play, D'Alton leaves no room for ambiguity, be it through strong reproaches like the above, or on a more mordant level, achieved through comedy. An obvious example of the latter is the fact that Crispin would have had no chance of securing Kilgarrig Manor had the nuns bid against him. As McRoarty says, 'If the nuns want it they'll get it if there was to be fifty Englishmen biddin'.' (6) Indeed, the only reason Crispin acquires Kilgarrig is that it turns out to be too small for the nuns who instead buy a castle from a bankrupt duke in the next county.

Even the memorial hall dedicated to Carberry's memory upsets the local priest, not because of the hypocrisy it represents, but because it will encourage dances. Early in the play Devereaux predicts the priest's reaction to the hall:

> *Devereaux*: I can almost hear the Canon when you tell him that *(Mimicking)* 'it's too much recreation the people are getting. All the time seekin' pleasure and the whole time wantin' more. They were better off in the days when they were risin' with the dawn and goin' to bed with the dusk, and doin' an honest days work for fewer pennies!' (7)

Indeed, Devereaux' anticipation is proved correct as we see when the Canon tells Crispin:

> *Canon*: I'm not in favour of pampering the people too much, Mr Crispin. It's too much is being done for them. Things were far better

> in the old days when they did a hard days work for fewer pennies, went to bed at dusk and rose up with the dawn. This new Memorial hall that's being built, what'll be the result of it. Dancin' two or three times a week if I'm not able to stop it, and young women paradin' the countryside at all hours of the night. How are they to avoid the occasions of sin with the like o' that goin' on? (26)

Thus, yet again, a notion raised in Louis' earlier writings, in this case in his first play *The Mousetrap*, returns in *This Other Eden*. Written almost fifteen years after Louis first approached this issue, *This Other Eden* shows us that contemporary Ireland still has a long way to go before recanting its insular, conservative attitudes and accepting its place in a more modern world. The modern art statue, deplored and misunderstood by the community, testifies to this fact.

It is interesting to note the progression of women in D'Alton's plays also, as Maire is in many ways an amalgamation of D'Alton's female characters in his earlier dramas. Like Molly Whalen, she is a modern-thinking young woman, but she still shows some of the guilt that consumes Jane Sheridan. Indeed, it is Maire's stay in England that allows her experience the freedom that provincial Ireland denies to D'Alton's other female characters. However, the progress that is afforded to Maire is checked by D'Alton at times. Unlike Hessy, she has an independence which allows her make her decisions for herself and not for others, and unlike Mary Sheridan, she can choose her own match and even mock and subvert the made-match by coyly depriving her father of a good bargain.

However, she still has to fight constantly against the patriarchal opinions that surround her. When she tells her father that she wants to return to England because 'I like the feeling that I can go to the devil in my own way if I feel like doing that … And because I like the feeling of being able to talk to a man, or even half a dozen men, without being suspected of wanting to go to bed with them!' (70), we read in the stage directions that *'The assembly is literally paralysed by this astonishing utterance.'* (70) Moreover, her father's exasperated attempts to mute her, 'Silence. I tell you. Silence! Silence! Silence!!!' (70) encapsulate yet an unresolved issue, that a woman's dissent was simply not permitted in Ireland at this time.

Christopher Murray points out that Maire's outburst 'was a daring set of preferences for the year 1953 in Ireland, where sex was still a taboo subject'.[56] Indeed, the subject matter and even the language used in the play worried two of the Abbey Readers, Richard Hayes and Robert Farren. Farren worried about the fact that the play would 'arouse some hostility, and there is a touch of wantonness in places – the stuff about the bastard in the last act, for example, which might be moderated without artistic loss.'[57] And Hayes wrote that 'the dialogue too would require censoring here and there – e.g. whore's ghost; praise-God-Barebones (describing the Canon), excellent example of Nonconformist conscience (describing the Canon)'. He concluded, 'the play can afford such and other omissions'.[58] But given he was a censor these remarks are hardly surprising.

Ironically, it was attitudes like these that D'Alton was writing against in *This Other Eden*, and the character that he uses as a vehicle to express his own sentiments is Devereaux. Described in the stage directions as *'a man of first-class ability whose life has been wasted in a backwater like Ballymorgan'* we are told that he has *'shed the illusions of his youth, but is still at heart something of an idealist.'* (6) As Devereaux admits himself, 'The world is full of frustrated idealism' (38), and tells Conor, laughing bitterly, at the close of the play not to become like him, 'One o' the fools that stayed to build the new Ireland.' (79) It is Devereaux that voices D'Alton's theme in the play when he tells Conor, 'It's not our sins we should fear in Ireland. Our decent silences and pious conspiracies are more deadly than any sins', but D'Alton can not provide Devereaux with a place in 'this other Eden' because he cannot take part in a Utopian world whose very foundations are built on lies. As he says, Conor should pity him as 'to be an exile is the saddest of all things' (81).

Thus, while *This Other Eden* ends happily for the other characters, there is a strong note of disillusion at the end of the play. The *Irish Independent* focused on this fact in its review of the play written under the heading 'Bitterness mars the humour of Abbey play'. Describing *This Other Eden* as 'funny to the point of farce' it noted that 'its wit is bitter with disillusionment, and it does not really give us the opportunity it promises of healthy laughter at ourselves'. Despite this audiences yet again chose to focus on the humour of the play, and although the *Irish Independent* attributed the blame to the Abbey company which failed to 'achieve a balance between the surface farce and the underlying tragedy', the fact remained that many of the play's subtleties were 'lost in surface laughter'.[59] D'Alton's final attempt to show the underlying tragedy in Irish society was thus also, once again, lost in laughter.

This Other Eden was a huge box office success running for a staggering twenty-three weeks at the Queen's Theatre. Its success led it to be included in the repertoire of the Abbey's Belfast tour in 1954 where it played alongside O'Casey's *The Shadow of a Gunman* and Shaw's *Village Wooing* in the Grand Opera House in Belfast. Blythe noted in his Manager's Report that the reception of *This Other Eden* was so good that it 'actually would have been better if we had retained the play for a second week', and the only reason that prevented him from originally doing this was that 'it would have not been desirable for us on our first visit to Belfast for sixteen years to have presented only one play'.[60] He felt so strongly about this that he repeated these sentiments in a manager's report written two and a half years later where he commented that is was a 'misjudgement' that 'we allowed ourselves to be persuaded that we should put on one of our old plays in Belfast instead of running *This Other Eden* for two weeks, the consequence was that we lost £93.0.0 there.'[61]

When *This Other Eden* was preparing to visit Belfast in May 1954, the *Irish Press* reported on its front page a controversy that apparently was effecting the tour's preparation. Under the headline 'Abbey Actors Protest over the British Anthem', the article reported, 'The question whether the Abbey Players should stand to attention and honour the British national anthem on their two week visit to Belfast, beginning 24 May, is causing difficulties in making preparations for the Belfast season'. The cast of the Edward-MacLiammoir Company had recently presented plays in the Opera House in Belfast, but when, as was customary, the British national anthem was played after the curtain calls with the players still on stage, Michael Dunne had walked off the stage in full view of the audience.[62] The *Irish Press* went on to report that the casts of both D'Alton's *This Other Eden* and O'Casey's *Shadow of a Gunman* had sent a memorandum to Blythe 'protesting that they should have to honour the anthem', but that the players were still awaiting his reply.[63] Blythe's perspective on this controversy is quite different:

> I have already written to the Directors about the alarm set going by the *Irish Press* and its malicious snooper in connection with the Belfast trip. Fortunately the effect on our actors of the story published was most salutory [*sic*] and some of those who wanted to avoid being visible on the stage when God Save The Queen was being played now prefer that exactly the same procedure should be followed when the Edwards-MacLiammhoir [*sic*] Company were in Belfast. I have explained the situation to Mr Lodge the Managing Director of the Grand Opera House and left it to him to make his decision. I presume that his attitude will be that the God Save the Queen is always played while the actors are acknowledging the applause of the audience and before the curtain goes down, but that there is no compulsion on any individual actor to take the call. The only member of the cast who has asked to be excused is Michael Hennessy; and the others have agreed that his behaving differently will cause no embarassment [*sic*] to them.[64]

The controversy was resolved successfully, but less than six months later when *This Other Eden* was due to be broadcast on Radio Eireann, Blythe faced more problems when the Abbey players demanded a flat payment from Radio Eireann of £20 each. Despite the fact that Blythe thought this to be 'unreasonable', when he returned from a holiday the broadcast had gone ahead and the demands had been met because the players had gone on strike and missed a rehearsal of the play. On Blythe's return he found a letter from Equity awaiting him, which stated that they had instructed the company to take part in no further broadcasts until the following matters had been discussed with the representatives of the players:

> (A) Flat Rate payments;
> (B) Consent of Players to Broadcasts;
> (C) Separate contract [*sic*] for each player.[65]

However, the players subsequently went back on their demands for a flat rate and decided that payment for any future broadcasts arranged by the Abbey should be on the basis of a percentage of a weekly salary. Blythe concluded the matter by commenting, 'It can now be said that the idea of a flat payment is not only dead but buried', and by noting that he had 'retained £11 for the Theatre'.[66]

Two years later *This Other Eden* yet again presented a dilemma for Blythe. However, this time it was a personal problem between Maire O'Donnell and her husband Geoffrey Golden which was brought to Blythe's attention, and which he subsequently charted in his manager's reports. Blythe had decided to revive the play, and as he had given permission to Doreen Madden to take a part in the film version of *The Rising of the Moon,* he decided that Maire O'Donnell should play the part of Maire McRoarty. Apparently however, upon hearing this news, O'Donnell 'wept copiously' and sent a plea to Blythe that she should not be asked to resume this part. Blythe ordered her to come and see him, and reported that during this meeting O'Donnell informed him that her reluctance to play the part was due to the fact 'that when the part was taken from her and given to Miss Madden at the time of our Belfast visit she had was told that she had been absolutely no good in it'. Blythe recounts in a rather condescending manner how the manner was solved: 'After I had spoken the necessary quantity of soothing and flattering words, she agreed to do her best to re-memorise the part'.[67] The play went ahead as billed although Blythe comments that it did 'rather badly'.

However, for Maire O'Donnell, this was a particularly difficult time, and her rationale for not wanting to be in the play was not as straightforward as the initial explanation she afforded Blythe. Indeed, as the play finished its rehearsal period, O'Donnell felt obliged to re-visit Blythe, where 'in great distress' she told him that matters between herself and her husband, Geoffrey Golden, had reached breaking point. The previous night he had 'put her out on the street in her nightdress in the middle of the night' and when she had returned via the back door and put on her clothes, 'he tore most of them off her and shoved her out on the street again'. Blythe continues, 'The point of most immediate interest to me was, however, that he had told her that if she appeared in her part of Maire McRoarty in *This Other Eden* last night he would not go on stage'.

In fact, Golden did not turn up on 17 April to play his part and Patrick Layde had to stand in and read the part, a part he took over and was able to play without the aid of a script the following night. As far as Blythe was concerned, Golden had 'dismissed himself' and he saw it as 'most improbable that the Directors will ever consent to let him back as deliberate refusal to play is an almost unpardonable theatrical sin'. As far as his treatment of his wife was concerned, Blythe concluded that Golden was 'a mental case' and he ended his report thus:

> His jealously is definitely insane. His wife has disclosed that over the past six or seven years he has beaten and put her out several times. Now that he is gone I have heard much more than I ever heard before about his offensive behaviour (which I think I once mentioned to the board) to nearly every actor who had to embrace or kiss Maire on the stage. All are delighted at the thought that he will plague them no more.[68]

Less than a month later, Blythe wrote that Golden was in St John of Gods as a voluntary patient and that he had received a certificate from Golden's doctor stating that the reason he failed to appear in *This Other Eden* was because of mental illness. Blythe realized 'I don't think that we can take it that he dismissed himself', but in spite of this doctor's certificate decided he 'should like to get rid of him if it could be done without actually driving him insane or without cancelling the possibility of reconciliation with his wife'.[69]

In October of the same year the first steps were taken to set up a film industry in Ireland which would result in *This Other Eden* being filmed in 1959. It is interesting to chart the development of this project for a number of reasons: the fact that *This Other Eden* would be one of the first films made in Ireland is an achievement in itself, and one which would have pleased D'Alton greatly had he lived to see this. However, it is also worth noting just how many of D'Alton's plays were considered by the directors of Ardmore when they were deciding which plays could be adapted into films, a sign not just of D'Alton's popularity but of the quality of his writing which would require very little re-writing in order for a screen-play to be produced.

In October 1956 Hilton Edwards, Louis Elliman and Emmett Dalton (no relation to Louis) approached Blythe about their idea to set up a film industry with the participation of the Abbey, where Abbey actors would be used for parts and the Abbey name would be credited. Blythe was reticent about 'the future and reputation of the Theatre', but when he received a draft agreement, although he felt it contained 'nothing that we should like to accept', he realized, 'I feel pretty certain that Mr Elliman's scheme is one which might go on even without us and might involve us without our consent.'[70] This issue was again debated in Blythe's subsequent Manager's Report where he recounted:

> It is suggested that a Management Company be registered on the Board of which there would be a representative of Mr Elliman and Emmett D'Alton [*sic*]. The idea is that themes and general treatment of the films would be subject to the approval of the Management Company, that such Abbey actors as might be required for the films would be engaged through the Management Company, thus ensuring consideration of the theatre's work in selecting a particular player at a particular time. The plan is that after a pilot film has been made in England, for the purpose of getting an order for the series in America the other films shall be made in Dublin. I am convinced from all that Mr Elliman has said that the scheme is one in which we ought to participate. If we do not do so it will probably go on without us.[71]

Blythe goes on to note the financial proposals, which stated that apart from payments to actors, the Abbey would be paid £200 per half-hour film, 'on the understanding that there will be no interference with the ordinary theatre rehearsals by taking away actors who should be engaged in them'.

The following year Emmett Dalton began to secure the filming rights for some of the Abbey plays. Among the plays to be considered were Shiels' *The Jailbird* and *Grogan and the Ferret;* MacNamara's *Look at the Heffernans*; and D'Alton's *The Devil a Saint Would Be* and *Lovers' Meeting.* A month later Emmett Dalton added *They Got What They Wanted* and *This Other Eden* to his list, but when it was realized that they would not be able to secure the rights for *They Got What They Wanted* as a film had already been made of it (*Talk of a Million*), it was decided that *This Other Eden* be produced. A location just outside Bray was secured where a studio would be built, and it was expected that the first stage would be ready for occupation on 15 January 1958 when shooting of *This Other Eden* would begin.[72] However, the American producers decided that seeing as two comedies had already been filmed (*Professor Tim* and *Boyd's Shop*), a serious play should be next produced and so it was decided that Walter Macken's *Home Is the Hero* be filmed before *This Other Eden.*

The film version of *This Other Eden* was eventually made in Ardmore in 1959, the fifth film to be made in the joint venture between the Ardmore Studios and the Abbey Theatre. Shiels' *Professor Tim* and *The New Gosoon* (re-titled *Sally's Irish Rogue*); Macken's *Home Is the Hero;* and Leonard's *The Big Birthday* (re-titled *Broth of a Boy*) were the four films that preceded D'Alton's *This Other Eden,* though Kevin Rockett notes that 'these four films pale in comparison with the most complex of the theatrical adaptations made at Ardmore … *This Other Eden*.'[73] Adapted for the screen by Patrick Kirwan and Blanaid Irvine, and produced by Alec C. Snowden, *This Other Eden* set a new precedent in Irish film in that it became the only feature film to be made at Ardmore that was directed by a woman, Muriel Box.[74] The film is faithful to the play in many ways; however, some interesting alterations do occur, most noticeably at the beginning of the film where a prologue to the main action of the film takes place during the War of Independence. In this short scene we see Carberry and Devereaux driving to a rendezvous with Crispin's father (renamed Brown in the film), where Carberry is shot by a Black and Tan.

In Rockett's appraisal of the film he makes an interesting speculation on the relationship of *This Other Eden* to Emmett Dalton's own life. Dalton was a hero in the War of Independence and was with Michael Collins when he was shot at Bealnablath. He then drifted into relative obscurity until his involvement with Ardmore, and Rockett wonders if *This Other Eden* was 'a signal from his past, an attempt to redress, if not re-write, history?' (109–10)

This Other Eden received mixed reviews in England following its release. *Kinematograph Weekly* noted that it 'represents reliable mass pleasure', its 'characters are skilfully drawn, its dialogue is fluent and detail and atmosphere convince, but a few of the situations are overplayed'.[75] However, the *Monthly Film Bulletin*'s review was less complimentary:

> The complexity of motives surrounding the plot drastically reduce the film's impact. It aims at too many satirical targets and in the events hits none. Problems touched on but never pursued include Irish hatred of the English, anti-Catholicism, newspaper morality, glorification of the IRA, to mention nothing of the many personal attachments and motivations. Even the Abbey Players, forced to

> oscillate between seriousness and humour, fail to disguise a poor script, and Crispin Brown is a caricature of embarrassing proportions. If all else fails, the gap is filled by Irish whimsy, and the resultant mixture is only made palatable by the acting of such stalwarts as Niall MacGinnis and Hilton Edwards.[76]

This review is rather too critical of a commendable production, and much of the satire that percolated from the play to the film was obviously missed by the reviewer. Even more interesting, however, is that there are no reviews whatsoever of the film's premiere in Cork, a fact which Rockett attributes to 'the sensitivity of the issues explored in the film'. He points out that *This Other Eden* was made during a period of transition within Fianna Fáil. Indeed, de Valera, having headed the government for twenty-one years, in 1959 was elected to become president, and was replaced as Taoiseach by Sean Lemass who 'represented the new out-ward looking world'. Thus, the premiere of *This Other Eden,* according to Rockett, 'might have been the occasion for an assessment of the film's critical look at the past and at the present.' However, the Cork Film Festival extolled instead *Miss Eire,* the film which celebrated the struggle for Independence up to 1918, and seemingly ignored *This Other Eden.* As Rockett remarks, 'Perhaps *This Other Eden* was made too early and, indeed, may have been seen as too cynical for even the Lemass era' (110).

D'Alton's final play *Cafflin' Johnny* was submitted to the Abbey by his widow, Eithne D'Alton, in August 1957. By all accounts the play was unfinished as although the drama had a beginning, middle and an end, there were no stage directions written on the script, and no descriptions of scenes or characters. This led the reader, E. Patrick, to conclude that it was 'probably written for the radio',[77] a possibility, especially when we read Blythe's Reader's Opinion: 'A few lines of dialogue will have to be written to bring characters on to the stage or get them off. In one or two places there will need to be a darkening of the stage or a momentary lowering of the curtain to indicate a lapse of time and the commencement of a new episode.'[78] However, it is just as likely that D'Alton was still working on this play when he died and that what was sent to the Abbey was an initial draft. It is unlikely that he would have switched to writing radio scripts at this late stage in his career, and far more plausible that he had intended to fill in stage directions at a later draft. Robert Farren's report on *Cafflin' Johnny* is interesting if we look on the play as being a draft, as not only does he note that the bridges between scenes are omitted, and entrances and exits undetermined, but he also remarks that had D'Alton lived, 'he would probably have tried to enrich his play with sub-plots and inset single scenes apart from the main

ABBEY THEATRE

— DUBLIN —

Playing at

THE QUEEN'S THEATRE

Pending Rebuilding and Enlargement of the Abbey

Monday, 7th April, 1958 and following nights at 8

First Production of

CAFFLIN' JOHNNY

A Comedy in Three Acts by Louis D'Alton

Characters:

HONORIA FORTUNE	**Bríd Ní Loinsigh**
SEAMUS FORTUNE	**Liam O Foghlú**
JOHNNY FORTUNE	**Rae Mac An Ailí**
NICKY FORTUNE	**Uinsionn O Dubhlainn**
LIZ	**Máire Ní Chatháin**
GUARD FEERY	**Pilib O Floinn**
FINUALA GOGAN	**Eithne Ní Loideáin**
MRS. MARY HALPIN	**Máire Ní Dhomhnaill**

The action takes place in the parlour behind Seamus Fortune's shop in a small town in Ireland.

The time is the present.

SMOKING WILL NOT BE PERMITTED IN THE AUDITORIUM

The inside pages of the programme for the Abbey production of *Cafflin' Johnny*.

ACT I: A forenoon in August.

ACT II: Scene I An hour later.
Scene II Three hours later.

ACT III: Scene I Evening of the same day.
Scene II Later the same evening.

There will be Intervals of Ten Minutes between Acts

Play produced by RIA MOONEY
Setting by TOMÁS MacANNA
Stage Manager SEÁN O MAONAIGH

ORCHESTRA

The Orchestra under the direction of John Reidy, Mus. Bac., will perform the following selections :

Overture	Tancredi	Rossini
1st Interval	Suite of Greek Folksongs	Reidy
2nd Interval	Petite Suite	Debussy
3rd Interval	Ceol Gaolach	Reidy

FORTHCOMING FIRST PRODUCTIONS

A CHANGE OF MIND by John O'Donovan
THE SCYTHE AND THE SUNSET by Denis Johnston
THE RISEN PEOPLE by James Plunkett
GREEN DUST by Pauline Maguire
SEVEN MEN AND A DOG by Niall Sheridan

COFFEE COUNTER NOW OPEN IN STALLS BAR

In the interest of public health this Theatre is disinfected with JEYES' FLUID and sprayed with JEYES' FLORAL SPRAY

plot.'[79] Indeed, judging from D'Alton's previous dramas, it seems unlikely that he would have left sub-plots unexplored, most glaringly Nicky's role in the play which is undeveloped and, as Lennox Robinson points out, his accident, and his relationship with Fiona.[80]

It is thus safe to assume that had D'Alton lived, he would have developed the satire in the play in order to reprove the society he was writing about. Even in what must be considered this draft version,[81] a 'skeleton of the author's prospective play',[82] there are signs of a typical D'Alton subtext, and it is this facet of the play that I wish to draw out.

By January 1958 some of the difficulties that the script presented in its raw state were resolved. Blythe, in consultation with Ria Mooney, 'by means of a little transportation of dialogue here and there and by adding an occasional phrase or sentence', had 'joined the various scenes together' and had managed to 'get the characters on and off stage without their entrances or exits seeming unnatural or unnecessary'. However, the editing of the play was proving more problematic to Blythe:

> The difficulty here is that several scenes are obviously too long and if played as written would tend to bore the public. On the other hand all the dialogue in them is pretty good and none of it is irrelevant and very little is wholly repetitious. It is difficult therefore, to decide what should go and make sure that we shall not cut out pieces which would evoke hearty laughter while leaving in sections that would be less amusing.[83]

By February Blythe was more optimistic. *Cafflin' Johnny* had been read to the cast, and although more cutting needed to done as the reading had taken over two hours, he concluded his Manager's Report, 'Judging by the reaction of the players I should say that *Cafflin' Johnny* will most probably amuse and interest audiences.'[84] Later on that month, when rehearsals of the play got underway, Blythe was even happier, especially with the performance of Ray MacAnally who would play Johnny Fortune: 'I shall be surprised if he is not outstandingly good, and if he does not carry the play to considerable popularity.' Blythe was equally proud of the fact that when he re-typed the play the actors were 'unable to identify' the dialogue that had been added. He hastened to add however, 'Of course, if D'Alton had lived to complete the script he would have written additional dialogue which would have been a positive benefit to the play instead of being merely harmless.'[85]

By March 1958 *Cafflin' Johnny* was ready to be staged; however, Blythe decided to postpone the production until after the Easter holiday, because to 'endure a break of three days before Easter might be to kill its chance of a good run.' By this stage however, Blythe was beginning to feel nervous about the play, undoubtedly because of the small part he took in constructing it, and although he was 'influenced by the contradiction between the producer's and players' conviction that unless it had exceptionally bad luck *Cafflin' Johnny* would be popular and run for at least six weeks', his own feeling was that 'in spite of its clever dialogue it might easily fall flat'.[86]

Unfortunately Blythe's fears were proved correct. *Cafflin' Johnny* opened in the Abbey on 7 April 1958 and, despite good reviews, by the end of its first week Blythe reported that it would be unlikely to do any better than 'a bare three weeks all told'. Blythe's view was that the play had been staged at the wrong time of the year, and had it had performed in July it may have lasted five or six weeks. However, he also noted that despite the fact that the play was being well-acted, and that the cast were doing as best as they could with the play, the problem was that though, 'it appears to be thoroughly enjoyed by people when they are at it', it didn't have, 'enough substance to make them speak about it afterwards to induce their friends and acquaintances to decide that they must also see it'.[87]

When we compare this comment to previous reactions of Abbey audiences to D'Alton's plays, it is impossible not to see the irony. The very fact that this comedy slots in nicely with the whole notion of popular drama, suggests that D'Alton was once again writing a drama to please Abbey audiences, and the fact that even the Reader's Opinions are sated with adjectives such as 'hilarious', 'delightful', 'witty', 'highly diverting', and 'most amusing', testifies to this. For many years Irish audiences had insisted on seeing only the comedy in his plays and had effectively forced D'Alton into writing light comedy in order to retain and promote his popularity. Now, seven years after his death, the Abbey was finally presented with a play that was pure comedy, and where D'Alton, due to his untimely death, had not added the subplots or satire he undoubtedly would have had he lived. If Irish audiences were finally seeking plays with 'substance' as Blythe suggests, then it can only be lamented that while he lived, D'Alton's ideas were before his time, and that he had not lived long enough to advance these ideas in plays which would have been appreciated by future audiences.

Cafflin' Johnny was reviewed in the *Irish Independent* as a 'seasonably light holiday entertainment of smart – I might almost say smart aleck – repartee to delight an audience.'[88] Johnny Fortune, the local playboy or 'caffler', returns to a small town in Munster after eighteen years to find out he has become a legend. His brother Shaymus, his exact opposite, and aptly described by his mother as 'steady and reliable',[89] gets engaged to the girl he has wanted to marry for the past eighteen years, but his plans are temporarily upset when Johnny returns and seduces her. Johnny's counterpart in the play is his nephew Nicky, who has imitated him throughout his life because for as long as he can remember the community have compared him to his uncle, and have expected him to follow in his footsteps.

Despite *Cafflin' Johnny* being a light comedy, there are certain themes which parallel those written about in earlier plays, especially the themes of fantasy and reality around which this play is constructed. Drawn from the theatrical Irish tradition of playboys, Johnny and Nicky are 'cafflers', a caffler according to D'Alton's prologue being someone who 'sounds sincere when he is telling the biggest lies, and phoney when he is sincere. A humbug, a rogue and a cod'. However, society is as much to blame for the validation of this role as Johnny is of its construction. Indeed, Nicky is not comfortable with this role which he feels has been imposed on him. He tells Johnny that he has been his 'evil genius', and that he has never been able to 'escape his influence', because he was, 'expected to grow up like him and act like him' from the moment it was noticed that he had Johnny's nose: 'I declare to me God, but the first minute ever I put my gob over the side of me pram suckin' a bottle, they all had it taped that I was the spittin' image of Uncle Johnny.' (38) Nicky remembers that growing up, 'I only had to lift my little finger and they'd roar their bloody heads off and say I was a born caffler. An' after a while they'd get to standin' around with their eyes poppin' till I couldn't stand the looks of disappointment an' I'd break out an' do something desperate.' (38)

Thus, it is perfectly clear that, in Nicky's case, it is the community that has created his character, a fact which we see even before we meet him. Honoria notes how Nicky is 'Johnny Fortune all over again', and how he is 'cuttin' the same pattern as his Uncle Johnny' (8), and even Guard Feery proudly assets that Nicky has 'the makin's of an exceptionally outstandin' young caffler' (16), and acknowledges *admiringly* 'Isn't he a divil?' (15) Indeed, when we first meet Nicky, Liz insists on roaring with laughter every time he opens his mouth which eventually drives him to exclaim, 'I know, I know, I'm a wit an' a caffler ... God help me!!! and everything I say an' do is funny. I declare to God if I dressed myself in a hair shirt and did the double journey to Lough Derg on my two knees, flogging myself with a length of cart chain ... They'd laugh their bloody heads of. *(Liz shrieks with delight).*' (25)

Johnny, on the other hand, seems comfortable and happy with the impression he has constructed of himself, and from the moment we meet him he validates that persona. But the fact is, eighteen years on, his reputation has grown without him and he has become 'more than just a caffler' but 'a tradition'. (39) Not only have the playboy riots in the Abbey been attributed to him, but he has also been accredited with holding up the police barracks single-handedly during the 'trouble times', taking Dublin Castle single handed during the Civil War, and filling the empty tank of his motor bike with two bottles of whiskey and driving forty miles on it. However, even Johnny is vaguely uncomfortable with the fact that he has now become 'some sort of abstraction, or an historical character'. (48)

Thus, *Cafflin' Johnny* is as much about the fantasies of a society as it is about the fantasy of one man, a fact which can be attributed to the difficulties of transcending the restrictions of Irish culture. Indeed, in a village where the only excitement is a local whist drive, where even on a young girl's wedding day the most she can look forward to is a trip to the pictures (and where this trip is not repeated in seventeen years of marriage), it is understandable that reality is so easily shunned and fantasy so eagerly welcomed in its place.

Further, those characters that don't indulge in fantasy are seen as dull and without spirit, Johnny's brother Shaymus, the self-professed 'freak o' the Fortune family' (9), being the obvious example. Even Mary acknowledges that she has resorted to a form of caffling when she coerces the passionless Shaymus into agreeing to marry her, knowing that he will never get around to this and that her childbearing years are running out. Yet when Johnny proposes to Mary, she is swept away with his charm and accepts, despite the fact that she realizes soon after that he was not sincere.

Mary is just one member of the community who willingly embraces the fantasy that Johnny represents, despite knowing better. In this society, reality is repudiated and when it does emerge, even momentarily, the mood that accompanies it is melancholic and sombre. We see this when Guard Feery realizes that Johnny could not have possibly achieved all that was claimed he did: '*(Disparagingly)* But sure I suppose the best part of it is romance.' (73) Not realizing that he is talking to Johnny he tells him, 'I'd like to have met Johnny, mind you. But sure I suppose I'd be disappointed if I did.' (73) When Guard Feery does eventually suspect who the man he is talking to is, he tells Johnny, 'I was thinking you were him …. Cafflin' Johnny', but the reality he sees is not as interesting as the romance that has been constructed, and he opts instead to ignore the truth, declaring, 'Oh, no. He'd be somethin' of the style of Wolfe Tone and John Mitchell, [sic] I'd say. A reckless divil of a man with a touch of Parnell and Captain Blood!!!!' (75)

Thus, Johnny's veil of deceit is thin enough to be seen through, should one want to. Certainly his mother admits, albeit in a moment of frustration, that she will no longer validate Johnny's fantasies for him: 'Johnny Fortune, who do you think you're codding, me or yourself?' (51), and in a poignant final scene, gives her son the money she would have left him in her will knowing he needs it, despite Johnny's talk of his millionaire status. Mary too, although previously carried away by Johnny's sweet talking and dream making, tells him, 'Yourself and your million dollars and your orange groves and your bald pate and your Spanish American Princess!!! Ha!!!' (64) Even dull, unmotivated Shaymus, manages to outsmart Johnny by not telling him that Mary has changed her mind about marrying him, and in so doing earns respect indeed from his mother, 'secretly inside your own mind you're a greater caffler than Johnny' (57). It seems then that, in the end, Johnny manages to deceive nobody but himself; but by encouraging Johnny to unleash his fantasies, society has a fantasy created for it which is more bearable than its reality.

It is not until the end of the play that Johnny finally allows his real self, albeit momentarily, to emerge to his young double, Nicky:

> *Johnny*: Imagine to find yourself, Nicky, on a dirty winter's night in Manchester at closing time, to make the discovery that you weren't a witty caffler after all, but a bum in a bar clowning for drinks. (66)

Interestingly, even in this description Johnny exaggerates by painting himself as a tragic figure, 'a martyr' instead of 'a hero' (66). The real Johnny can never fully emerge because he has been repressed for so long:

> *Johnny*: *(Appealing to him solemnly)* ... Try to picture it, try to visualise the squalor of my surroundings, the abyss of my despair. Think of me grappling fearfully with that awful sense of degradation, huddling in a doorway against the bitter, slashing rain, hopeless ... wretched. Nicky, d'ye think I would tell you all this if it wasn't true. Would I reveal to you that I'm a fake and a failure if it wasn't true? *(Urgently)* Would I? All right, don't say it ... I would!!!! (67)

Finally Johnny has to admit that he will never change: 'I'm a humbug and a fool and a failure. I'm a clown, in short I'm a caffler, and this is my Waterloo.' (68) Even his fictitious identity is lost, and when he returns from the pub where he had sought refuge after his conversation with Nicky, he tells his mother, 'I listened entranced of things I never did and feats of the most amazing divilment I never performed ... They had me in roars with the witty things I never remember saying!' (70) Interestingly, it is at this stage that he starts to talk about himself, not only in the past, but in the third person: 'Uncle Johnny is filled with immortal longings. His raw material was life and though he may have botched a part of it, he created ... he was born to create

... The legend of Cafflin' Johnny.' (71) He thus decides to remain a thing of the past, a legend. There is no place for him in the community and he realizes that if he were to stay there, 'The spell would be broken. They'd see Johnny was an ordinary middle-aged man drifting peacefully in senility. The Legend would be destroyed.' (71) He tells Nicky, 'I am of the past!!! I am a thing of the future. What I'm not is a thing of the present.' (72) And when we see him cock his hat on his head, and leave the house, we know that his fate will be to continue to transcend time the only way possible, through fantasy.

D'Alton was influenced by the type of comic rogue Boucicault created in his melodramas. But this play is no melodrama, and though D'Alton's playboy may be similarly central to the romantic plot, here there is no happy ending, but a resignation. Furthermore, while *Cafflin' Johnny* is a sympathetic study of the comic rogue, it also seeks to expose the society that creates these playboys. However, true to form, the Abbey audiences chose to see only the benign humour in the play. As the *Irish Times* reported on 8 April, the play 'convulsed the customers' adding, 'and the customers can't possibly be wrong.' Blythe accredited the short run of *Cafflin' Johnny* to a number of reasons: the 'unbroken jocularity'; the fact that there is 'only one real cafflin' scene'; and the lack of one 'pathetic scene in which Johnny, perhaps as a result of drink, had let his mother and the audience see clearly what a futile failure he had been.'[90] The latter argument is surprising, as the scene between Johnny and Nicky clearly shows the audience that Johnny is a failure, even if the many other less obvious hints throughout the play are ignored. Even the *Independent*'s reviewer noted, 'Nothing, however, can spoil the mute pathos of Johnny's final scene with his mother, a moving piece of entertainment and a perfect crystallization of the often misunderstood mother-and-son relationship.' (8 April 1958).

Despite Blythe's attestations that 'the kind of change required was such as only the author could have made', it is unlikely that D'Alton would have amended *Cafflin' Johnny* along the lines Blythe suggested. D'Alton may have tailored his plays to please the desires of contemporary Abbey audiences, but as I have argued, in most of them he resisted succumbing wholly to their intent to ignore the criticisms inherent in them. It is this factor that led the *Irish Independent* critic to lament, 'The pity is that a potentially strong psychologically strong theme should be so often and so ruthlessly shattered by gusty laughter.' Indeed, it was the Abbey audience who refused to see the blatant theme of the play, a fact D'Alton surely would have predicted given his past experiences. And thus, it is not unreasonable to suggest that *Cafflin' Johnny* was a direct parody of this deliberate refusal to acknowledge the truth. If this is the case, then D'Alton's last play can be seen as a final gesture of defiance from a playwright who had at times allowed himself become a victim of popular taste.

CHAPTER EIGHT

The final collaborator is the audience[1]

In an unpublished short story written by Louis D'Alton, the narrator gives a new slant to the legend of St Kevin. The introduction to this story, 'The Saint and the Woman', sets the tone for this comic piece of narrative:

> An Irish legend of St Kevin of Glendalough tells how he was tempted to amorousness by the beautiful Cathleen, how he fled from her and she pursued him. In the end to rid himself of her persistent attentions, it is said that he threw her into a river in flood where she was drowned. The story here is re-told but from a new standpoint, since tradition appears to have been unfair to St Kevin who was not, as far as is known, a ruthless character.[2]

In this story, the whole notion of sainthood and holiness is satirized. As the narrator tells the reader, 'What class of a saint is it that would go commit a murder? An' how would he lay claim to bein' a saint if he did?' (3–4) However, criticized also are those who uphold these legends: 'Dhrownin' is a hangin' job an' what's more 'tis certainly no qualification for deckin' your pole with a halo.' (4) The narrator adds, ''Tis not much of a compliment to him [St Kevin] to say he thrun a woman into the river sooner than oblige her with a bit of a squeeze' (3), thus casting doubt on his Irish contemporaries who insist on emphasizing the 'sanctity an' pi'seness' (3) of Irish saints. If such legends have become misconstrued, according to the narrator, ''Tis not the story-tellers is at fault at all but the construction is put on the stories by intherested parties.' (3) It seems then that, yet again, D'Alton is satirizing society's veneration of a religious fervour which not only considered celibacy a virtue, but applauded the fact that Kevin retained his celibacy at all costs, even at the price of murder. And while this legend must necessarily be seen as a fantasy, as far as D'Alton was concerned, a fantasy that so proudly flaunted the importance of abstinence at any price, deserved to be parodied.

In D'Alton's version of this legend, Kevin is presented as being a rather foolish and naive young man, even though:

> In the opinion o' some that are well up in the goin's on of theology Saint Kevin was the boyo that left them all standin'. For penances an' austerities an' lacerations an' mortifications o' the flesh he put them all in the ha'penny place. 'Tis beyone the mind o' man to know the discomforts he put on himself in the intherests of superior holiness. (2)

In this story Kevin moves to a cave in Co. Louth, which has 'every inconvenience' (4), to pursue a life of discipline and penance. One morning, as he is thinking of arguments 'for confoundin' the heretics, local an' provincial', and wearing 'nothin' but a little bit if a loincloth for the sake of decency, even though he was alone' (5), a beautiful young woman approaches him. The woman is 'mother naked' (5), which the narrator tells us was a pagan custom, and not at all uncommon, but Kevin is deeply offended and tells her, 'But for the fact o' me bein' a man o' exceptional holiness ... the sight o' you would be the ruin o' me an' put ideas into me head.' (8) Caithlin, the woman, is eventually sent on her way by Kevin who is convinced she is a devil sent by hell to tempt him, and though he is struck by her beauty, he is intent on 'livin' up his saintliness an' apin' the heavy manner of the older clergy' (11).

Over the next few days Kevin begins to realize he is 'thinkin' far too much o' the lassie's good looks' (12), and fearing that his 'saintship' (12) is in terrible danger, he travels forty miles to a new cave, 'puttin' more penances on himself than if he was afther ravishin' the whole counthryside' (12). However, Caithlin follows him, and this time, despite his intention to save her from her pagan state, he allows her to kiss him. Regretting this act, he runs away to Glendalough, and though he spends two years 'half-hopin' to see her' (17), the narrator informs us, 'his aspirations for holiness were that great he exceeded all that was ever known in the way o' mortifications o' the flesh an' the fame of the penances an' endurances were scatthered throughout the land' (18). So it is that Caithlin hears of his whereabouts and follows him there. The following morning she waits for him on a little hill above the river that is ready to overflow due to the heavy rains. When he sees her he clasps her in his arms, 'an' kissed her madly' tells her, 'Tis little I care for prayin' an' fastin' or anythin' but yourself.' (20) Caithlin is so shocked with this change of heart that she steps back in surprise, the ground beneath her crumbles, and she is swept away by the river below her. The final page of this manuscript is missing, and the last we read of Kevin is that he makes no attempt to rescue Caithlin, even though he can hear her calling for him. So Kevin does not push Caithlin into the lake as the legend goes, but vows instead to give up his saintly ways for her.

This incomplete manuscript, its lack of conclusion, mirrors D'Alton's life: his premature death, his unrealized potential as a writer, and his fragmented life, never settling in one place for long (a manifestation of the fit-up lifestyle). Neither did his relationships ever achieve fulfilment, his first marriage ending in divorce, his second one cut short by his untimely death. That there is no complete collection of his plays, that some of them are unpublished and others simply lost, that his biography has hitherto been neglected, and that his writings have been all but ignored by producers, theatre historians and academics alike, are all symptomatic of the inconsistent achievement that was D'Alton's.

D'Alton never published 'The Saint and the Woman'. Given the fact that he had experienced what it was like to have had a novel censored – his novel *Rags and Sticks* was banned in 1938 – it is likely that he realized this short story would not have received a good reception, given the conservative times he was living in and the fact that his contemporaries, especially the clergy, were so sensitive about the public image portrayed of Ireland through its literature. Indeed, although this short story is a delightful piece of humour, its irony is biting, and the portrayal of Kevin, with his 'strong body' and 'hairy chest' as an eager but arrogant young man 'with a good opinion of himself', (5) trying his best to be a saint, would surely have been viewed as offensive.

We know that humour formed an important part of Louis D'Alton's play writing; nonetheless, as we have seen, the humour in his plays, as in this short story, is often cynical and employed to exploit the attitudes of what he believed to be an antiquated society. Yet this society sought only to be entertained by the humorous side of his plays, and refused to see their more serious undertones. It is, however, important to contextualize these attitudes. Most of his plays were written in the 1940s, a period in Irish history that was particular for many reasons. The traditionalism of the 1930s, most marked in Ireland by its antagonism to modernism, did not begin to be challenged until the 1940s, and the conservatism that D'Alton writes against in his plays and novels can be directly linked to a post-Independence mentality in Ireland, where the notion of self-sufficiency was advanced vigorously. The prevailing ethos was that since foreign subjugation had been finally dislodged, Ireland's future depended on her ability to cultivate a national detachment. So assiduously was this ideology pursued though, Ireland became antagonistic to any cosmopolitan influences, good or bad, and began to mature in an isolated, inhibited environment.

As we have seen, D'Alton's first novel, *Death Is So Fair* (1937) is a diatribe against the idealism that prevailed about Ireland's revolutionary years. The principal character, Marcus Considine, is punished by D'Alton for his revolutionary romanticism in a novel that exposes the popular myths of revolution that had percolated into 1930s Ireland, and that had helped engender Ireland's isolation and fear of modernism. 1930s Ireland was characterized by a nationalism that was at once political, economic and cultural. This nationalism quickly diffused into protectionism, primarily religious, and one that was propagated in an essentially draconian manner. When D'Alton began his writing career, he was writing against the xenophobic scepticism that swept the country, whereas most artistic representations of the day echoed this attitude of suspicion to outside influences; indeed, art forms that attempted to break new ground were treated with scorn. As Terence Brown notes of the 1930s:

> The theme of Irish tradition was staunchly reiterated in reviews of plays, exhibitions and concerts … An almost Stalinist antagonism to modernism, to surrealism, free verse, symbolism and the modern cinema was combined with prudery (the 1930s saw opposition to paintings of nudes being exhibited in the National Gallery in Dublin) and a deep reverence for the Irish past.[3]

It was exactly this prudery that resulted in the passing of the Censorship Act in the 1920s. In the 1930s some 1200 books had been banned, D'Alton's *Rags and Sticks* (1938) among them, most likely because the heroine of the novel engages in pre-marital sex. The Censorship of Publications Act (1929), initiated to safeguard Ireland's traditional values, set up a board (consisting of five members whose make-up at one point was: one Protestant layman, three Catholic laymen, and a Catholic priest who was the chairman), to prohibit the sale or distribution of books or periodicals it considered 'indecent or obscene'.[4] The Censorship of Publications Act was just one of several measures set up by the governments of the day to maintain traditional Catholic values, if necessary by legislation. Other measures included the Censorship of Films Act 1923, which could refuse a licence to films which were viewed as being subversive; the Intoxicating Liquor Act 1924, which reduced the hours of opening for public houses; and the Intoxicating Liquor Act 1927, which made provision for reducing the number of licensed premises in Ireland. But as John Whyte observes, there is no evidence to suggest that pressure from the hierarchy was needed to instigate any of these acts. He notes that the two major political parties, who differed on constitutional or economic issues, were at one on moral issues:

> Mr Cosgrove refused to legalise divorce; Mr de Valera made it unconstitutional. Mr Cosgrove's government regulated films and

> books; Mr de Valera's regulated dance halls. Mr Cosgrove's government forbade propaganda for the use of contraceptives; Mr de Valera's banned their sale or import. In all of this they had the support of the third party in Irish politics, the Labour party.[5]

Whyte goes on to say that during this period, the policy of giving Catholic moral standards the backing of the state was systematically opposed by only one quarter – a small group of literary men which included W.B. Yeats, Sean O'Casey, Oliver St John Gogarty, Lennox Robinson, George Russell, and from the younger generation, Frank O'Connor and Sean O'Faolain. In the 1920s the main vehicle for their attacks was the weekly *Irish Statesman,* and when this ceased publication in 1930, Yeats established an Irish Academy of Letters to encourage young writers and, at the same time, 'discourage the Catholic Church from suppressing them'.[6] The group's main campaign was waged against the Censorship of Publications Bill of 1929, yet when Yeats died a decade later in 1939, censorship was still an engulfing force in Ireland.

Less than a year after Yeats' death Sean O'Faolain edited a new journal, *The Bell,* which was intended to keep this liberal criticism alive. O'Faolain's aim in *The Bell* was to present an honest picture of Ireland, based on actual life rather than on abstractions so that, 'When Ireland reveals herself truthfully, and fearlessly, she will be in possession of a solid base on which to build a superstructure of thought.'[7] Each issue of the journal was a mixture of stories, poems and articles, O'Faolain's biographer, Maurice Harmon, noting, 'The range of material covered in the factual, informative, investigative articles was impressive.'[8] Indeed, these articles ranged from reviews of current theatre, exhibitions, concerts or literature, to expositions which covered an impressive range of such diverse topics as 'Sex, Censorship and the Church', 'Anti-Clericism', 'Women in Politics', 'Two Dublin Slums', 'The Life of a Country Doctor', and 'Insanity in Ireland'.

As far as O'Faolain was concerned, 'Those who examine nothing and question nothing end up knowing nothing and creating nothing',[9] and so he persisted in sustained attacks on censorship in *The Bell* as well as through other forums. When Halliday Sutherland's *The Laws of Life* was banned by the censorship board, despite the fact that it had received the imprimatur of the diocese of Westminster, O'Faolain argued that the censors were abusing the law. And when Eric Cross's *The Tailor and Ansty* was banned in 1942 (presumably due to one sentence which referred to homosexual practices), O'Faolain protested to the Minister through the Irish Academy of Letters and, along with Frank O'Connor, wrote a protest letter to the *Irish Times.* This sparked a controversy which resulted in a debate in the Senate. The motion expressing criticism of the act was lost by 34 votes against to 2 votes for, which led an indignant O'Faolain to comment, 'How the hell can anyone work in a country where the mob creates an atmosphere of bigoted ignorance?'[10] Indeed, as Terence Brown remarks, the event itself was 'curious' considering that Europe was at war and the Senate had 'occupied itself with four full days on this issue'.[11]

When D'Alton's *The Money Doesn't Matter* was criticized in 1941 for caricaturing a public figure in a tasteless manner, O'Faolain faced a serious problem in *The Bell.* Frank O'Connor had attended the play, but had walked out because he believed Denis O'Dea was playing the part of Philip Mannion as a caricature of Lennox Robinson. O'Connor was infuriated by this, and on 24 April sent an incensed letter to R.M. Smyllie, editor of the *Irish Times*, castigating the directors of the Abbey for allowing one of their members to be so unfavourably portrayed. Written in a note accompanying this letter was an explanation of his protest: 'Whatever Robinson's faults may have been, he was a distinguished figure, and for the directors of the theatre to permit one of their members to be portrayed as a dipsomaniac and thief is the foulest treachery, which shows what little respect they have for their responsibilities.'[12]

O'Connor followed up his letter to Smyllie with a letter to *The Bell*, which not only criticized D'Alton and the Abbey, but *The Bell* itself as being a dog that did not bark. O'Faolain wrote to O'Connor stating that D'Alton was entitled to caricature Robinson as long as he did not do so stupidly, and he told O'Connor that he would only print his letter if he toned down his 'rhetorical exaggeration'.[13] The editorial board of *The Bell* further decided that the caricature of Robinson should not be brought out into the open, and O'Faolain had O'Connor's letter checked by the solicitor, Herman Good, who decided that a certain passage should be changed, to avoid the possibility of the Abbey Directors taking legal action. O'Connor's statement was only printed when O'Faolain was content that the risk of financial loss was minimized.

Louis D'Alton's first retort to O'Connor's attack was to write a lengthy letter to the *Irish Times.* Asking permission to 'reply to an attack made elsewhere', D'Alton sets about discrediting O'Connor's criticisms: 'I am accused' he writes, 'in somewhat unrestrained terms, by Frank O'Connor, of putting a public character on the stage. This is untrue.'[14] He then proceeds to give a full and logical argument to counteract O'Connor's 'monstrous assertion'. He notes how when he attended the dress rehearsal of the play, O'Dea's interpretation was not his idea of the part, but since 'it seemed good of its kind', he told O'Dea to 'go ahead on his own lines.' He then gives his reasons for his not having objected to this interpretation: 'I saw nothing to object to – no resemblance to the person supposed to be caricatured. I saw a playing of a rather aesthetic type of young male, instead of the furtive nervous person, at times inclined to adopt a rather grandiose manner, that I had imagined.'

D'Alton concedes that when, at the end of the third week of the play, it was pointed out to him that the mannerisms of 'the player were rather like that of so-and-so', he agreed with Ernest Blythe that, 'it would be a good thing to insist upon a different interpretation of the part.' Thus the role was subsequently played 'quite differently'. The letter then proceeds to defend his script:

> There is nothing in my script which remotely suggests the person supposed to be caricatured, and it is obvious that if there had been the Reading Committee of the Abbey Theatre would not have failed to see it ... The character I had in mind was devised in the usual way of writers, and is a composite portrait of at least four people, two of whom are dead ... a play is not the sole product of one person, but the result of a collaboration. Players and Producers go to work on the author's material, and that which proceeds from the joint efforts of those collaborators is not necessarily the thing the author originally envisaged, any more than the thing the author sets out to write is the thing he ultimately does write. The final collaborator is the audience which sees something that none of the previous collaborators has even thought of.

This ultimate point is not only an attack on O'Connor's reading of the part played by O'Dea, but an insightful observation which obviously pertains to D'Alton's previous play, *The Spanish Soldier,* where audiences read the play in an entirely different way to how it was intended to be viewed. He finishes his letter by stressing its objective: 'to acquit myself of the contemptible motive imputed to me – that of attempting to pillory a man with whom I have always been, and now am, very good friends.'[15]

D'Alton's next move was to reply to O'Connor's 'Stone Dolls' in *The Bell.* As Harmon notes, when he sent his initial letter to O'Faolain, O'Faolain decided that D'Alton's response 'would have exacerbated the row' he was trying to soften, and so he re-drafted D'Alton's response and returned it: 'To his relief D'Alton reacted mildly and wrote a humorously dismissive reply to O'Connor's criticism.' Nonetheless, Denis O'Dea went ahead and brought libel action against O'Connor, O'Faolain and *The Bell.* O'Faolain had to brief two senior counsels at a fee of £100 a day, and in a letter to O'Connor suggested that he pay off his part of the costs at the rate of one pound a week.

O'Dea won his case and J.J. O'Leary, the owner of *The Bell*, had to pay £250 pounds in damages, and *The Bell* £79.[16] O'Connor's attack on *The Bell* resulted in his already deteriorating relationship with O'Faolain reaching a nadir. In a letter to Denis Johnson in 1941, O'Faolain wrote that he was 'furious and miserable at the way he [O'Connor] is getting sour and cockeyed ... just now even I, and I've stood years and years of him, couldn't stand another hour.'

On the other hand, D'Alton seemed to hold no grudges, going on to produce O'Connor's play *The Invincibles* at the Gaiety Theatre in February 1943, before taking it on tour in Ireland.[17] And, in *An Only Child* (1961), O'Connor relates the story of how an old friend of his from Cork believed he had been caricatured in *The Invincibles*. Though this accusation upset O'Connor somewhat, he notes, 'the characters in whom we think we recognize ourselves are infinitely more revealing of our real personalities than those in which someone actually attempts to portray us' (193). Perhaps O'Connor could, after all, empathize with D'Alton's position.

In June 1945 O'Faolain decided to give up his post of editor of *The Bell*. For five years it had been the forum for many attacks on contemporary Ireland's continuing inward-looking defensive stance, but the current state of Ireland under de Valera was now deplorable to O'Faolain who wrote in an editorial: 'The truth is that people have fallen into the hands of flatterers and cunning men who trifle with their intelligence and would chloroform their old dreams and hopes, so that it is only the writers and artists of Ireland who can now hope to call them back to the days when these dreams blazed into a searing honesty.'[18] O'Faolain was disillusioned with his nation. In fact, he concluded the editorial saying that there was no such thing as an independent nation, pronouncing, 'it took a war to teach me that obvious fact.' He, who had for so long and emphatically argued that Ireland's future lay in a European Federation, finally had to accept that the war years, and Ireland's neutrality at this time, had only added to Ireland's isolation from the rest of the world. As he remarked in *The Bell*, 'Life is so isolated now that it is no longer being pollinated by germinating ideas windborne from anywhere.'[19]

Interestingly, Louis D'Alton did not believe that Ireland would be able to maintain her neutrality during the war. In an unpublished document, D'Alton poses the question:

> What will Ireland's position be when war comes, as come it will? Mr O'Faolain says that neutrality will be dishonourable. Let me assure him, also, that it will be impossible. The American ruling class is no altruistic body, but a ruthless driving power which will permit nothing to mar its efficiency. It will allow no gap in the Atlantic Defenses, nor

> will it forgo the excellent 'unsinkable aircraft carrier' that we provide. We shall willy–nilly be Taken Over. Poor old second-rate England has lost the 'Nelson Touch' and will not this time be able to stand between us and 'much heat'. America is prepared to pay for the strategic (sic) she will secure by having us on her side. And obviously to fight on any side would find us in the wrong camp. America is willing to pay our price. But the point is – our price is not eighteen million dollars. 'By all means throw me to the English wolves' Parnell told us once, 'but when you do, make sure that you get your price for me'.[20]

However, Terence Brown notes a certain cultural change in Ireland during this wartime. He points out that the years of 'the emergency' saw a significant increase in the number of books borrowed from public libraries, and also remarks on the increased popularity of amateur dramatic festivals.[21] Indeed, Michael Farrell, who wrote for *The Bell,* reported after fifteen months of recording rural theatre:

> The striking fact is that dramatic activity in the country is abundant and enthusiastic, and that it is not necessary to list among the difficulties of the Country Theatre a lack of talent. Possibly at no time has there been so much of it; or so much talk of drama and plans for drama. Clearly, the long lull which followed the palmy and piping days of Redmondite Ireland has given place to a period of greater vigour than ever.[22]

We have seen how in April 1940, D'Alton acted as manager and took the Abbey Company on a four-month tour of provincial Ireland. And when the tour ended the following August, he settled back into a life of play writing – *The Money Doesn't Matter* premiered six months later at the Abbey, followed by *Lovers' Meeting* in October 1941. However, the prominence of Ernest Blythe at the Abbey during these years, and his dissatisfaction with D'Alton's *Lovers' Meeting* in 1941, served to propel D'Alton back to a touring life where he could produce and direct his own plays, emphasize his own ideas, and manage his own actors. The war years saw D'Alton back on the road touring provincial Ireland once again, and while he was quick to take advantage of the renewed interest in drama in the provinces, this would not have been a purely mercantile move. As I have emphasized, D'Alton was so attuned to life on the road, having grown up in the fit-ups, it was obviously more satisfying for him to tour rural Ireland during this period than to remain in Dublin writing plays for the Abbey.

It was not just provincial Ireland that witnessed an upsurge in theatrical activity during the war. Dublin also saw a change in attitude that resulted in theatregoers setting standards and governing change. Terence Brown quotes an interesting insight by Patrick Campbell who remarked, 'Dublin almost seemed to have a special duty, in a world gone grey and regimented, to preserve the gaieties and pleasures that we felt had vanished from everywhere else.'[23] It was exactly this mood that posed for D'Alton his biggest dilemma. A stern critic of the conservative, isolated society he was living in, he wanted his plays to expose, and no doubt change, the attitudes that governed the multitude. However, the onset of the war only heightened Ireland's isolation, and while Ireland's neutrality ensured that one's social life could continue, the effect the war had on theatregoers was that they wanted to be amused through wholly humourous drama; theatre which encouraged circumspection or which was in any way critical of its audiences' attitudes was simply not entertained. Theatregoers wanted diversion, escapism – they needed to laugh. The enormity of change in the world around them had only served to deepen their conventionality, and while D'Alton's plays had attempted to open his audiences' eyes to the faults inherent in their country's conservatism, his audiences had no desire to be thus enlightened.

Wartime Ireland can thus be viewed as a time where the country's traditionalism was merged with new social demands resulting from its neutrality. We can now begin to understand why D'Alton's audiences insisted on being entertained through comedy. As Nicholl purports, 'Laughter is indeed predominantly social',[24] and in a society that demanded amusement and distraction, comedy could provide this. Serious plays, or tragedies, would have sparked resignation, and this was the last thing Irish audiences wanted at this time. Comedies, on the other hand, helped create a celebratory ambiance, which, no matter how temporary, was a much more attractive condition. And if laughter can result in 'the liberation of the natural man from the ties and conventions of society',[25] and provide even a fleeting liberation from repression, then D'Alton's audiences' demands for comedy can be viewed as a subconscious desire for a temporary escape, not only from the consequences of war, but from the binds of Puritanism that fed off the insular, parochial Ireland of the 1940s.

On St Patrick's Day in 1943, de Valera broadcast a speech that famously recorded his hopes for Ireland:

> That Ireland which we dreamed of would be the home of a people who valued material wealth only as a basis of right living, of a people who were satisfied with frugal comfort and devoted their leisure to

> the things of the spirit; a land whose countryside would be bright with cosy homesteads, whose fields and villages would be joyous with sounds of industry, the romping of sturdy children, the contests of athletic youths, the laughter of comely maidens; whose firesides would be the forums of the wisdom of serene old age.[26]

Paradoxically, the ideologies expressed here, the same ideologies that D'Alton was writing against in his dramas, were in many ways closer to fantasy than D'Alton's fictional writings. *The Mousetrap* (1938), published five years previous to de Valera's speech, showed how this idyllic vision was impossible, as it is precisely this veneration of the past, coupled with a deep-rooted fear of modernism, that caused the insurmountable problems depicted in this play.

De Valera's speech emphasizes the importance of frugal comforts, cosy homesteads, comely maidens, and serene old age. Almost hidden among these rural ideals is a reference to 'the sounds of industry', making fields and villages 'joyous'. Modernism, represented by industry, is only a sound, one that de Valera places alongside the reverberations of the children, the youth, and the old. Yet as D'Alton shows in *The Mousetrap*, it is a troubled juxtaposition if conservative attitudes refuse to accommodate change. The Hartnett family are described in this play as being 'too decent'. (245) Like many Irish people at this time, the Hartnett parents react against new leisure activities, in particular the growing influences of cinema and dance halls. Yet when a new factory opens in Farraghnore, competition is kindled among the community members who are all eager to work in the factory to earn money. Indeed, we hear that a neighbouring town is 'in a state o' revolution over not getting the facthry', (160) and that even the Canon of Farraghnore had rallied the local men to put up the money needed for the factory. However, modernization is only welcomed because of the financial benefits it brings to the community, and the remainder of *The Mousetrap* exposes the narrow attitudes of a community fearful of change.

That modernism and traditionalism cannot meet in this play is not wholly surprising; what is remarkable is that the same rift dominates D'Alton's *This Other Eden*, written over a decade later. As we have seen, *This Other Eden* is a play which focuses on the protectionism still dominant in Irish society. The complicity of church and state is still prevalent, and the overriding influence of the Catholic church central to this community which hides Conor's illegitimate origins from him, which still debates the dangers of dance halls, where censorship remains a dominant force, and where emigration is often the only exit for the youth of the village to escape the stifling conservatism. *This Other Eden*, in many ways a continuation of some of the themes written about in D'Alton's first novel, *Death Is So Fair,* criticizes the Irish Free State and a religion that blesses hypocrisy. D'Alton's other plays reiterate this view, notably *The Spanish Soldier* which refuses to deal with the physical horrors of war, as its title would suggest, but concentrates instead on the domestic problems caused by religious fervour; and *Lovers' Meeting,* a domestic tragedy which focuses on the consequences of marriages contracted on purely materialistic grounds, like many of his plays, exposes the faults inherent in a society which refuses to release itself from the powerful grip of moral conservatism. D'Alton's plays are undoubtedly a fervent portrayal of the times he lived in, unusual in that they invited his audiences to question their settled beliefs; however, as we have seen, his audiences steadfastly refused to accept this invitation.

The plays D'Alton wrote before 1942 were predominantly experimental in both theme and form and, although influenced by melodrama, aspired to a psychological depth that transcended melodrama. None of his characters rise to heroic action like their melodramatic predecessors, and reconciliation, a dominant feature of melodrama, is not afforded a place here. What D'Alton does it to use melodrama, and his audiences' knowledge of this dramatic mode, to his own ends. Deliberately inverting his audiences' expectations, he undermines the very conventions he sets up and attempts to propel his audiences into a world that is far removed from the popular conventions and beliefs upon which melodrama is based, a world where the dangers of traditionalism is critiqued. However, his audiences refused to acknowledge anything that disrupted their already formed opinions. They had no desire to acknowledge such criticism in any shape or form, and when faced with it simply ignored it.

The Spanish Soldier and *Lovers' Meeting* marked a watershed in D'Alton's writing career, when he was forced to concede that he was fighting a losing battle. Here were two plays that were powerful in their condemnation, so stern, in fact, that D'Alton felt the need to balance the seriousness of his arguments with some comic relief. Yet, not only did audiences focus on the comic aspects of these plays but, particularly in the case of *Lovers' Meeting,* they also interpolated comedy where none was indicated.[27] Audience and Press reaction to *Lovers' Meeting* and *The Spanish Soldier* convinced D'Alton that if he were to build on his popularity he would have to give his audiences what they wanted. As a dramatist this was an onerous task, as it would mean modifying his plays to his audiences' desires; and as a liberal who had fought so hard in his writings not only to expose the dangers of complacency, but also to advance the urgency of a change of attitude, this pill was even harder to swallow. But D'Alton, with his experience of fit-up theatre, and his knowledge of city theatre, knew the importance of pleasing his audience and understood that he, a commercial playwright, came in a poor second behind them. As William Fay, who acknowledged Louis D'Alton's father, Frank, as being influential in his career, notes:

> Drama is a trinity composed of author, actor and, last but by no means least, audience, who are the most important of the trio, for if they don't want the play thirty pages of explanatory preface in the printed edition will not bring ten shillings to the box office.[28]

After a long period touring Ireland, D'Alton returned to the Abbey in 1947 with the aptly titled *They Got What They Wanted,* a play that set the standard for his subsequent dramas. It is the arrival of an outsider from America which spurs the action in this comedy. This is an ironic comment on the ethos of self-sufficiency that still prevailed in Ireland at this time, because this outside influence is presented as a positive one – the arrival of the American attorney, and the subsequent opportunity to make easy money, inciting the lazy Bartley Murnaghan to action. *They Got What They Wanted* was viewed as a fast-moving comedy, 'a delightful piece of entertainment',[29] which satisfied the demands of Irish audiences and re-enforced D'Alton's status as a popular playwright. Nonetheless, hidden beneath the comic surface is a biting satire that mocks the greed and hypocrisies of parochial Ireland.

D'Alton's remaining plays follow in this vein, and go some way to solve the dilemma of this playwright who needed to entertain, but who wanted to make his audiences think. His use of satire allowed him to find this balance, on the one hand quenching his public's thirst for comedy; on the other hand, exploiting the conditioned attitudes his audiences brought to the theatre by voicing his views to those who were willing to see beyond the comedy. His final three plays, *The Devil a Saint Would Be, This Other Eden* and *Cafflin' Johnny* are all comedies which still manage to criticize sternly certain aspects of Irish life. In *The Devil a Saint Would Be* neither the law, the church nor the state escape the satirist's biting tongue; *This Other Eden* uses humour to expose the hypocrisies inherent in many aspects of Irish life; and *Cafflin' Johnny* manages to parody D'Alton's audiences in their refusal to face the realities that surrounded them in order to worship a tradition that was never much more than a fantasy in the first place. D'Alton's first play, *The Man in the Cloak* produced in 1938, was a play that focused on the necessity of confronting one's past honestly. That D'Alton felt the need to reiterate this message in his final play, *Cafflin' Johnny,* indicates his conviction that the attitudes he was denunciating in his earlier plays were still the norm two decades later.

By 1958, when *Cafflin' Johnny* was premiered, times were slowly beginning to change as Ireland progressed from a rural, agricultural society complete with its ideological de Valerian reverberations, to an industrial, urban one where the attitudes and values of urban consumerism were slowly beginning to be fostered. The first sign of a new economic order in Ireland was the First Programme for Economic Expansion launched by the government in 1958. However, Ireland in the 1950s had not experienced the effects of the post-war economic revival; on the contrary, this decade was a time of economic recession and heavy emigration. Indeed, Tobin points out that even by the late 1950s Ireland had no national television station, no supermarkets or shopping centres, no native pop industry, and few restaurants of any quality.[30]

Irish attitudes were clearly beginning to change as the nineteen sixties arrived. In 1961 Cardinal D'Alton of Armagh wrote in a pastoral, 'We no longer enjoy our isolation of former days',[31] a statement that says much about the psychological change that was emerging in Ireland at that time. Tobin sees the nineteen sixties as a time of 'contempt for tradition', but we cannot assume that this change surfaced from a void; rather, the public image of Ireland that had previously been officially extended to the world, finally had given way to reality. If we continue to read Cardinal D'Alton's pastoral statement, we can see one of the main reasons for this change of image – the rise of television: 'In this distorted world, through the medium of the press, the radio and the television, we are subject to the impact of views wholly at variance with Catholic teaching.' Television, in particular, was treated with suspicion by many, especially as Ireland was soon to have her own television channel, the fear being that it would be a demoralizing influence. However, as Tobin points out, 'Television was a metaphor. It was the most blatant, and yet the most intimate, agent of that international culture which offered a direct threat to the official culture of Irish-Ireland.'[32] Because television was a commercial product, those that watched it could demand what they wanted, a feature D'Alton would have understood all too well. As Tobin notes, the secure childhood of the Gaelic myth had given way to a noisy adult world of cosmopolitan consumer capitalism.[33] And sure enough Irish theatregoers began to want different things to what they had demanded when D'Alton was writing for them; ironically, they now sought what D'Alton had tried to offer them.

The revelation that television helped uncover, that the image officially portrayed of Ireland and her people was not the reality, may well have been, 'a painful business for the cultural acolytes of traditional Ireland', but out of this 'came the possibility of national self-knowledge and national maturity'.[34] Here was an Ireland D'Alton would have felt more at home with, and had he lived we may have witnessed a third phase in his dramas, where finally he could have written for an audience who understood his grievances, and who shared his vision. Indeed, by 1967 literary censorship was finally amended, and D'Alton's banned works were among the five thousand titles of those works banned before 1955 that were now automatically released. However, like many writers of his generation, he did not live to witness and experience the more benevolent climate that was developing for Ireland's creative artists.

The question to be posed now is why D'Alton's plays have been so neglected by theatre producers since the 1960s? Heinz Kosok states that 'at least four of his plays – *They Got What They Wanted,* a farcical comedy; *Lovers' Meeting,* a tragic problem play; *Cafflin' Johnny,* a satirical comedy; and *This Other Eden,* a play of ideas – are models of their type within the range of Irish drama.'[35] Yet it would seem that there is no place for his plays in the modern repertoire as theatre producers are quick to pigeonhole them as outmoded Abbey comedies. However, the themes and subtexts of many of these plays are sufficiently strong to merit production, and with a little creativity many of them could still entertain theatregoers, and at the same time enlighten modern audiences to the cultural conditions of the Ireland D'Alton was writing about.

Outside of amateur productions, the only recent revival of a D'Alton play has been Garry Hynes's 1990 production of *Lovers' Meeting.* The approach Hynes took to this play is exemplary. She had noted the 'extremely strong psychological basis to the characters' in *Lovers' Meeting,* and while she recognized a different 'theatre grammar' in D'Alton's writing, she was willing to see beyond the restrictions of naturalism.[36] Hynes approached *Lovers' Meeting* by concentrating on its production values, by modernizing its conventions, and by transforming its setting. Her approach was successful, her revival of *Lovers' Meeting* described by the *Irish Times* as an 'utterly compelling production' of a 'faded play'.[37]

One way that Hynes made this play more accessible to modern audiences was to build a 'completely non-naturalistic set':

> The basis of it was that it was taken from inside the character's head rather than from the outside social situation which is so recognizable and triggers so many clichéd reactions in relation to Irish life that the play could have ended up in a production in nineteen-ninety looking like a piece of clichéd Abbey kitchen drama.[38]

The set created was very simple and stark (far removed from the more cluttered, naturalistic look D'Alton had advocated), Hynes dressing the actors entirely in black to reflect the darkness of the theme of the play. Hannie and

Mary were the only characters who wore white, and while this contrast presented 'a rich visual picture', it was also Hynes's intention to highlight that these were the only two characters in the play who refused to 'play the darkness' by allowing society dominate and repress them.

Hynes notes how writers like D'Alton 'struggled' with the form they were expected to use, and how they lacked the resources to develop their craft sufficiently to deal with the subject matter they were writing about. What she wanted to emphasize in this production was 'the darker side' of the play: 'In the course of rehearsals, after the first or second week, the cast uniformly felt that there was a time bomb ticking under this play, and the more we worked at it, the more we felt that we revealed things that were very dark.' Her aim was to somehow liberate the message of the play, which she felt was being hidden by the naturalistic form it was written in:

> I think it's true of many of those plays in the older repertoire, as I think a lot of what Irish writers had to say at that time, or where they might have gone, was being constricted by a kind of naturalism ... which theatres like the Abbey did nothing to advance ... it's as if they got suffocated.[39]

By transforming the setting and shifting the conventions of the play, Hynes managed to make *Lovers' Meeting* accessible to a modern audience. Even the comic scenes, so misjudged in the play's first production, were carefully constructed into this production. The humour in the jocular, but nonetheless threatening role of Batt Seery, and the risible but poignant role of Hannie, were highlighted to balance the play's more sinister aspects, a move which D'Alton would surely have approved of. But whereas D'Alton's audience would not look behind the comedy, and were thus shocked by the play's tragic ending, the audience that attended Hynes's revival acknowledged the darker sides of these play.

Of course, society today is more open to plays like *Lovers' Meeting*, but the right balance still has to be found between humour and pathos in a play like this, and it is up to the director to create this equilibrium. Take the role of Hannie: Hynes saw Hannie as 'a beautiful, warm, fragile person', and although she recognized that there 'is some humour in the role', she chose to emphasize the relationship between Hannie and Mary, as she felt Hannie's tragedy mirrored Mary's tragedy. Ingrid Craigie's portrait of Hannie was described by the *Irish Times* as 'memorable', the reviewer noting that though Hannie 'may be "cracked", [she] is the wisest character in the play, knowing that there is nothing more important than love even if only briefly experienced.' D'Alton would have been happy with this interpretation.

The same review sums up the difficulties inherent in a modern production of a 'faded' play, but notes that these pitfalls can be overcome:

> D'Alton larded the piece with much comedy, posing hazards that could unbalance his obviously serious intent. Ms Hynes and her players succeeded admirably in maintaining the genuinely tragic tone of the play while not neglecting the comic elements, and, even more difficult, also manages to keep the mind of the audience distracted from some of the melodramatic happenstance inherent in the writing.

Surely then, if a modern revival of one of D'Alton's plays can be so successful, there is scope to revive other D'Alton plays with equally efficacious results. As Hynes notes, to approach a repertoire like his, given the times he was writing in and the conventions he was restrained by, one simply has to 'look underneath the text rather than on top of it'.[40]

G.B. Shaw may have advised D'Alton to 'Put your stuff in the fire; and don't bother me with it',[41] but modern-day producers should not be influenced by this opinion. Listen instead to Gabriel Fallon who noted in D'Alton's obituary, 'He just couldn't write an ineffective play, and his many good ones seemed always on the verge of greatness.'[42] Or note D'Alton's obituary in the *Irish Times* which recorded how he, 'fashioned and polished his works to the last degree of technical perfection, resulting in plays so competently made, so true in characterization and so complete in production details that they almost acted and produced themselves.'[43]

D'Alton's premature death undoubtedly was a great loss to the Irish stage. Cyril Cusack, who acted in his early plays, wrote to me about D'Alton shortly before his own death concluding, 'He should not be forgotten.'[44] Hopefully my work has gone some way in remembering Louis D'Alton, the playwright and the man.

Appendices

Appendix A: Louis D'Alton's Abbey Plays

This lists the first production dates and original cast members of those Louis D'Alton's plays produced at the Abbey Theatre.

The Man in the Cloak
A play in two acts.
First produced at the Abbey Theatre on 28 September 1937.

James Clarence Mangan	Cyril Cusack
James Mangan	Fred Johnson
Kate Mangan	Ann Clery
John Mangan	Malachi Keegan
Bridie Gilheaney	Josephine Fitzgerald
Marty Phelan	W. O'Gorman
Con Colgan	Seamus Healey
Mick Fogarty	Eric Gorman
Cis Carmody	Shela Ward
Catherine Hayes	Shelah Richards
Laurence Tighe	Tom Purefoy
Blythe	Jim Winter
Messenger	P.J. Considine
Doctor	Cecil Barror

Production by Hugh Hunt. Settings by Tanya Moiseiwitsch.

To-Morrow Never Comes
A play in three acts.
First produced in the Abbey Theatre on 13 March 1939.

Lar Broderick	Louis D'Alton
Mary Broderick	Ria Mooney
Ned Claffey	Cyril Cusack
Mick Hennessy	Denis O'Dea
Cornelius D'Arcy	W. O'Gorman
Guard Bannon	Seamus Healy

Sergeant Harrigan	Austin Meldon
James McEvelly	Michael J. Dolan
Mrs Cousins	May Craig

Production by Louis D'Alton. Settings by Anne Yeats.

The Spanish Soldier
A play in three acts.
First performed at the Abbey Theatre on 29 January 1940.

Mrs McMorna	Eileen Crowe
Moses Furlong	F.J. McCormick
Hugh McMorna	Denis O'Dea
Kevin McMorna	Cyril Cusack
Hessy McMorna	Ria Mooney
Davey Deasy	Fred Johnson
Nanno Deasy	Phyllis Ryan
Father Conn	Michael J. Dolan

Production by Lennox Robinson.

The Money Doesn't Matter
A play in three acts.
First produced at the Abbey Theatre on 11 March 1941.

Tom Mannion	W. O'Gorman
Harvey Mannion	Brian O'Higgins
Norah Mannion	Bríd Ní Loingsigh
Philip Mannion	Denis O'Dea
Veronica Hogan	Ria Mooney
Mick Kenirons	F.J. McCormick
Father Maher	Liam Redmond
Michael Harney	Joseph Linnane
Mrs Kinsella	Eileen Crowe
Maid	Cathleen Fawsitt

Production by Frank Dermody.

Lovers' Meeting
A play in three acts.
First produced at the Abbey Theatre on 20 October 1941.

Tom Sheridan	W. O'Gorman
Jane Sheridan	Eileen Crowe
Mary Sheridan	Phyllis Ryan
Hannie Martin	Ria Mooney

Frances Linehan	Maureen Delaney
Mossy Linehan	Michael J. Dolan
Joe Hession	Denis O'Dea
Sergeant Toolin	F.J. McCormick
Batt Seery	Seamus Healy

Production by Frank Dermody. Setting by Michael Walsh and Sean Barlow.

They Got What They Wanted
A play in three acts.
First produced at the Abbey Theatre on 18 February 1947.

Bartley Murnaghan	F.J. McCormick
Bessie Murnaghan	Eileen Crowe
Sally Murnaghan	Maureen Toal
Norah Murnaghan	Doreen Madden
Jack Murnaghan	Geoffrey Goldne
Derry Murnaghan	Ronnie Walsh
Peter Murnaghan	Michael O'Briain
Owney Tubrity	Harry Brogan
Matty McGrath	Brian O'Higgins
Joe McGrath	Sean Mooney
Tom Cassidy	Pádraig Ó Dulchonta
Lorcan	Micheál Ó Duinn

Play produced by Michael J. Dolan.

The Devil a Saint Would Be
A play in three acts.
First produced at the Rupert Guinness Hall on 10 September 1951.

Stacey	Bríd Ní Loinsigh
Ellie	Ite Ní Mhathúna
Sean	Micheál Ó hAonghusa
Father Johnny	Pilib Ó Floinn
Guard Herrity	Rae Mac an Áili
Dr Nolan	Seathrun Ó Goili
Paddy Cassidy	Micheál Ó Briain
Moll	Máire Ní Chathain
The Saint	Eamonn Guailli
Attorney Mowran	Harry Brogan
Voice of St Peter	Brian O'Higgins

Production by Ria Mooney. Setting by Vere Dudgeon.

This Other Eden
A play in three acts.
First produced at the Queen's Theatre on 2 June 1950.

John McRoarty	Seathrun Ó Goili
Pat Tweedy	Micheál Ó Briain
Humphrey Clannery	Harry Brogan
Mick Devereaux	Liam Ó Foghlu
Sergeant Crilly	Brian O'Higgins
Maire McRoary	Máire Ní Domhnaill
P. McNeely	Micheál Ó hAonghusa
Canon Moyle	Eamonn Guailli
Roger Crispin	Christopher Cassin
Conor Heaphy	Raghnall Breathnach

Production by Ria Mooney. Setting by Vere Dudgeon.

Cafflin' Johnny
A play in three acts.
First produced at the Queen's Theatre on 7 April 1958.

Honoria Fortune	Bríd Ní Loinsigh
Seamus Fortune	Bill Foley
Johnny Fortune	Ray MacAnally
Nicky Fortune	Vincent Dowling
Liz	Máire Ní Catháin
Guard Feery	Philip O'Flynn
Finuala Gogan	Eithne Ní Loideain
Mrs Mary Halpin	Máire O'Donnell

Production by Ria Mooney. Setting by Tomas MacAnna.

Appendix B: Fit-up companies

The following list is an inventory of fit-up companies that visited or toured Ireland in the nineteenth and twentieth centuries. I have tried to make this list as comprehensive as possible, but due to the lack of information on strolling players, it must be assumed that what we see here is only a sample of the many companies that performed in provincial Ireland during these times.

This information has been compiled mainly from newspaper reports and advertisements for provincial shows and from the papers of Gearóid Ó Briain. Included here are circuses, menageries, drawing room entertainment, moving pictures, magic shows etc., documented to indicate the wide variety of entertainment companies that travelled Irish roads in the eighteenth and nineteenth centuries.

Nineteenth-century touring companies

NAME	TYPE OF ENTERTAINMENT
African Roscius	Drama
W.J. Allen's Company	Irish Drama
The American Circus	Circus
The Anglo Americans	Minstrel Troupe
Batty's Circus Royal	Equestrian/Zoological Hippodrome
Belfast Dramatic Company	Drama
Bells Circus	Circus
C. Bernard's Legitimate Drama Company	Drama
Signor Bosco	Magic
Miss M. Bourke Drawing Room	Entertainment
The Brahams	Variety
The Buckley Brothers	Minstrel Show
Bullock's Marionettes	Marionettes
Carlton's Dramatic Company	Drama
Carroll and Desmond	Drama
Charles Cooke	Drama
Christy's Eclipse Constellation	Minstrel Show
Real Original Christy's Minstrels	Minstrel Show
A. Condon Operetta & Comedy	Comedy and Opera
M.G. Cooke	Drama
Cooney's Circus	Circus
A. Dashwood's Company	Mesmerist
Henry Davenport	Drama
Davies Circus	Circus
Gratton Dawson Drawing Room	Entertainment
Diorama	Diorama
Diplomacy Company	Drama and Variety
Charles Du Val	Drama and Variety

Duck's William 'Our Boys'	Drama and Variety
Edward's Company	Panorama
Joseph Eldred's Opera Company	Opera and Burlesque
Ethiopian Serenaders	Minstrel Show
Charles Eustace	Comedy
Falconer and Sharpe's Company	Variety
Female American Serenaders	Minstrel Show
Female Christy's	Minstrel Show
The Fitzgeralds	Drama
Fizroy Wallace's Comedy Company	Comedy and Burlesque
Forsyth's	Drama
Gaiety Company (Charles Wybert)	Drama
Gallagher V	entriloquism
M. Gardner	Comic Opera
Captain Gascoine	Drama and Variety
Ginnette's Great French Circus	Circus
Gratton Dawson Drawing Room	Entertainment
Great American Combination Company	Variety
Great Australian Circus	Circus
Great Hippodrome Japanese Circus	Circus
Great United States Circus	Circus
E. Grieve's Dramatic & Concert Company	Drama and Variety
The Fay Brothers	Drama
Master A. Grossmith	Drama and Imitation
Hague's Minstrel's	Minstrel Show
Harbuster, King of Wizards	Wizardry
Harvey & Bowtell's Comedy and Drama	Comedy and Drama
James Hicks	Variety
Monsieur Hoginis's Circus	Circus
Howes & Cushing Great American Circus	Circus
Hutchinson Brothers	Variety
Infant Power	Variety
Infant Rosciae	Drama
Japanese Tannakeri	Variety
Albert Jones	Lectures on Education
Jim Johnson	Variety
T.C. King	Variety
Herr Alfred Koening	Diorama of the War
Lacy and O'Brien	Drama and Variety
Jennie Le Tellier Drama and Opera	Drama and Opera
John Levey & the Garryowen Company	Drama and Variety
Lewis's World Renowned American Company	Drama
Harry Liston	Variety
Andrew Lloyd and his Comic Company	Comedy and Variety

Lloyd's Grand New Mexican Circus	Circus
William Lynch	Lectures on the Phonograph
W. Lyndon's Comedy and Burlesque	Comedy and Burlesque
Dr Lynn's Oriental Workers	Variety
Lyster and Company	Drama and Variety
Macarte & Clarke's Champs Elysses Circus	Circus
Magpie Minstrels	Variety
Miss Marie Majiliton's Company	Drama
Mander's Mammoth Hippodrome	Circus
M.A. Manning and Company	Variety
Mr C. Matthew Drama and	Variety
Mr McCormack	Magic
Miller and Browning	Drama and Variety
Professor Miller	Magic
Mr J. Mortimer and Miss K. Bell	Drawing Room Entertainment
Myrton Hamilton Company	Drama
O'Sullivan's American Minstrels	Minstrel Show
Ormonde Family	Variety
The Original Professor Pepper's Ghost	Special Effects Drama
Paganini Redivus	Variety
Pell's American Minstrels	Minstrel Show
Professor Pembroke	Magic
Phillipsons Imperial Hand Bell Ringers	Bell Ringing
Pinder's Great American Circus	Circus
Powell and Clarke's Paragon Circus	Circus
Professor Pepper's Ghost	Special Effects Drama
Professor Raymond	Magic
E.P Reardon	Drama
Reid's Pepper's Ghost Special Effects	Drama
Royal Hand Bell Ringers	Bell Ringers
Mr Russell	Magic
Scott's Great Continental Circus	Circus
Mr Seymour	Drama
Signor Soz	Magic
Silvestor's Company	Drama and Variety
Madame Sinco's Opera Company	Opera and Concert
Fred Smith's Burlesque Company	Burlesque
Snowden's Company	Panoramas
St Peter's Total Abstinence Society	Drama
Emma Stanley	Drama
Mr Stanley and Company	Drama
Stephen's Royal Menagerie	Menagerie
Mr and Mrs Charles Sullivan	Drama
Barry Sullivan	Drama

Miss Tempest and her London Company	Drama
Thorn's French Marionettes	Variety
Miss Rosa Towers	Drama and Variety
Mr A. Tucker	Diorama
United States Circus	Variety
Vance Variety	
Valentine Vousden (Valentine Vox)	Variety
Mr Ward	Drama
Miss Florence Warde and Company	Drama
Professor Whitworth	Variety
Whitworth's Charity Minstrels	Minstrel Show
Wombell's Royal Menagerie	Menagerie and Circus

Companies that toured in both the nineteenth and twentieth centuries

Baker's Great American Circus	Circus
Bostock and Womsweills	Menagerie
Carrickford's Repertory Company	Drama
William Dobell	Drama
Mr and Mrs Hubert O'Grady	Drama
Wright's Comedy Party	Comedy and Variety

Twentieth-century touring companies

Ira Allen's Irish Company	Drama
Arts League of Service	Drama and Variety
Harry Bailey's Comedy Company	Drama and Variety
Bernardo and Preston	Living Pictures
Benton Edward	Magician
Bertram Mills	Circus
Bohemian Players	Drama
The Brooklyn Players	Living Pictures
Brother's Variety Show	Variety
Buff Bill's Circus	Circus
N. Cannon & Miss Hope Trust	Drama
Carl Clopet Productions	Variety
The Carmel Players	Drama
Castlerea Players	Drama
Norman Chanrty and Company	Drama
Chipperfield's Circus	Circus
Cody's Grand Variety Company	Variety and Boxing
John Coleman	Drama
Costello's Bohemian Players	Drama
Carl Craichton	Magician
Cyril Cusack	Drama
Louis D'Alton	Drama
Anne D'Alton's Irish Players	Drama

George Daniels	Drama and Variety
Duskie Dan's Company	Variety
Democratic Dramatic Productions	Drama
Jack Doyle	Variety
Dublin City Players	Drama and Variety
Dublin Travelling Company	Living Pictures
Duffy's Circus	Circus
John Durrant's Dramatic Company	Drama
Edison's New Animated Pictures	Films
Emerald Players	Drama and Variety
Equity Productions	Drama
Falosa, the Great Indian Magician	Magic
The Flash Parade	Variety
Fossett's Circus	Circus
Foster-Grime Opera Company	Opera
J.F. Foster	Living Pictures
J. Gabriel and his Maker's Variety Company	Variety
GEM Animated Picture Company	Showed the Burns-Johnson Fight
Paul Goldin	Variety and Hypnotism
Gormley's Tours	Variety
Madame Grafton's Company	Drama
Ronald Grierson	Drama
Guest's Star Variety Company	Variety
Hanneford's Circus	Circus
H. Harrison's Standard Repertoire Company	Drama
The Edwin Heath Show	Variety
Heckenberg's Berlin Tower Circus	Circus
Hibernian Players	Drama
Pat Holmshaw	Variety
Hurley's London Company	Drama
The Hustlers	Variety
Jameson and Sons	Living Pictures
Jeserich's Celebrated Circus	Circus
Miss Eloise Juno	Drama
Kays Brothers	Circus
T.P. Keenan's Irish-American Minstrels	Minstrel Show
Walter Kirton	Lecture's on the War
The Jim Larkin Dramatic and Concert Company	Drama and Variety
Harold Lloyd's Company	Drama and Variety
Lynton's Touring Hippodrome	Hippodrome
J.C. Mack's Show Stars	Variety
Mack's Original No. 1 Repertoire	Drama
George Mallin's Pantomime Company	Pantomime
Marist Brothers	Variety

Anew McMaster	Drama
McFadden's Stages	Drama and Variety
Mr Francis McMahon	Drama and Variety
The Mercury Players	Drama
The Midland Players	Drama
Kenneth Miller's Irish Company	Irish Drama
Tom Moore	Concerts and Sketches
Mozard Wilson Family	Farces and Operettas
Navan Pioneer Players	Drama
The New Irish Players	Drama
James O'Brien	Drama
Jimmy O'Dea	Variety
Frank O'Donovan	Variety
Victor O'Donovan Power	Drama
Breffni O'Rourke	Drama
O'Rourke McGlynn	Animated Pictures
Onlookers Variety Company	Variety
Original Irish Animated Picture Show	Animated Pictures
Original Irish Animated Production Company	Animated Pictures
Dr Ormonde	Variety and Film
The Patriotic Players	Variety
Petterson's Circus	Circus
Payne Seddon	Drama
The Reco Brothers	Circus
Rodeo Frolics Revue	Variety
The Royal Italian Circus	Circus
Alf Saunder's Celebrated Dramatic Company	Drama and Variety
Sharpe and Preston	Films
A. Sinclair and his Irish Players	Irish Drama and Farces
Six Jolly Pigeons Dramatic Society	Drama
St Michael's Players	Drama
The Starlight Players	Drama and Variety
The Strolling Players	Drama
Sundrive Players	Drama and Variety
Madame Sylvester and Company	Variety
The Travelling Variety Company	Variety
Toft's Company Travelling	Amusements
Toft and Sons	Living Pictures
The Unknown Players	Drama
Weston's Theatrical Company	Drama
Whitbread's Drama Company	Drama
World's Animated Pictures and Variety	Animated Pictures and Variety
Mark Wynne and his Celebrated Repertoire	Drama and Variety

Appendix C

The draft agreement between Elliman, Dalton and Edwards and the Abbey Theatre Company concerning the participation of the Abbey with a television film industry in Ireland.[1]

HEADS OF TERMS OF AGREEMENT

PARTIES:

(1) A Private Company to be incorporated in Ireland with the powers of a management company for the entertainments generally (hereinafter called the 'Management Company').
(2) The Abbey Theatre Company.

RECITING:

1. The desire of the Management Company to arrange for the production of motion picture and television films for worldwide distribution.
2. The agreement of the Abbey Theatre Company to enter into an Agreement by which the name of the Abbey Theatre and the right to engage artistes under contract shall be granted exclusively to the Management
Company for Television on the terms below.

AGREEMENT:

1. The Management Company shall during the continuance of the Agreement be entitled
(i) to the exclusive use of the name of the Abbey Theatre or Abbey Theatre Company for the production of motion picture and television films.
(ii) to the exclusive right to engage artistes under contract to the Abbey Theatre to appear in such motion picture and television films.
2. The Management Company shall be entitled to enter into an Agreement for the production of such films with a company to be incorporated for that purpose (hereinafter called 'Dublin Film Productions').
3. The Management Company to be entitled to arrange with Dublin Film Productions for the production of a Pilot film to be produced in England and to be ready for delivery by the end of February 1957.
4. The Management Company to have a series of options to extend this Agreement year by year from 1st June in any one year by notice in writing to be given to the Abbey Theatre.
5. The Management Company to pay to the Abbey Theatre a royalty of £200 for each half hour film produced pursuant to this Agreement and a proportionate royalty for films of greater length.

DATED the day of 1956.

For and on behalf of

For and on behalf of
THE ABBEY THEATRE COMPANY.

Notes

INTRODUCTION

1 Gabriel Fallon, *Standard,* 2 May 1941.
2 R. Hogan and N. Sahal have done much to re-introduce this period of Irish drama to academics. N. Sahal in *Sixty years of realistic Irish drama* charts the 'realists' of Irish drama from 1900 to 1960 but lists Louis D'Alton among those playwrights he 'had to neglect' (Introduction, p. x). Hogan, in *After the Irish Renaissance,* allocates a chapter to the Abbey dramatists from 1926 to 1945, and another to Abbey dramatists from 1946 to 1965.
3 Tomas MacAnna, 'Ernest Blythe and the Abbey' in E.H. Mikhail (ed.), *The Abbey Theatre: interviews and recollection* (Basingstoke, 1988), p. 168.
4 In a letter to the *Irish Times* on 28 July 1944 Liam Collins writes, 'Sir – The trouble with the Abbey Theatre is that half the players are down in the Gaeltacht learning Irish and the other half are up in Dublin learning English.'
5 Author's interview with Phyllis Ryan, 29 April 1995.
6 'Meet Mr Blythe' in Mikhail (ed.), *The Abbey Theatre,* p. 162.
7 *Irish Times,* 19 June 1951.

CHAPTER ONE

1 Louis D'Alton was the first of his immediate family to add an apostrophe to his name. His sister, Babs, and brother, Noel, followed suit, but his parents were 'Daltons'.
2 *Evening Herald,* 9 September 1922.
3 *Theatre Magazine,* October 1923.
4 *Evening Herald,* 9 September 1922.
5 *Freeman's Journal,* 16 October 1906.
6 'Small-Change and Boucicault', *Dublin Magazine,* 1 (November 1923), p. 280.
7 *Irish Times,* 18 October 1880.
8 *Evening Herald,* 9 September 1922.
9 Unpublished personal interview with Babs D'Alton, 18 February 1994.
10 *Evening Herald,* 9 September 1922.
11 *Tuam Herald,* 4 June 1887. Advertisement for the company's five-day visit to Tuam where Boucicault's *The Shaughraun, The Octoroon* and *The Colleen Bawn* were to be performed commencing on Monday 6 June.
12 *Irish Times,* 1 March 1887.
13 *Evening Mail,* 1 March 1887.
14 Ibid.
15 *Wexford Independent,* 11 May 1887.

16 *Westmeath Independent*, 28 May 1887.
17 *Freeman's Journal*, 5 September 1887.
18 W.G. Fay and Catherine Carswell, *The Fays* (London, 1935), p. 52. Fay specifically compliments Frank's portrayal of Danny Mann in *The Colleen Bawn.*
19 Fay and Carswell, *The Fays of the Abbey Theatre*, pp 52–3.
20 David Krause, *Sean O'Casey and his world* (London, 1976), pp 9–10. There are some inconsistencies in this account. For example, Krause refers to Frank Dalton as Charles Dalton (as he also does in his editions of O'Casey's letters), and states that Dalton's son, Louis, was also in the company, and that it was he who called in O'Casey. However, this is impossible, as Louis was not born until 1900. O'Casey himself refers to this incident in some detail in his autobiography *Pictures in the hallway: autobiographies*, vol. 1 (London, 1963), pp 201–19.
21 See the *Westmeath Examiner*, 23 April 1898 for an example of an advertisement for the company.
22 Louis D'Alton, *Rags and sticks* (London, 1938), p. 41.
23 See advertisement in the *Chatham, Rochester and Gillingham News*, 9 March 1912.
24 Ibid.
25 Unpublished interview with Babs D'Alton, 18 February 1994.
26 Unpublished letter from John Cowley to author, 29 April 1995.
27 Untitled, undated report held in Charles Carey's scrapbooks which are housed at the Irish Theatre Archives, TA/107/54.
28 Ibid.
29 Unpublished letter from John Cowley to author, 29 April 1995.

CHAPTER TWO

1 Letter of 24 July 1943 from Sean O'Casey to Louis D'Alton in David Krause (ed.), *The letters of Sean O'Casey 1942–1954*, vol. 2 (New York, 1980), p. 136.
2 A detailed list of the names of these companies, the dates they toured and the type of entertainment they offered can be found in Appendix B of this book.
3 'Tatler's Leader Page Parade', *Irish Independent*, 29 April 1956, p. 6.
4 Fay papers pertaining to the life of W.G. Fay: National Library of Ireland, MS 5,974–76.
5 Fay papers: Material for a Second Edition of *The Fays of the Abbey Theatre*, by W.G. Fay: National Library of Ireland, MS 5,982.
6 Ibid.
7 Eleanor Elder, *Travelling players: the story of the Arts League of Service* (London, 1939), p. 14.
8 *The Fays of the Abbey Theatre*, p. 40.
9 Bob Bickerdike, 18 June 1995. Irish Theatre Archive. Author's interview with Paddy Dooley, 14 October 1996.
10 *The Green Room*, p. 472. Quoted in Michael Sanderson, *From Irving to Olivier: a social history of the acting profession in England, 1880–1983* (London, 1984), p. 61.
11 *Recollections of the life of John O'Keeffe*, vol. 1 (London, 1862), p. 225.
12 Elder, *Travelling players*, pp 37–8. The Company travelled twice to Ireland in April 1926 and May 1927. These trips were organized by Judith Wogan, who joined the company in 1920 having spent her early career touring Ireland with Madame Markievicz and her husband.
13 Louis D'Alton, *Rags and sticks* (London, 1938), pp 74–5.
14 'Report on Prospective Provincial Tour', Blythe Papers, Archives Department, University College Dublin, P/24/771.
15 Author's interview with Shela Ward, 25 May 1994.

16 Author's interviews with Babs D'Alton, 18 February 1995, and Shela Ward, 25 May 1994.
17 John O'Keeffe, *Wild oats, or The strolling gentlemen* (Dublin, 1791), p. 27.
18 *Memoirs of the countess of Derby*, pp 12–13, quoted in 'Strolling players and provincial drama after Shakespeare', *P.M.L.A.* (1922), 243–280, p. 265.
19 Act IV, iii, *The complete works of William Shakespeare*, ed. B. Hodek (London, 1958), p. 254.
20 O'Keefe, *Wild oats*, p. 35.
21 *Chambers's Journal*, [3rd Section], vol. 1 (London, 1854), p. 322.
22 Unpublished interview with Bob Bickerdike, 18 June 1995. Irish Theatre Archive.
23 *The Fays of the Abbey Theatre*, pp 49–50.
24 'Report on Prospective Provincial Tour', Blythe papers, Archives Department, University College Dublin, P/24/771. Blythe goes on to say that, 'D'Alton also thinks that two men are necessary to assist with the unloading of scenery and to act as scene shifters, and that preferably one of them should have acknowledge of electricity.'
25 Albert B. Daniels, *Five and nine: recollections of the touring shows in Ireland* (Donegal, 1991), p. 3.
26 *Wexford Independent*, Saturday 18 June 1898.
27 *Westmeath Independent*, 26 August 1871.
28 From the private collection of Brendan O'Brien. Apart from *Uncle Tom's cabin*, the company also produced Boucicault's *Arrah-na-Pogue*,and *Foul Play*, Col. Tony Clarke's melodrama *Cruel Slavery*, Reade's *'It's Never Too Late to Mend'* and Buchanan and Jays' *Alone in London.*
29 *Clare Journal*, 27 July 1896.
30 1926 programme advertising Dobell's 'La Comedie Irlandaise Company'. Brendan O'Brien's unpublished papers: 'Dobell', p. 18.
31 *Athlone Times*, 19 November 1892.
32 Poster reproduced with the permission of David Costello.
33 These include favourites such as *East Lynne, The Face at the Window, Hawk Island, His Mother's Rosary, Maria Martin, Pal o' My Cradle Days, Three Leaves of a Shamrock, Smiling Thro', Sweeney Todd, Noreen Bawn, The Wearin' o' the Green* and *The White Sister.*
34 Irish Theatre Archive: ITA 54. Undated.
35 Ibid., ITA 102. Undated.
36 Ibid., ITA 102. Undated.
37 *Rags and Sticks*, pp 13–14.
38 Author's interviews with David Costello, 2 April 1997, and Shela Ward, 25 May 1994.
39 *Cork Constitution*, Thursday 16 March 1837.
40 *Sligo Independent*, 4 August 1855.
41 *Wexford Guardian*, 20 January 1855.
42 *Wexford Guardian*, 27 January 1855.
43 *Freeman's Journal*, 1 March 1851.
44 Samuel Wild, *Old Wilds: a nursery of strolling players* (London, 1888), pp 12–13.
45 Author's interview with Babs D'Alton, 24 October 1993.
46 Author's interview with David Costello, 2 April 1997.
47 'Donnybrook Fair', William Hogarth, From the John Johnson Collection, Bodleian Library.
48 *Bentley's Miscellany*, vol. 11 (1841). Quoted in Jane Traies, *Fairbooths and fit-ups* (Cambridge, 1980), p. 29.
49 See Samuel Wild, *Old Wilds: a nursery of strolling players* (London, 1888), p. 70.
50 Quoted in Clarke, *The Irish stage in the county towns, 1720–1800* (Oxford, 1965), p. 266.
51 From public meetings held in Athlone. From the Brendan O'Brien personal papers. The Father Mathew Hall, which seated up to five hundred people, was finally opened on 26 November 1897.

52 Author's interview with Bob Bickerdike, November 1995, Irish Theatre Archive. Compare this to Parker's memory of a seventeenth-century village performance where the ale-house served as the ladies' dressing rooms, the blacksmith's shop as the men's; the doors of the alehouse and forge were entrances to the theatre, the curtain consisted of bed curtains strung on pack thread and the black cloth was made out of furniture paper. See George Parker, *A view of society and manners*, 1781, quoted in Sybil Rosenfeld, *Strolling players and drama in the provinces, 1600–1765* (Cambridge, 1939), p. 22.
53 Unpublished interview with Billy Hayden, December 1995, Irish Theatre Archive. Unpublished interview with Shela Ward, 25 May 1994.
54 Albert Daniels, *Five and nine*, pp 6–7.
55 Ibid. p. 6.
56 Thomas Hardy, *Far from the madding crowd* (London, 1994), p. 318.
57 Clark, *The Irish stage in the county towns, 1720–1800*, pp 7–8.
58 Tate Wilkinson, *Memoirs of his own life*, vol. 3 (York, 1790), p. 164.
59 Carl Falb, 'A world elsewhere: the stage career of Anew McMaster' (Ohio State University, PhD, 1974), p. 23.
60 Goldsmith, *Essays* (London, 1794), p. 115.
61 *Waterford News*, 28 October 1881; *Westmeath Independent*, 26 November 1898.
62 Peter Paterson, *Glimpses of real life as seen in the theatrical world of Peter Paterson, a strolling comedian* (Edinburgh, 1864), p. 39.
63 'A world elsewhere', p. 25.
64 Author's interview with Shela Ward, 25 May 1994.
65 Albert Daniels, *Five and nine*, p.34.
66 *Westmeath Independent*, January 4th, 1913.
67 'Spice of Life', RTE Sound Archives: JVT313.
68 Elder, *Travelling players*, p. 171.
69 Daniels, *Five and nine*, p. 36.
70 Val Vousden, *Val Vousden's caravan* (Dublin, 1941), p. 12.
71 Interview with Cecil Davies, quoted in Peter George Billingham, 'Theatres of conscience: a study of four British regional theatre companies, 1939–1950', PhD dissertation (Leeds University, 1994), p. 115.
72 W. Wetherburn, 'The stroller or All in the dark'. This manuscript was sent to R.B. Sheridan at the Theatre Royal in 1799, and is now housed in the Manuscripts Room of the British Library, Add 25,946.
73 Thomas Hardy, *Far from the madding crowd*, pp 320–1.
74 O'Keeffe. *Recollections*, vol. 1, p. 336.
75 Mrs Martha Mc Tier, *The Drennan correspondence*, no. 163, quoted in *The Irish stage in the county towns, 1720–1800*, pp 254–56.
76 W.G. Fay, Untitled essay, 8 October 1928, National Library of Ireland Manuscript, MS 5891, p.6.
77 Fred Spangle, *Fred Spangle or The life of a strolling player* (London, 1873) vol. 1, p. 110.
78 Author's interview with Tony Glass, Undated, Irish Theatre Archives.
79 Author's interview with Vikki Jackson, 9 November 1996.
80 'Spice of Life', RTE Sound Archives: JVT-313. Interviews with Treasa Davidson, Vernon Hayden and Hal Roach.
81 See Aubrey Gwynn, 'The origin of Anglo-Irish Theatre', *Studies* (Dublin), 38:10 (June 1939), p. 268. This prohibition lasted until the sixteenth century.

82 See the *Galway Vindicator*, 20 October 1884

83 The Theatrical Notebooks of T.H. Wilson Manley. Held at the British Museum Manuscript Room. Reference Number: Add MSS 41073–4.

84 See J.B. Lippincott, *Hawkers and walkers* (Philadelphia, 1927).

85 One Man in his Time, Wednesday 29 1846 (month not noted), and 14 June 1846.

86 Author's interview with Vikki Jackson, 9 October 1996.

87 Other examples of showman's argot include: Scrid – church; Mumming – drama; mumming booth – drama booth; Tober – the ground a tent was fitted on, Letty or letta Casa – lodgings; to Scarper – to run away without paying; Strummel – hay; Clone – girl; Fiellier or Chaaver–child; Ohmis – man; Polones – woman; Jossers – the Public; Trick of the Loop – somebody in Show Business; Medzus or Danales – money; Parlarey – talk; Mungari – food; Multy – bad; Multy cateever – very bad; Bona – good.

88 Author's interview with David Costello, 7 April 1997.

89 Unpublished interview with Lawrence Hayes, 12 December 1995, Irish Theatre Archive.

90 Author's interview with Babs D'Alton, 25 October 1993.

CHAPTER THREE

1 Peter Brooks, *The melodramatic imagination: Balzac, Henry James and the mode of excess* (New York, 1985).

2 Barry Jackson, 'Barnstorming days', in Muriel St Clare Byrne (ed.), *Studies in English theatre history*, pp 120–1.

3 Thaler, 'Strolling players and provincial drama after Shakespeare', PMLA (1922), p. 267.

4 Reminiscences, vol. 1, p. 70, quoted in Thaler, 'Strolling players', p. 267.

5 Jackson, 'Barnstorming days', p. 120.

6 John O'Keeffe, *Wild oats* (Dublin, 1791), p. 27.

7 Quoted in Billingham 'Theatres of conscience', pp 181–2.

8 *Spectres of the Past* is just one example of the many fit-up plays that included songs and dances, and it is interesting to note that, according to the reviewer, the dances were 'well applauded' and the 'first rate topical songs [...] introduced to new and catchy airs are likely to become popular'. See *Freeman's Journal*, Monday 30 January 1893. Even melodramas such as *East Lynne* contained music and when Cooke played this play in Ballinasloe in 1878, it was reviewed as containing 'good soul-stirring music executed with a correctness and style that would do merit to a first class orchestra', *Tuam Herald*, 26 September 1878. Songs and music continued to be included in fit-up dramas until the end of the fit-up era, as can be seen in the 1960s versions of *The Wearing of the Green* and *Pal o' My Cradle Days*. Both of these plays will be analyzed in this chapter.

9 Michael R. Booth, *English melodrama* (London, 1965), p. 14.

10 Seamus de Burca, *The Queen's Royal Theatre Dublin, 1829–1969* (Dublin, 1983), Introduction.

11 Peter Brooks, *The melodramatic imagination*, p. 36.

12 *Goldsmith essays* (London, 1794), p. 115. This essay is also reproduced in Arthur Friedman, *Collected works of Oliver Goldsmith*, vol. 3 (Oxford, 1966), pp 133–42.

13 Quoted in Peter Brooks, *English melodrama*, p 15.

14 Ibid. p. 197.

15 *Mullingar Guardian*, 1 November 1851.

16 D'Alton, *Rags and sticks*, pp 103–4.

17 Jackson, 'Barnstorming days', pp 120–1.

18 Frank Rahill, *The world of melodrama* (Pennsylvania, 1967), p. 251.

19 Maud and Otis Skinner, *One man in his time: the adventures of H. Walkins, strolling player 1845–1863, from his journal* (London, 1938).
20 *The world of melodrama,* p. 252.
21 Unpublished playbill from Brendan O'Brien's personal collection, advertising *The Love That Lasts for Ever* which played in the Father Mathew Hall on Tuesday 27 August 1912.
22 Ibid.
23 *Carlow Nationalist,* 1 December 1883, and *Kilkenny Journal,* February 1886.
24 John Oxenford, *East Lynne,* in Michael Kilgarrif (ed.), *The golden age of melodrama: twelve nineteenth century melodramas* (London, 1974). A fit-up working script of East Lynne is available to view in the Irish Theatre Archive, ITA/128/4/10.
25 See Kilgarriff (ed.), *Golden age of melodrama.*
26 Cheryl Herr (ed.), *For the land they loved: Irish political melodramas, 1890–1925* (New York, 1991), p. 4, p. 19.
27 David Krause, *The Dolmen Boucicault* (Dublin, 1964), pp 33, 171–2
28 *For the land they loved,* p. 20.
29 *The Wearing of the Green,* unpublished anonymous version, p. 5. Further references to this play shall be taken from this version and the page number shall be given after quotations in the text.
30 *Arrah-na-Pogue,* in David Krause, *The Dolmen Boucicault,* p. 166.
31 Author's interview with Paddy Dooley, 27 January 1998.
32 I shall be quoting from an anonymous version, held at the Irish Theatre Archive. The play is also known to have toured England under the title *Over the Hill.* Paddy Dooley remembers this play being performed right up to the demise of fit-up drama: 'It was one of the most popular plays in the 1940s and 1950s – almost every company must have performed it regularly.' Author's interview with Paddy Dooley, 27 December 1997.
33 Unpublished, anonymous version of *Pal o' My Cradle Days* held at the Irish Theatre Archive. All quotes shall be taken from this version, to which the page numbers refer.
34 Unpublished interview with Lawrence Hayes, 12 December 1995, Irish Theatre Archive.
35 Boucicault, 'The decline of drama', *North American Review* (September 1877). If Thaler's assertion that Shakespeare 'played with his company in the provinces' is correct, then this quote bears even more significance. 'The travelling players in Shakespeare's England', p. 122.
36 Colm Tobin, *The best of the decades: Ireland in the 1960s* (Dublin, 1974), p. 64.
37 Unpublished interview with Bob Bickerdike, November 1995, Irish Theatre Archive.

CHAPTER FOUR

1 Gabriel Fallon, 'Experiment in the Theatre', *Irish Monthly,* 65 (June 1937), 406.
2 See the *Irish Times* and the *Irish Independent* in their reviews of Moses Furlong's role in *The Spanish Soldier,* 30 January 1940.
3 On 1 April 1936, Louis received a letter from Máire Lynch who worked at William Heinemann (Great Russell Street, London) who would later publish Louis's two books. Two things are interesting about the letter. Firstly, Lynch refers to the dedication of *Death Is So Fair* and tells Louis, 'I should be very much honoured, but I simply don't know whether it would be etiquette or not. I must consult someone.' It seems that Louis was considering dedicating his novel to Máire Lynch, despite never having met her. In the end, *Death Is So Fair* was dedicated to D'Alton's father, Frank. Secondly, Lynch suggests a title for the novel, *The Holy Gunman,* informing D'Alton, 'To be honest, I don't like any of yours'. Seemingly, D'Alton didn't like hers any better. Information quoted from a letter dated 1 April 1936, from Máire Lynch to Louis D'Alton, author's own collection.

4 Louis Lynch D'Alton, *Death Is So Fair* (London, 1936), p. 39. Further references to this novel shall be taken from this edition and the page number shall be given after quotations in the text.
5 *Dublin Magazine* (Jan–May 1937), p. 96.
6 Author's interview with Babs D'Alton, 24 October 1993.
7 It is Manus' brother who is attracted to Norah and when she becomes pregnant with his child, she tells Manus, after having seduced him, that the child she is carrying is his.
8 D'Alton, *Rags and sticks* (London, 1938), p. 17. Further references to this novel shall be taken from this text and the page number shall be given after quotations in the text.
9 Interestingly, *Rags and sticks* was described by its publishers as the Irish *Good companions*, but there is little in common between the two except the shared thespian background. Priestley's novel has no definite theme and is a rather dull portrayal of a touring company. However, D'Alton would have been aware of this novel, especially since it was dramatised in 1931.
10 *Rags and sticks* was listed in the half year report of books prohibited (1 April to 30 September 1938) under the Censorship of Publications Act of 1929.
11 'Barn Stormers in Ireland', *The Birmingham Post*, 15 February 1938.
12 *Times Literary Supplement*, 26 March 1938.
13 The copy is in my possession and on its first page is written, *The O'Hagan*, by Louis D'Alton.
14 Original cast: The O'Hagan, Count De Marnay – Louis Dalton; Mac Namara – Noel Dalton; Sheila O'Malley – Annette Mulhall; Mahony, Innkeeper and Lord Clanmoynagh – Sean Longford; Manners [First name indecipherable] – Mona Macdonald; Robert Clanmoynagh and Sir James Braithwaite – Kenneth Raymond.
15 Louis Lynch D'Alton, *Two Irish plays: The Man in the Cloak* and *The Mousetrap* (London, 1938). (Note that Louis was still writing under the name Louis Lynch D'Alton at this time.) Further references to these plays shall be taken from this edition and the page number shall be given after quotations in the text.
16 Flann O'Brien, 'The Dance Halls', *The Bell*, 1:5 (February 1941), p. 45.
17 Ibid. pp 44–52.
18 *Irish Catholic Directory, 1925* (8 April 1924).
19 'Why there are so many bachelors: Archbishop's warning to the modern girl', *Irish Times*, 12 May 1931, p. 6.
20 'Mixed bathing and beauty contests deplored', *Irish Times*, 11 May 1931, p. 5.
21 M.P.R.H., 'Illegitimate', *The Bell*, 2:3 (1941) 79.
22 In one case it was reported that the defendant was allowed out on bail to get married to the child's father. See *Irish Times*, 30 April 1931, p. 3.
23 See M.P.R.H., 'Illegitimate', p. 86.
24 Taken from the Reader's Opinion files housed at the Abbey Theatre Archives.
25 Ibid.
26 John Desmond Sheridan, *James Clarence Mangan* (Dublin, 1937).
27 Although it was well known that Mangan referred to himself as 'the Man in the Cloak.' See D.J. O'Donoghue, *The life and writings of J.C. Mangan* (Dublin, 1897), pp 100–2. There are many other reasons which lead me to believe D'Alton had read this biography, which I shall footnote as they arise. In Gabriel Fallon's critique of *The Man in the Cloak*, he criticizes D'Alton for taking 'Mangan's opinion of Mangan' at his word, especially the low opinion he had of his father: 'In this, of course, Mr D'Alton may or may not have been justified; the biographers can say'. See Gabriel Fallon, 'Sitting at the play', *Irish Monthly*, 65 (December 1937), 839–46 at 838. Yet Sheridan also emphasizes in his biography the resentment Mangan felt for his father.

28 Louis D'Alton, *The Man in the Cloak* (Dublin, 1971), p. 27. Further references to this play shall be taken from this edition and the page number shall be given after quotations in the text.

29 The character of Melancholy also appears whenever Mangan is confronted by the ghost of his father. Melancholy always takes the side of the father, often repeating what he has said. Obviously D'Alton wanted his audience to see what drove Mangan into depression, and the blame lies clearly with his father's treatment of him. Neither Melancholy nor Drunkeness appear in the published version of *The Man in the Cloak.*

30 See the working script of *The Man in the Cloak* housed at the national Library of Ireland, MS 21, 327. Interestingly, The *Evening Herald* reviewer considered that the play 'would have been more successful if the superfluous figures of Melancholy and Drunkenness were cut out' as they were 'not merely crude ... but boring'. *Evening Herald,* 28 September 1937.

31 Ibid.

32 Tanya Moiseiwitsch designed the settings for the play and Hugh Hunt produced it.

33 *Evening Herald,* 28 September 1937. *Irish Press,* 28 September 1937.

34 'Sitting at the Play' 65 (December 1937), 839.

35 Sheridan, *James Clarence Mangan,* p. 110. O'Donoghue claims that Mangan 'had a pronounced leaning towards Spiritualism', that he 'assured his friends that he was in communion with forms from the unseen world' and that he 'had a notion that his father often came to him in the night and troubled his rest'. See p. 116 of D.J O'Donoghue's *Life and writings of James Clarence Mangan.* In a biographical note in Sheridan's biography of Mangan, he notes that he was indebted to O'Donoghue's biography. It is thus possible that D'Alton also read this account of Mangan's life and that his idea for writing a dream sequence was also inspired by this biography.

36 Sheridan, *James Clarence Mangan,* p. 62.

37 This poem is quoted in Sheridan's biography of Mangan. In a chapter which deals with Mangan's interest in translating poems, and his love affair with Catherine, Sheridan notes that 'Catherine's early death left Mangan disconsolate. It seemed to him but another gesture of a malign fate whose constant sport it was to wreck his dreams.' (39) Sheridan also notes that Mangan was 'hugely pleased that she [Catherine] should show interest in his development' (39) and that when he would present translations of poems to her 'like a couple of children they [would] turn to the back of the page, and add their laughing signatures to the souvenir' (39) This action is seen in D'Alton's *The Man in the Cloak* on p. 33.

38 In the Abbey working script for the play, Drunkenness and Melancholy once again make an appearance at this point. Mangan despairs, 'Oh God, if only I could escape all this ...' to which Drunkenness and Melancholy reply that they will give him the secret. The act ends with Drunkenness imploring Mangan to come with him, Melancholy adding 'He will show you the way to peace and happiness'. At this point Mangan recites the poem 'Where shall I find rest, alas', and the act ends. 'The masked figures come forward and gather about him mocking him with pointed fingers. He backs away from them. He tries to beat them off and they retreat away on one side and close in on another. He is gradually driven back towards the pallet. When he reaches it they rush forward and close about him. The voices die and the masked figures withdraw into the darkness. Mangan is seen lying upon the pallet.' (See *The Man in the Cloak* working script housed at the National Library of Ireland, MS21, 327.) However, Drunkenness and Melancholy are cut from the printed version of the play, presumably because D'Alton felt their presence led the audience to focus too much on Mangan's drink problem and his depression whereas D'Alton wanted the audience to look for what caused these problems.

39 Sheridan notes in his biography that Mangan was convinced that he would be one of cholera's victims but that 'he was quite resigned – the 'hand in the darkness' had no terrors for him' (see

Sheridan, *James Clarence Mangan*, p. 121) D'Alton emphasises throughout the final act of *The Man in the Cloak* just how resigned Mangan was, which is made all the more clear when contrasted with the panic and fear of the other characters in the doss house. Mangan did not in fact die of cholera but of malnutrition (although it was at first thought that he had cholera) and though it is not stated in D'Alton's play that Mangan did die of cholera, the other characters in the doss-house believe that this is what he is dying from. In the Abbey production of *The Man in the Cloak*, Colgan realizes that Mangan in fact dying of malnutrition, but D'Alton cut these lines in his published version of the play. This was probably to heighten the atmosphere of dread that forms the basis of the final act of *The Man in the Cloak*.

40 *Irish Times*, 28 September 1937.

CHAPTER FIVE

1 *Irish Independent*, 14 March 1939.
2 *Irish Independent*, 14 March 1939.
3 Louis D'Alton, *To-Morrow Never Comes* (Dublin, 1968), p. 39. Further references to this play shall be taken from this script and the page number shall be given after quotations in the text.
4 *Irish Times*, 14 March 1939
5 Ibid. 30 January 1940.
6 Aodh de Blacam, 'Can Ireland help Spain?', *Irish Monthly*, 64 (1936), 645–51 at 645.
7 'The Religious revival in Spain', *Irish Monthly*, 64 (1936), 653–7 at 653–4.
8 Louis D'Alton, *The Spanish Soldier* (unpublished: Working script housed at the National Library of Ireland, MS 21,328, p. 6. Further references to this play shall be taken from this script and the page number shall be given after quotations in the text.
9 Michael Farrell, 'Plays for the country theatre', *The Bell*, 2:1 (1941), p. 81.
10 *Irish Independent*, 30 January 1940; *Irish Times*, 30 January 1940.
11 *New York Times*, 4 and 5 February 1941.
12 Author's interview with Babs D'Alton,
13 *Irish Times*, 11 March 1941.
14 Louis D'Alton, *The Money Doesn't Matter* (Dublin, 1980; first published 1942), p. 10. Further references to this play shall be taken from this script and the page number shall be given after quotations in the text.
15 When *The Money Doesn't Matter* was staged by the Mullingar Little Theatre Group at the Tullamore Festival in 1950, the Pioneer Organization were congratulated by the reviewer in *The Standard* 'on the praise-worthy work of its members in the cause of rural drama'. However, the reviewer also notes that 'the stage of Tullamore literally bustled with Pioneer emblems', and his questions this practice: 'Is it dramatically correct, so to speak, to wear the emblem as an integral part of every theatrical costume? The appearance of the dipsomaniacal [*sic*] Philip Mannion, complete with emblem, pouring "finger" after "finger" of whiskey may present an unintended risibility.' *Standard*, 2 June 1950.
16 *Irish Independent*, 11 March 1941; *Irish Times*, 11 March 1941; *The Bell*, 2 (April 1941), p. 91.
17 Hugh Hunt, *The Abbey: Ireland's national theatre, 1904–1978* (Dublin, 1979), p. 169.
18 Gabriel Fallon, 'No rest for the critic', *Irish Monthly*, 69 (May 1941), 268–74 at 269.
19 See Frank O'Connor, 'Public opinion: the stone dolls', *The Bell*, 2:3 (June 1941), pp 61–7.
20 Louis Lynch D'Alton, 'Public opinion', *The Bell*, 2:4 (July 1941), pp 72–6. D'Alton also wrote a letter to the *Irish Times* printed on 3 June 1941 about this issue. For a discussion of this see chapter 8.

21 Denis Ireland, 'The Abbey Theatre', *The Bell*, 2:3 (1941), pp 67–8.

22 Denis Johnston, 'The Theatre', *The Bell*, 2:4 (July 1941), pp 76–81.

23 Reader's opinion on *Lovers' Meeting* by Richard Hayes, dated 30 July 1941, housed in the Abbey Theatre Archives.

24 Author's interview with Phyllis Ryan, 29 April 1995.

25 Phyllis Ryan, *The company I kept* (Dublin, 1996), p. 86.

26 Louis D'Alton, *Lovers' Meeting* (Dublin, 1964), p. 7. Further references to this play shall be taken from this edition and the page number shall be given after quotations in the text.

27 *Irish Times*, 21 October 1941.

28 Ibid.

29 Ibid. However, I would argue that D'Alton did not intend the figure of Hannie 'as comic relief'. This comment reminds us of O'Casey's *Juno and the Paycock* when, because of the final scene's juxtaposition of 'high tragic sentiment' and 'knockabout comedy' the play was deemed 'artistically indefensible' by critics. See Stephen Watt's discussion of this in *Joyce, O'Casey and the Irish popular theatre* (Syracuse, 1991), pp 177–8.

30 Christpoher Murray, '*Lovers' Meeting* and the national dream-life', Druid Theatre Company Programme for *Lovers' Meeting*, October 1990.

31 *Irish Times*, 21 October 1941.

32 F.S.L. Lyons, *Ireland since the Famine* (Glasgow, 1971, revised edition 1973), pp 557–8.

33 Quoted in Gabriel Fallon, 'Not forgetting the audience', *Irish Monthly*, 68 (June 1939), 419–24 at 420–1.

CHAPTER SIX

1 Abbey Theatre minute book (26 May 1939–14 November 1940). Unpublished.

2 Ernest Blythe, 'Report on Prospective Provincial tour', Blythe papers, P/24/771, Archives Department, University College Dublin.

3 'Report on Prospective Provincial Tour'.

4 Ibid.

5 Abbey Theatre minute book (26 May 1939–14 November 1940).

6 'Report on Prospective Provincial Tour'.

7 *Kilkenny Journal*, 4 October 1941.

8 Phyllis Ryan, *The company I kept* (Dublin, 1996), pp 88–9. Note that F.J. Mc Cormick was sent to perform with the company in Sligo for the week beginning 27 May 1940.

9 *Northern Standard*, 12 April 1940.

10 *Tyrone Constitution*, 10 May 1940.

11 *Clare Champion*, 15 June 1940.

12 F.S.L. Lyons, *Ireland since the Famine* (Glasgow, 1973), p. 557.

13 *Tyrone Constitution*, 19 May 1940.

14 *The Money Doesn't Matter* was also advertised in the *Cork Examiner* for its matinee and evening performance on Saturday 21 February 1942, but it was not reviewed in subsequent editions of the newspaper. It must be noted that the aforesaid review may have been a puff.

15 D'Alton did well to perform to 'full houses' in Wexford, considering that Local cinemas the same week were screening *Keeping the Company* starring Frank Morgan, and *Danger Rides the Range*, James Cagney in *City for Conquest*, Denis Morgan, Merle Oberon and Rita Hayworth in the romantic comedy *Affectionately Yours*, and Michael Laynard in the romance and robbery *The Lone Wolf Takes a Chance*. A mystery show, *The Night of January 16th* was also to be screened during this week.

16 Unpublished letter from Sean O'Casey to Louis D'Alton, 20 August 1942. Author's private collection.
17 Ibid.
18 Ibid.
19 Unpublished letter from Sean O'Casey to Louis D'Alton, 21 October 1942. Author's private collection. The letter goes on to contemplate the changing world, the war, the demise of the aristocracy and the growth of Communism.
20 Unpublished letter from Sean O'Casey to Louis D'Alton, 23 November 1942. Author's private collection. D'Alton's tour was not mentioned in the local newspapers. However, on 10 October 1942 the *Mayo News* carried articles which reported on Castlebar's new dance hall that was granted a licence for dances on Wednesday and Saturday nights. Indeed, the bulk of advertisements relating to entertainments were for local dances, so it could be postulated that these dances enticed audiences from D'Alton's performances. O'Casey's letter to D'Alton continues with him lamenting that he had to part with the rights for *Juno and the Paycock* ('half of them') to French 'in a damned bad patch', and that he had to argue with the company 'to prevent them charging five guineas a performance (the usual fee), and managed to get them down to three guineas – a big figure to ask from a little amateur co, and a littler town.'
21 'I am very glad that Waterford gave you such a welcome welcome,' wrote O'Casey to D'Alton on 29 April 1943. Unpublished letter from Sean O'Casey to Louis D'Alton, 29 April 1943. Author's private collection.
22 Author's interview with Phyllis Ryan, 29 April 1998.
23 Letter to author from John Cowley, 29 April 1995.
24 See Michael Sanderson, *From Irving to Olivier*, pp 257–9.
25 See Peter Noble, *British theatre* (London, 1946).
26 W. MacQueen Pope, *Ivor* (London, 1974), p. 462, quoted in Michael Sanderson, *From Irving to Olivier*, p. 261.
27 *Actors' Church Union Call Board*. September 1941. Letter from an anonymous member in ENSA. Quoted in Michael Sanderson, *From Irving to Olivier*, p. 260.
28 The papers of Mrs C.M. Lowry, p. 69. Ref: 86/12/1. Held at the Imperial War Museum, London.
29 The letters of Gracie Fields. 27 August 1945. Ref: 76/23/1. Held at the Imperial War Museum, London.
30 The diary of Lieutenant Commander A. Hughes. 16 November 1944. Ref: 93/1/1. Held at the Imperial War Museum, London.
31 The memoirs of Mrs B.H. Holdbrook, p. 37. Ref: 95/27/1. Held at the Imperial War Museum, London.
32 Brian Rix, *Tour de Farce: a tale of touring theatres and strolling players* (London, 1992), p. 118.
33 For example, Major Harper Nelson stated in a letter written in Italy on 17 November 1944, 'I have never in my life seen such an unprofessional and incompetent organization overseas as ENSA', and in another letter written on 25 November 1943 comments, 'There seems to be no drive behind the ENSA [...] the wretched artists are left largely to their own devices [...]. They [ENSA] don't give a damn what kind of entertainment the troops get provided they don't have to work too hard to provide it.' See the letters of Major Harper Nelson. Ref: 85/34/1. Held at the Imperial War Museum, London.
34 Peter Noble, *British theatre*, p. 106.
35 Walter Hudd, 'New audiences for the old', *CEMA Bulletin*, January 1944. Quoted in Michael Sanderson, *From Irving to Olivier*, p. 265.

36 John Casson, *Lewis and Sybil* (London, 1972), p. 216. Quoted in Michael Sanderson, *From Irving to Olivier*, p. 264.
37 1946–1947 CEMA Annual Report, p. 11. Held at the Public Record office of Northern Ireland. (Portadown is mentioned twice in this list.)
38 *Derry Standard*, 1 May 1946. Barry Cassin notes that Ryan became revered for her role in *Shadow and substance*, that she had 'hit Dublin like a storm' when the play first opened, and that 'She had an extraordinary ethereal quality as Brigid'. Unpublished interview with Barry Cassin, 5 May 1995.
39 *Derry Journal*, 3 May 1946.
40 *Derry Standard*, 3 May 1956.
41 Indeed, it is well documented that Yeats, in a letter to Synge on 21 August 1904, having seen a rehearsal of *The Well of the Saints*, asked Synge to 'cross out a number of the Almighty Gods'. Synge replied that he would only make changes to improve the play artistically, but refused to rewrite the language of his characters to make it conform to common notions of decency. (For a discussion of this, see David Krause, *The profane book of Irish comedy* ,p. 227.)
42 *Derry Standard*, 3 May 1946.
43 Ibid.
44 Unpublished personal Interview with Barry Cassin, 5 May 1995.

CHAPTER SEVEN

1 Louis D'Alton, *They Got What They Wanted* (first edition, Dublin, 1962; this edition Dublin, 1982).
2 *Irish Times*, 19 February 1947; *Irish Independent*, 19 February 1947.
3 Allardyce Nicoll, *The theatre and dramatic theory* (London, 1962), p. 118.
4 *The Times*, 20 July 1950.
5 Blythe papers, Manager's Report for fortnight ending 22 February 1950, P/24/749. Archive's Department, University College Dublin.
6 Blythe papers, P/24/749 (5).
7 Norma Phillips, 'No Keys for Carstairs', in 'The Cinema Studio', supplement to *The Cinema*, September 1950, p. 19.
8 See post-production copy of *Talk of a Million*, housed at the British Film Institute, Special Materials Unit.
9 'Talk of a Million', *Picturegoer*, August 1951.
10 'Talk of a Million', *To-day's Cinema*, June 1951.
11 'You Can't Beat the Irish', *Variety*, May 1952.
12 'Talk of a Million', *To-day's Cinema*, June 1951.
13 'You Can't Beat the Irish', *Variety*, May 1952.
14 'Talk of a Million', *To-day's Cinema*, June 1951.
15 Ibid.
16 Manager's Report for four weeks ended 7 March 1951, P/24/750 (3), Archives Department, University College Dublin.
17 Reader's Opinion on *The Devil a Saint Would Be*, Richard Hayes, 9 March 1951, Abbey Theatre Archives.
18 Ibid., Robert Farren, 13 March 1951.
19 Ibid., Lennox Robinson, 21 March 1951.
20 Ibid., Ernest Blythe, 4 March 1951.

21 Letter dated 10 April 1951 to Louis D'Alton, Abbey Theatre Archives.
22 Author's interview with Babs D'Alton, 4 February 1994.
23 Blythe papers, Manager's Report for the fortnight ending 4 April 1951, P/24/750, p. 4.
24 Author's interview with Babs D'Alton, 4 February 1994.
25 The last will of Louis Francis Dalton, extracted from the Principal Registry of the Probate Divorce and Admiralty Division of the High Court of Justice.
26 D'Alton, *The Devil a Saint Would Be* (Dublin, December 1952), p. 7. Further references to this play shall be taken from this edition and the page number shall be given after quotations in the text.
27 Anthony Cronin, 'Theatre', *The Bell* (October 1951), 18:7, pp 59–60.
28 *Irish Times*, 11 September 1951.
29 Blythe, Manager's Report for four weeks ending 19 September 1951, p. 9.
30 Anthony Cronin, 'Theatre', *The Bell*, p. 60.
31 Blythe, Manager's Report for four weeks ending 19 September 1951, p. 9. When the play was first submitted, Eileen Crowe's name was mentioned for the part, but according to Blythe he could not see her 'making nearly as good a fist of the part of Stacey' as Ní Loinsigh did.
32 Blythe, Manager's Report for fortnight ending 3 October 1951, P/24/750 (10), p. 3. In Dudgeon's defence, it should be noted that this report makes reference to the fact that a doctor's certificate had been submitted to Blythe by Dungeon which stated that he needed a fortnight's rest.
33 Ibid. p .2.
34 Blythe, Manager's Report for fortnight ending 17 October 1951, P/24/750 (11), p. 2.
35 Blythe, Manager's Report for four weeks ending 19 September 1951, P/24/750 (9), p. 2.
36 Blythe, Manager's Report for fortnight ending 3 October 1951, P/24/750 (10), p. 2.
37 Ibid. p. 3.
38 Blythe, Manager's Report for fortnight ending 17 October 1951, P/24/750 (11), p. 2.
39 Blythe: 'I spoke to Mr Bailey about the complaint that whiskey had been watered. I have arranged with him, as Odeon did, we shall take samples from the whiskey bottles in the bar at intervals and have them tested [...] As soon as I have made enquiries about the cheapest way of getting the whiskey tested I shall have samples taken from all bars.' See Manager's Report for fortnight ending 17 October 1951, P/24/750 (11), p. 2.
40 Ibid.
41 See the Abbey Account Books, housed in the Abbey Theatre Archives, Dublin.
42 Blythe, Manager's Report for fortnight ending 23 April 1952. P/24/751 (8), p. 1.
43 See Blythe, Manager's Report for three weeks ending 14 May 1952, P/24/751 (9), p. 1. Take the 1952 reproduction of *The Money Doesn't Matter* at the Queen's. In the weeks that it played at the Queen's it received more people than would have packed the Abbey theatre for the equivalent time period.
44 P24/750/ (14), pp 1–2.
45 P24/750/ (14), pp 1–2.
46 *Irish Times*, 11 September 1951.
47 Robert Hogan, *After the Irish Renaissance* (London, 1968), p. 49.
48 Ibid.
49 Louis D'Alton, *This Other Eden* (Dublin, 1954), p. 19. Further references to this play shall be taken from this edition and the page number shall be given after quotations in the text.
50 Lennox Robinson, Reader's Opinion on *This Other Eden*, 20 January 1953, Abbey Theatre Archives.
51 Blythe, Second Opinion on *This Other Eden*, 25 February 1953, Abbey Theatre Archives.

52 Ibid. See also Reader's Opinion of 20 January 1953.
53 Kevin Rockett and Luke Gibbons, *Cinema and Ireland*, p. 109.
54 Ibid. p. 108.
55 See F.S.L Lyons, *Ireland since the Famine*, rev. edn (Glasgow, 1973), p. 625.
56 Christopher Murray, *Twentieth-century Irish drama: mirror up to nation* (Manchester and New York, 1997), p. 145.
57 Robert Farren, Reader's Opinion on *This Other Eden*, Undated, Abbey Theatre Archives.
58 Richard Hayes, Reader's Opinion on *This Other Eden*, 22 January 1953, Abbey Theatre Archives. Interestingly, none of these examples appear in the published version of *This Other Eden*.
59 *Irish Independent*, 2 June 1953.
60 Blythe, Manager's Report for five weeks ending 16 June 1954, P/24/753 (5), p. 1.
61 Blythe, Manager's Report for fortnight ended 28 November 1956, P/24/ 755 (13).
62 See Blythe, Manager's Report for three weeks ending 14 April 1954, P/24/753, p. 4. In this report Blythe describes Michael Dunne as 'a slightly cracked individual whom de Valera had in prison throughout practically the whole of the last war'.
63 *Irish Press*, 7 May 1954.
64 Blythe, Manager's Report for fortnight ended 12 May 1954, P/24/753 (4), pp 1–2. Blythe's own view was that they should not ask for the Opera House to revise its practice with reference to the Anthem.
65 See Blythe, Manager's Report for fortnight ending 3 November 1954, P/24/753 (12), p. 4.
66 Ibid. p. 7.
67 Blythe, Manager's Report for fortnight ending 4 April 1956, P/24/755 (2), p. 4.
68 Ibid. pp 3–4.
69 See Manager's Report for three weeks ending 9 May 1956, P/24/755 (4).
70 See draft agreement in appendix. Blythe, Manager's Report for fortnight ending 31 October 1956, P/24/755 (11), pp 4–5.
71 Blythe, Manager's Report for fortnight ending 14 November 1956, P/24/755 (12), pp 3–4. Blythe goes on to note the financial proposals which stated that apart from payments to actors, the Abbey would be paid £200 per half-hour film 'on the understanding that there will be no interference with the ordinary theatre rehearsals by taking away actors who should be engaged in them.'
72 Blythe, Manager's Report for two weeks ending 11 December 1957, P/24/756 (19), p. 3.
73 K. Rockett, L. Gibbons and J. Hill, *Cinema and Ireland*, rev. edn (London, 1988), pp 107–108.
74 Muriel Box (1905–91) was a British director and scripter who directed twenty-four films between 1946 and 1964. See the International Film Index at the British Film Institute, London.
75 *Kinematograph Weekly*, 26:309 (October 1959), p. 140.
76 *Monthly Film Bulletin*, 2708 (August 1959), p. 28.
77 E. Patrick, Reader's Opinion on *Cafflin' Johnny*, 10 August 1957, Abbey Theatre Archives.
78 Ernest Blythe, Reader's Opinion on *Cafflin' Johnny*, 12 August 1957, Abbey Theatre Archives. Blythe's first reaction to the play was that 'it was not at all as good as *This Other Eden* but it seems to be as good as *They Got What They Wanted* and may be a possibility for us.' See Blythe's Manager's Report for fortnight ended 14 August 1957, P/24/756. In his next report Blythe noted how he told D'Alton's widow when sending her the contract for the play that 'not merely would we have to cut a good deal of it' but 'little scenes would have to be written in to provide links'. See Manager's Report for three weeks ended 11 December 1957, P/24/756 (19).
79 Robert Farren, Reader's Opinion on *Cafflin' Johnny* ,4 November 1957, Abbey Theatre Archives.
80 Lennox Robinson, Reader's Opinion on *Cafflin' Johnny*, 20 August 1957, Abbey Theatre Archives.

81 I have found no working script of this play, and the published version I am quoting from has been added to and edited by Blythe, as we have seen. However, judging from Blythe's Manager's Reports, any added dialogue seems to serve the purpose of facilitating entrances and exits for the characters, and we must assume that little if any changes were made to the themes and storyline of the play.

82 As was concluded by Richard Hayes in his Reader's Opinion on *Cafflin' Johnny,* 23 August 1957, Abbey Theatre Archives.

83 Blythe, Manager's Report for the fortnight ended 21 January 1958, P/24/757 (2), Archives Department, University College Dublin.

84 Ibid. the fortnight ended 2 February 1958, P/24/757 (3).

85 Ibid. the fortnight ended 26 February 1958, P/24/757 (4).

86 Ibid. the fortnight ended 2 April 1958, P/24/757 (6).

87 Ibid. the fortnight ended 16 April 1958, P/24/757 (7).

88 *Irish Independent,* 8 April 1958.

89 Louis D'Alton, *Cafflin' Johnny* (Dublin, 1966), p. 8. Further references to this play will be taken from this edition and the page number shall be given after quotations in the text.

90 Blythe, Manager's report for fortnight ended 30 May [*sic*] 1958 (this should probably read 30 April 1958), P/24/757 (8), Archives Department, University College Dublin.

CHAPTER EIGHT

1 Louis D'Alton, letter to the *Irish Times* written on 2 June 1941 and published on 3 June 1941.

2 Louis D'Alton, 'The Saint and the Woman', undated, National Library Manuscripts, Dublin, MS 29,162, p. 1. Further references to this short story will be taken from this manuscript and the page number will be given after quotations in the text.

3 Terence Brown, *Ireland: a social and cultural history, 1922–1985* (Glasgow, 1987), p. 147.

4 Censorship of Publications Act 1929, ss 3,6,7.

5 John Whyte, *Church and state in modern ireland 1923–1929,* 2nd ed. (Dublin, 1984), p. 60.

6 Frank O'Connor, *My father's son,* revised ed. (Belfast, 1994), p. 98.

7 Sean O'Faolain, quoted in Maurice Harmon, *Sean O'Faolain* (London, 1994), p. 132.

8 Ibid. p. 133.

9 Sean O'Faolain, *The Bell,* 1:1 (October 1940).

10 Sean O'Faolain, Diary, 1942, Quoted in *Sean O'Faolain,* p. 139.

11 Brown, *Ireland,* p. 197.

12 Quoted in James Matthews, *Voices: a life of Frank O'Connor* (Dublin, 1983), p. 178. Matthews has taken this quote from a carbon of O'Connor's letter to R. M. Smyllie stored in the Frank O'Connor Collection at Mugar Memorial Library, Boston University. Although Matthews claims that this letter was published in the *Irish Times,* I have been unable to locate it. D'Alton's letter which was published in the *Irish Times* in June 1941, suggests that D'Alton was replying to the article written by O'Connor that would have been just published in *The Bell* (2:3, June 1941). D'Alton's opening ('Sir – May I ask the courtesy of your columns to apply to an attack made *elsewhere?*') and his conclusion to his letter ('I cannot trespass further upon your limited space, but I propose to deal with the rest of Mr O'Connor's remarks *in the journal in which they appear.*') support this view. [Italics mine]

13 See Harmon, *Sean O'Faolain,* p. 144.

14 Louis D'Alton, letter to the *Irish Times* written on 2 June 1941 and published on 3 June 1941.

15 Ibid.

16 Harmon, *Sean O'Faolain*, pp 146–7.
17 See Matthews, p. 414, footnote 43, who quotes a letter from Louis D'Alton to Frank O'Connor, 27 February 1943, showing box office receipts of £557 for the week just ended.
18 Sean O'Faolain, 'Principles and propaganda', *The Bell*, 10:3 (June 1945), p. 204.
19 Sean O'Faolain, 'Ulster', *The Bell*, 2:4 (1941), p. 9.
20 Unpublished, undated document written by Louis D'Alton. Author's own collection.
21 See Brown, *Ireland*, p. 178. Brown notes that by 1944 twenty-four out of twenty-six counties in Ireland had a public library.
22 Michael Farrell, 'The country theatre', pp 387–8.
23 Quoted in *Ireland: A social and cultural history*, p. 177.
24 Allardyce Nicoll, *The theatre and dramatic theory* (London, 1962), p. 118.
25 Allardyce Nicholl, *Theory of drama* (London, 1931), p. 196.
26 *Irish Press*, 18 March 1943.
27 The fact that critics also misread these plays would have frustrated D'Alton further. Indeed, not only did this happen in Ireland, but in America also where *Taynard Street* was dubbed 'a modern miracle play' by the *New York Times*, 5 February 1941.
28 William Fay, 'A Spot of Acting', unpublished manuscript, National Library of Ireland, MS 5981.
29 *Irish Independent*, 19 February 1947.
30 F. Tobin, *The best of decades* (1984), p. 3.
31 Quoted in Tobin, *The best of decades*, p. 40.
32 Ibid. p. 67.
33 Ibid. p. 235. Some examples of this given by Tobin are 'the kids who abandoned Dromcondra for Manchester United'; 'the old ladies who watched *Coronation Street*'; and 'the bourgeois who discovered continental food'.
34 Ibid. p. 67.
35 Heinz Kosok, *Plays and playwrights from Ireland: an international perspective* (Trier, 1995), p. 222.
36 Author's interview with Garry Hynes, 8 December 1993.
37 Michael Finlan, 'Lovers Meeting at Druid, Galway', *Irish Times*, 4 October 1990.
38 Author's interview with Garry Hynes, 8 December 1993.
39 Ibid.
40 Ibid.
41 Unpublished letter to Louis D'Alton from G.B. Shaw, Ayot Saint Lawrence, Welwyn, Herts, dated 15 June 1947. Author's own.
42 Gabriel Fallon, 'The late Louis D'Alton', *The Standard*, 22 June 1951.
43 *Irish Times*, 19 June 1951.
44 Unpublished letter from Cyril Cusack to author, 20 April 1993.

APPENDICES

1 The following draft is copied from Blythe's Manager's Report for the fortnight ending 31 October 1956, P/24/755 (11), pp 5–6. Housed at the Archives Department, University College Dublin.

Bibliography

MANUSCRIPT SOURCES

Abbey Theatre Archive, Props lists, Readers' Opinions, Cast Lists, Programmes and accounts for various productions of D'Alton plays.

Anonymous scripts of *The wearing of the green* and *Pal o' my cradle days*, Irish Theatre Archive.

Blythe, Ernest, 'The Blythe Papers', Archives Department, University College Dublin, Ref: P/24.

Carey, Charles, Scrapbooks, ITA/107, Irish Theatre Archive.

Cusack, Cyril, 'The Cyril Cusack papers', volumes of press cuttings: Theatre, 1931–1978; Theatre Productions, 1945–1959, the National Library of Ireland [henceforth NLI].

Louis D'Alton, *The Spanish soldier*, Working script. NLI, MS 21,329.

—— *To-morrow never comes*, Working script. NLI, MS 21, 320.

—— *The man in the cloak*, Working script. NLI, MS 21,327.

—— *The devil a saint would be*, Working script. NLI, MS 21, 326.

—— Typescript of *The man in the cloak*. NLI, MS 21,327, N6369, P7373.

—— Typescript of *To-morrow never comes*. NLI, MS 21,329, P.7373, N 6369.

—— Typescript of *The Spanish soldier*. NLI, MS 21,328, P6369, N7373.

—— Typescript of *The devil a saint would be*. NLI, MS 21,326, N6369, P7373.

—— Manuscript of 'The saint and the woman'. Undated, NLI, MS 29,162.

—— Film script for 'Talk of a million' (1951), Filmed version of Louis D'Alton's *They got what they wanted*, The Special Materials Unit, British Film Institute.

Earnan de Blaghd papers, MS 20, 715, NLI.

The M.J. Dolan papers, MS 22,554; 22,555; 22,556; 22,559; 22,561, NLI.

The Fay papers (William and Frank), MS 5974–82, NLI.

Fields, Gracie, 'The papers of Mrs Gracie Fields', Imperial War Museum, London, Ref: 76/23/1.

Harper-Nelson, J., 'The papers of Major J. Harper-Nelson', Imperial War Museum, London, Ref: 85/34/1.

The Holloway papers, MS 22,404; 22,411; 22,416; 22,419; 22,425; 23,213; 23,214; 23,215, MS 1872, MS 1873, NLI.

Hughes, A.I., 'The papers of A.I. Hughes', Imperial War Museum, London, Ref: 93/1/1.

Irish Theatre Archive unpublished interviews with: Michael McFadden, Mona Courtney, Tom Casey, Billy Hayden, Lawrence Hayes, Vikki Jackson, Bob Bickerdyke, Charles McSherry, and Tony Glass.

Lamb, R.A. 'The papers of R.A. Lamb', Imperial War Museum, London, Ref: 79/2/1.

The T.C. Murray papers, MS 23, 511–13; MS 21,746, NLI.

The Brendan O'Brien papers, unpublished papers of the late Brendan O'Brien, relating to fit-up activity in Athlone. The author was given access to these papers by his son Gearoid O'Brian, Athlone.

The Mathew O'Mahony papers, MS 24,901; 24,902, NLI.

Mathew O'Mahony, 'Playguide for Irish amateurs' MS 25,283, NLI.
Mathew O'Mahony, 'Progress guide to Anglo-Irish plays' MS 25,283, NLI.
Taylor, G.E., 'The papers of G.E. Taylor', Imperial War Museum, London, Ref: 96/28/1
Vernon, Virginia, 'The Second World War papers of Mrs Virginia Vernon', Imperial War Museum, London, Ref: 75/47/1
W. Wetherburn, *The stroller* or *All in the dark*. Add. MSS 25,946, British Library Manuscript Room.
The Notebooks of T. Wilson Manley, Add. MSS 41073–41074, British Library Manuscript Room.

PRINTED SOURCES AND THESES

Adams, Anthony (ed.), *Rogues and vagabonds* (Oxford, 1969).
Adams, Michael, *Censorship: the Irish experience* (Dublin, 1968).
Ackland, Joss, *I must be in there somewhere* (London, 1989).
Arensberg, Conrad M., and Solon T. Kimball, *Family and community in Ireland* (Cambridge, Mass., 1968).
Billinham, P.G., 'Theatres of conscience: a study of four British regional theatre companies, 1939–1950'. PhD thesis (Leeds University, 1994).
Blanshard, Paul, *The Irish and Catholic power: an American interpretation* (London, 1954).
Booth, Michael, *English melodrama* (London, 1965).
Boylan, Henry, *A dictionary of Irish biography* (Dublin, 1978).
Brooks, Peter, *The melodramatic imagination: Balzac, Henry James and the mode of excess* (New York, 1985).
Brown, Terence, *Ireland: a social and cultural history, 1922–1985* (London, 1987).
Byrne, Muriel St Clare (ed.), *Studies in English theatre history* (London, 1952).
Cairns, David and Shaun Richards, *Writing Ireland: colonialism, nationalism and culture* (Manchester, 1988).
Carpenter, Andrew (ed.), *Place, personality and the Irish writer* (Gerrards Cross, Bucks., 1977).
Carlson, Julia (ed.), *Banned in Ireland: censorship and the Irish writer* (London, 1990).
Carstairs, Paddy, 'A director reflects on his worth', *Kinematograph Weekly*, 405.2268 (1950), 37.
Clark, William Smith, *The early Irish stage: the beginnings to 1720* (Oxford, 1955).
—— *The Irish stage in the county towns, 1720–1800* (Oxford, 1965).
Connolly, Rex, 'Censorship', *Christus Rex*, 13 (1959), 151–70.
Crane, Harvey, *Playbill* (Plymouth, 1980).
Cronin, Anthony, 'Theatre', *The Bell*, 17.7 (October 1951), 58–60.
Curtain Call: A complete review of the amateur stage in Ireland (Dublin, [n.d.]).
D'Alton, Frank, 'Ghosts of "Old Royal" ', *Dublin Magazine*, 1:3 (October 1923), 199–203.
—— 'Small change and Boucicault', *Dublin Magazine*, 1:4 (November 1923), 280–5.
D'Alton, Louis, *Death is so fair* (London, 1936).
—— *Two Irish plays: The man in the cloak; The mousetrap* (London, 1938).
—— *Rags and sticks* (London, 1938).
—— *The money doesn't matter: a play in three acts* (Dublin, 1942), repr. P.J. Burke 1980
—— *To-morrow never comes: a play in three acts* (Dublin, 1945), repr. P.J. Burke 1968
—— *The devil a saint would be: a morality in three acts* (Dublin, 1988).
—— *This other Eden: a play in three acts* (Dublin, 1954, repr., 1970).
—— *They got what they wanted: a three-act comedy* (Dundalk, 1960, new ed., 1982).
—— *Lovers' meeting: a tragedy* (Dublin, 1964).
—— *Cafflin' Johnny: a comedy* (Dublin, 1966).
—— 'Public opinion', *The Bell*, 2:4 (July 1941), 72–6.

Daniels, Albert B., *Five and nine: recollections of the touring shows in Ireland* (Donegal, 1991).
Davies, Andrew, *Other theatres* (London, 1987).
de Blacam, Aodh, 'Can Ireland help Spain?', *Irish Monthly,* 65 (December 1936), 645–651.
de Burca, Seamus, *The Queen's Royal Theatre, Dublin, 1829–1969* (Dublin, 1983).
Elder, Ellen, *Travelling players: the story of the Arts League of Service* (London, 1939).
Ellis-Fermor, Una, *The Irish dramatic movement* (London, 1939, 2nd ed., 1954).
Falb, Carl, 'A world elsewhere: the stage career of Anew Mac Master', PhD thesis (Ohio State University: 1974).
Fallon, Gabriel, *Sean O'Casey, The man I knew* (London, 1965).
Fallon, Gabriel, 'The theatre speaks', *Irish Monthly,* 64 (December 1936), 836–841.
—— 'The despondent sociologist', *Irish Monthly,* 65 (February 1937), 118–123.
—— 'Experiment in the theatre', *Irish Monthly,* 65 (June 1937), 406–411.
—— 'Mangan, Macbeth, invincibles, etc.', *Irish Monthly,* 65 (December 1937), 838–46.
—— 'Not forgetting the audience', *Irish Monthly,* 68 (June 1939), 419–18.
—— 'No rest for the critic', *Irish Monthly,* 69 (May 1941), 268–74.
—— 'Sitting at the play', *Irish Monthly,* 70 (July 1942), 289–95.
—— 'Full-house and empty theatres', *Irish Monthly,* 70 (July 1942), 155–61.
—— 'Some lessons of war-time theatre', *Irish Monthly,* 71 (June 1943), 249–255.
—— 'Some aspects of rural entertainment', *Irish Monthly,* 73 (July 1945), 286–92.
—— 'McMaster in Oedipus', *Irish Monthly,* 74 (December 1946), 530–7.
Farrell, Michael, 'Plays for the country theatre', *The Bell,* 2:1 (April 1941), 78–84
Fay, Gerard, *The Abbey Theatre: cradle of genius* (Dublin, 1958).
Fay, William George and Catherine Carswell, *The Fays of the Abbey Theatre: an autobiographical record* (London, 1935).
Fitz-Simon, Christopher, *The Irish theatre* (London, 1983).
—— *The Boys: a double biography.* London, Nick Hern, 1994
Foulkes, Richard, *The Calverts: actors of some importance* (London, 1992).
Foster, R.F., *Modern Ireland, 1600–1972* (London, 1989).
Friel, Brian, *Crystal and Fox* (London, 1984 [1970]).
Friedman, Arthur (ed.), *Collected works of Oliver Goldsmith,* vol. 3 (Oxford, 1966).
Gledhill, Christine (ed.), *Home is where the heart is: studies in melodrama and the woman's film* (London, 1987).
Goldsmith, Oliver, *Essays* (London, 1794).
Green, John and Gladys Clark, *The Dublin stage, 1720–1745* (London, 1993).
Grice, Elizabeth, *Rogues and vagabonds* (Lavenham, 1977)
Guinness, Bryan, *Potpourri from the thirties* (Burford, Oxon, 1982).
Gussow, Mel, *Conversations with Pinter* (London, 1994).
Gwynn, Audrey, 'The origin of Anglo-Irish theatre', *Studies,* 27 (June 1939), 260–274.
Hardy, Thomas, *Far from the madding crowd* (London, 1994).
Harmon, Maurice, *Sean O'Faolain: a life* (London, 1994).
Hartnoll, Phyllis (ed.), *Oxford companion to the theatre* (Oxford, 1983)
Hederman, Mark Patrick and Richard Kearney (eds), *The Crane bag of Irish studies* (Dublin, 1982).
Heilman, Robert Bechtold, *The iceman, the arsonist, and the troubled agent: tragedy and melodrama on the modern stage* (London, 1973).
Herr, Cheryl (ed.), *For the land they loved: Irish political melodramas, 1890–1925* (Syracuse, 1991).
Hickey, Des & Gus Smith, *A paler shade of green* (London, 1972).
Harmon, Maurice, *Sean O'Faolain* (London, 1994).
Hobson, Rodney, 'This is my story', *Picturegoer,* 12 November 1949.

Hogan, Robert, and M.J. O'Neill (eds.), *Joseph Holloway's Abbey theatre* (London, 1967).
—— *After the Irish renaissance: a critical history of Irish drama since 'The Plough and the Stars'* (London, 1968).
—— *Laying the foundations, 1902–1904* (Dublin, 1978)
—— and James Kilroy, *The Irish literary theatre, 1899–1901* (Dublin, 1975).
—— and James Kilroy, *The Abbey Theatre: the years of Synge, 1905–1909*, vol. 3, *The modern Irish drama: a documentary history* (Dublin, 1978).
—— and James Kilroy, Richard Burnham and Liam Miller, *Rise of the realists, 1910–1915* (Dublin, 1979).
—— *'Since O'Casey' and other essays on Irish drama* (Gerrards Cross, 1983).
—— & Richard Burham, *The art of the amateur, 1916–1920* (Portlaoise, 1984).
—— and Richard Burnham, *The years of O'Casey, 1921 –1926*: a *documentary history* (Gerrards Cross, 1992).
—— et al., eds., *Dictionary of Irish literature*, revised ed. (Westport, CT, 1996).
Howard Gordan, Leslie, *Play production and stage management for amateurs* (London, 1927).
Hume, Kathryn, *Fantasy and mimesis: responses to reality in western literature* (London, 1984).
Hunt, Hugh, *The Abbey: Ireland's national theatre, 1904–1978* (Dublin, 1979).
—— Kenneth Richards and John Russell Taylor (eds), *The revels history of drama in English: vol. 7, 1880 to the present day* (London, 1978).
Irving, Stanley, 'John Paddy Carstairs', *Film and Television Technician*, 37.308 (1971), 15.
Jackson, Rosemary, *Fantasy: the literature of subversion* (London, 1981).
Jeffares, A. Norman, *Anglo-Irish literature* (London, 1982).
Johnston, Denis, 'Plays of the quarter', *The Bell*, 2:1 (April 1941), 89–95.
—— 'More melodrama, being a discourse on a number of plays', *The Bell*, 2:2 (May 1941), 31–38.
—— 'The theatre', *The Bell*, 2:4 (July 1941), 77–81.
Ireland, Denis, 'The Abbey Theatre', *The Bell*, 2:4 (July 1941), 67–8.
Joyce, Alice Dwyer, *The strolling players* (London, 1975).
Kavanagh, Peter, *The story of the Abbey Theatre* (Tralee, 1946, repr. New York, 1950).
Kelly, Eamon, *The apprentice* (Dublin, 1995).
Kenneally, Michael (ed.), *Irish literature and culture.* Irish Literary Series 3 (Gerrards Cross, 1992).
Kiberd, Declan, *Anglo-Irish attitudes* (Derry, 1984).
—— *Inventing Ireland* (London, 1995).
Kilgarrif, Michael, *The golden age of melodrama: twelve nineteenth-century melodramas* (London, 1974).
Kilroy, Thomas, 'The Irish writer: self and society, 1950–1980', in Peter Connolly (ed.), *Literature and the changing Ireland*, Irish literary series 9.
Kosok, Heinz, *Plays and playwrights from Ireland: an international perspective* (Trier, 1995).
Krause, David (ed.), *The Dolmen Boucicault* (Dublin, 1964).
—— *The profane book of Irish comedy* (London, 1982).
—— (ed.), *The letters of Sean O'Casey, vol. 1, 1910–1941* (London, 1975).
—— (ed.), *The letters of Sean O'Casey, vol. 2, 1942–1954* (New York, , 1980).
—— (ed.), *The letters of Sean O'Casey vol. 3, 1955–1958* (Washington, 1989).
—— (ed.), *The letters of Sean O'Casey, vol. 4, 1959–1964* (Washington D.C., 1992).
—— *Sean O'Casey, the man and his work*, first published 1960; enlarged edition 197, 2nd edn (London, 1966).
—— *Sean O'Casey and his world* (London, 1976).
Levey, R.M. and J. O'Rorke, *Annals of the Theatre Royal, Dublin.* (Dublin, 1880).
Lloyd, David, *Anamalous states: Irish writing and the post-colonial moment*(Dublin, 1993).
—— *Nationalism and minor literature: James Clarence Mangan and the emergence of Irish cultural nationalism* (London, 1987).

Lyons, F.S.L., *Ireland since the famine* (Glasgow, 1973).

McAsh, Iain, 'Leslie's been "a Wolf" from the very start', *Film Review*, 26:3. (1976), 18–19.

Mc Cann, Sean, ed., *The story of the Abbey Theatre* (London, 1967).

McHugh, Roger, 'Too immoral for any stage', *The Bell*, 15:2 (November 1947), 60–3.

Mac Liammoir, Micheál, *All for Hecuba: an Irish theatrical autobiography* (London, 1947), revised edn, Dublin, 1961.

—— *Enter a goldfish: memoirs of an Irish actor, young and old* (London, 1977).

—— *Theatre in Ireland* (Dublin, 1950, revised edn 1969).

Mc Kechnie, Samuel, *Popular entertainment throughout the ages* (London, 1931)

McMahon, Sean, 'The Wearing of the Green: the Irish plays of Dion Boucicault', *Eire-Ireland*, 11:2 (1967), 98–111.

Macqueen-Pope, W., *The curtain rises: a story of the theatre* (Westport, CT, n.d.).

Mackenzie, Edward, *Rogues and vagabonds* (London, 1967).

Malone, Andrew E., *The Irish drama* (London, 1929)

Malone, Andrew E., 'From the stalls: propaganda and melodrama', *Dublin Magazine*, 2:11 (June 1925), 629–35.

—— 'The Irish theatre in 1930', *Dublin Magazine*, 6:2 (April–June 1931), 1–11.

—— 'The future of the theatre', *Dublin Magazine*, 7:1 (January–March 1932), 31–41.

—— 'The Irish theatre in 1935', *Dublin Magazine*, 11:1 (January 1936), 48–59.

Mathews, D. (ed.), *Glimpses of real life as seen in the theatrical world and bohemia: being the confessions of Peter Paterson, a strolling comedian* (Edinburgh, 1864)

Matthews, James, *Voices: a life of Frank O'Connor* (Dublin, 1983).

Maxwell, D.E.S., *A critical history of modern Irish drama, 1891–1980* (Cambridge, 1984)

Melford, Mark, *Life in a booth* (London, 1913).

Mercier, Vivian, *The Irish comic tradition* (Oxford 1962).

Mercier, Vivian, 'Irish comedy: the probable and the wonderful', *University Review*, 1:8 (Spring 1956), 45–53.

Mikhail, E.H. (ed.), *The Abbey Theatre: interviews and recollections* (Basingstoke, 1988).

—— *An annotated bibliography of modern Irish drama, 1899–1970* (New York, 1981).

Molin, Sven Eric and Robin Goodefellowe, 'Nationalism on the Dublin stage', *Eire–Ireland*, 21 (1986), 135–8.

Molloy, John, *Alive, alive oh! John Molloy's one man show* (Dublin, 1975).

Morse, Donald E. and Csilla Bertha (eds), *More real than reality: the fantastic in Irish literature and the arts* (Westport, CT, 1991).

M.R.P.H., 'Illegitimate', *The Bell*, 2:3 (June 1941), 78–87.

Murphy, C.B., 'Sex, censorship and the church', *The Bell*, 2:6 (1941), 65–75.

Murray, Christopher (ed.), *Selected plays of Lennox Robinson* (Gerrards Cross, 1982).

—— *Twentieth-century Irish drama: mirror up to nation* (Manchester, 1997).

Nagler, A.M., *A source book in theatrical history* (New York, 1952).

Nancollas, Richard, *Rhyming Dick and the strolling player* (London, 1815).

Nicoll, Allardyce, *The theatre and dramatic theory* (London, 1962)

—— *English drama, 1900–1930: the beginnings of the modern period* (Cambridge, 1973).

—— *Theory of drama* (London, 1931)

Noble, Peter, *British theatre* (London, 1946).

Nowlan, Kevin B., and T.D. Williams (eds), *Ireland in the war years and after, 1931–1951* (Dublin, 1969)

Ó hAodha, Micheál, *Plays and places* (Dublin, 1961).

—— *Theatre in Ireland* (Oxford, 1974).
—— *The importance of being Michael: a portrait of MacLiammoir* (Dingle, 1990).
—— *Siobhán, a memoir of an actress* (Dingle, 1994).
O'Brien, Flann, 'The dance halls', *The Bell*, 2:5 (August 1941), 44–52.
O'Brien, Johnson, Toni and David Cairns (eds), *Gender in Irish writing* (Bristol, 1991).
O'Callaghan, Margaret, 'Language and religion: the quest for identity in the Irish Free State, 1922–1932' MA thesis (University College Dublin, 1981).
O'Casey, Sean, *Autobiographies* : 2 vols (London, 1963).
—— Seven unpublished letters from Sean O'Casey to Louis D'Alton; author's own, a gift from Babs D'Alton.
O'Connor, Frank, *An only child.* Revised ed. (Belfast, 1993).
—— *My father's son.* Revised ed. (Belfast, 1994, first ed. 1968).
O'Connor, Frank, 'The stone dolls', *The Bell*, 2:3 (June 1941), 61–7.
O'Donoghue, D.J., *The life and writings of J.C. Mangan* (Dublin, 1897).
O'Driscoll, Robert, ed., *Theatre and nationalism in twentieth-century Ireland* (London, 1971)
O'Faolain, Sean, 'Standards and tastes', *The Bell*, 2:3 (June 1941), 5–46.
O'Keeffe, John, *Wild oats or the strolling gentlemen* (Dublin, 1791).
—— *Recollections of the life of John O'Keeffe*, 2 vols (London, 1826)
O'Neill, Michael J., *Lennox Robinson* (New York, 1964).
O'Neill, Michael J., 'The diaries of a Dublin playgoer as a mirror of the Irish Literary Revival' PhD thesis (University College Dublin, 1952).
O'Shea, Tom, *Encore: the Harry Bailey story* (Dublin: Magill Print, 1990).
O'Sullivan, Donal, *Carolan: the life, times and music of an Irish harper*, vol. 1 (London, 1958).
Parker, John (ed.), *The green room book, 1907–1909* (London, 1912).
Paterson, Peter, *Behind the scenes: confessions of a strolling player* (Edinburgh, 1859).
Pearson, Hesketh (ed.), *Who's who in the theatre*, 16th edn (London, 1912; repr. 1977).
Phillips, Leslie, 'Criticism follows success', *Films and Filming*, 7:8 (1961), 20.
Phillips, Norma, 'No keys for Carstairs', *The Cinema Studio*, (September 1950), 18–19.
Pine, Richard, 'After Boucicault: melodrama and the Irish stage', *Prompts*, 6 (September 1983), 39–50.
Pinter, Harold, *Poems and prose, 1949–1977* (London, 1978).
Pitt Lennox, William, *Plays, players and playhouses*, vol. 2. (London, 1881).
Plagicry, Peter, *The song smith* (London, 1818)
Priestley, J.B., *The good companions* (London, 1929)
Rabkin, Eric, S., *The fantastic in literature* (Princeton, 1976).
Rafroidi, Patrick, Raymond Popot and William Parker (eds.), *Aspects of Irish theatre* (Paris, 1972).
Rahill, Frank, *The world of melodrama* (University Park, PA, 1967)
Riordan, Eugene, 'The fatal night', *Limerick Association Yearbook*, 1981, 47–50.
Rix, Brian, *Tour de farce: a tale of touring companies and strolling players: from Thespis to Branagh* (London, 1992).
Robinson, Lennox (ed.), *The Irish theatre: lectures delivered during the Abbey Theatre Festival held in Dublin in August 1938* (London,1939).
—— *Curtain up: an autobiography.* (London, 1942)
—— *Ireland's Abbey Theatre: a history, 1899–1951* (London, 1951).
—— *I sometimes think* (Dublin, 1956).
Rockett, Kevin and Luke Gibbons, *Cinema and Ireland* (London, 1987).
Rosenfeld, Sybil, *Strolling players and drama in the provinces* (Cambridge, 1939).
—— *The theatres of the London fairs in the eighteenth century* (Cambridge, 1960).

Ryan, John, *Remembering how we stood: Bohemian Dublin at the mid-century* (Dublin, 1975).

Ryan, Phillis, *The company I kept* (Dublin, 1996).

Sahal, N., *Sixty years of realistic Irish drama: 1900–1960* (Calcutta, 1971).

Sanderson, Michael, *From Irving to Olivier: a social history of the acting profession in England, 1880–1983* (London, 1984).

Saxon, A.H., *Enter foot and horse: a history of hippodrama in England and France* (Yale University Press, 1968).

Schleifer, Ronald (ed.), *The genres of the Irish literary revival* (Dublin, 1980).

Shannon-Mangan, Ellen, *J.C. Mangan, a biography* (Dublin, 1995).

Shaw, George Bernard, unpublished letter from Shaw to Louis D'Alton, author's own, a gift from Babs D'Alton.

Sheridan, John Desmond, *James Clarence Mangan* (Dublin, 1937).

Simpson, Alan, *Beckett and Behan and a theatre in Dublin* (London, 1962).

Skinner, Maud and Otis (eds), *One man in his time: the adventures of H. Walkins, strolling player 1845–1863, from his journal* (London, 1938).

Slater, Michael, 'The Transformation of Susan: The stage history of Douglas Jerrold's *Black Eyed Susan* 1829–1994', *Theatre Notebook* (1996), L.3, 146–75.

Smyth, Patrick and Ellen Hazelkorn, *Let in the light: censorship secrecy and democracy* (Dingle, 1993).

Society for Theatre Research [n. ed.], *Studies in English theatre history: in memory of Gabrielle Enthoven* (London, 1952).

Spangle, Fred, *Fred Spangle or the life of a strolling player* (London, 1873).

Stratton, Clarence, *Producing in little theatres* (London, 1922).

Templeton, William, *The strolling player*, 3 vols (London, 1802).

Thaler, Alwin, 'Travelling players in Shakespeare's England', *Modern Philology*, 17 (1920), 121–45.

—— 'The Elizabethan dramatic companies', *PMLA*, 35 (1920), 123–59.

—— 'The players at court', *Journal of English and German Philology*, 21 (1920), 19–46.

—— 'Strolling players and provincial drama after Shakespeare', *PMLA*, 37 (1922), 243–80.

Tobin, Fergal, *The best of decades: Ireland in the nineteen sixties* (Dublin, 1984).

Traies, Jane, *Fairbooths and fit-ups* (London, 1980).

Vousden, Val, *Val Vousden's caravan* (Dublin, 1941).

Wallace, Adayle and Ross, Woodburn (eds), *Studies in honour of John Wilcox* (Detroit, 1958).

Watt, Stephen, *Joyce, O'Casey and the Irish popular theatre* (Syracuse, 1991).

Watters, Eugene and Matthew Murtagh, *Infinite variety: Dan Lowrey's music hall, 1879–97* (Dublin, 1975).

Watson, G.J., *Irish identity and the literary revival: Synge, Yeats, Joyce and O'Casey* (London, 1979, revised ed., Washington DC, 1994).

Watt, Stephen, 'The plays of Hubert O'Grady', *Journal of Irish literature*, 14:1 (1985), 3–13.

Weintraub, Stanley, ed., *Dictionary of literary biography*, vol. 10, part 1: *Modern British dramatists, 1900–1945* (Detroit, 1975).

Whyte, John, *Church and state in modern Ireland, 1923–1929*, 2nd edn (Dublin, 1984).

Wild, Samuel, *The original old Wilds* (London, 1888).

Wilkinson, Tate, *Memoirs of his own life*, 4 vols (York, 1791).

—— *Memoirs and letters*, 4 vols (York, 1791).

—— *The wandering patentee*, 4 vols (York, 1795).

Woodward, Zenka and Ian, *Strolling players: poems* (London, 1978).

Wright, Richardson, *Hawkers and walkers in early America* (Philadelphia, 1927).

Young, Charlotte & Christabel R. Coleridge, *Strolling players: a harmony of contrasts* (London, 1893).

Zach, Wolfgang & Kosok, Heinz (eds), *Literary interrelations: Ireland, England and the world*, vol. 1: 'Reception and translation' (Tubingen: Narr, 1986), vol. 3, 'National images and stereotypes' (Tubingen: Narr, 1987).

UNPUBLISHED INTERVIEWS (BY CIARA O'FARRELL)

Robert Carrickford: 17 May 1995

Barry Cassin: 5 May 1995

David Costello: 8 June 1996; 8 October 1996; 2 April 1997

John Cowley: 16 June 1995

Babs D'Alton: 24 October 1993; 18 February 1994; 19 September 1994; 4 January 1996; 19 February 1996; 4 March 1996; 22 March 1998

Eithne D'Alton: 15 February 1996

Paddy Dooley: 14 September 1996

Pauline Flanagan: 9 December 1997

Garry Hynes: 8 December 1993

Vikki Jackson: 9 October 1996

Milo O'Shea: 4 February 1998

Phyllis Ryan: 29 April 1995; 29 April 1998

Shela Ward: 25 May 1994

Index